Organised crime in Europe: the threat of cybercrime

Situation report 2004

Council of Europe
Octopus Programme

Council of Europe Publishing

For more information on the subject of this publication, please contact:

Department of Crime Problems
Directorate General I – Legal Affairs
Council of Europe
F-67075 Strasbourg Cedex, France
Tel: +33 (0) 3 90 21 45 06
E-mail: octopus@coe.int
Web: www.coe.int/economiccrime

Cover design: Graphic Design Workshop, Council of Europe
Layout: Department of Crime Problems

Council of Europe Publishing
F-67075 Strasbourg Cedex
http://book.coe.int

ISBN 92-871-5682-4

© Council of Europe, March 2005

Printed at the Council of Europe

Contents

Preface

Organised crime has been a major threat to European societies for decades, and – unfortunately – it is likely to remain a major threat in the future. While the face of organised crime may keep changing in the context of globalisation, technological transformation and European integration, its basic impact remains the same: it undermines democracy, human rights and the rule of law, which are the values on which Europe is based.

The Council of Europe has taken on this challenge by establishing common standards, by carrying out programmes to strengthen the capacity of member states to fight such crime, by documenting good practice and by preparing annual reports on the current situation.

The 2004 report helps member states to ensure that counter-measures are based on a thorough knowledge of the situation. Economic crime, drugs and the smuggling and trafficking in human beings are the main issues, while money represents the common denominator of organised criminal activities. New treaties on money laundering and trafficking in human beings are under preparation, and their early adoption and implementation by member states is of utmost importance.

The topical chapter on the threat of cybercrime shows that, while information and communication technologies provide states with unprecedented opportunities, states also become vulnerable, and this vulnerability is exploited by criminals, not only in Europe but globally. The report thus makes a strong case for the widest possible geographical implementation of the Council of Europe's Convention on Cybercrime and its Protocol on Racism and Xenophobia. I should like to take this opportunity to thank Professor Ulrich Sieber and his colleagues from the Max Planck Institute for Foreign and International Criminal Law in Freiburg and the University of Munich who prepared the chapter on the threat of cybercrime.

In view of the 3rd Summit of Heads of State and Government in May 2005, I believe that this publication is very timely and I am confident that it will provide a useful basis for the Council of Europe's work for the coming years.

Terry Davis
Secretary General of the Council of Europe
Strasbourg, February 2005

Chapter 1 – Organised crime in Europe: the framework

Background and purpose of the report

Organised crime has been on the agenda of the Council of Europe for at least two decades,[1] and in particular following the 2nd Summit in 1997 at which European heads of state and government tasked the Council of Europe to step up measures against organised crime, corruption and money laundering.

One of the results of the 2nd Summit was the establishment of a committee of experts[2] which, among other things, prepared seven annual reports on the organised crime situation covering the years 1996 to 2002. In 2003 it was decided to transfer this task to the Octopus Programme against organised crime and corruption in Europe.

Organised crime and other forms of economic and serious crime are likely to remain priority concerns of European societies for some time to come. However, as the nature of crime changes and as new threats emerge, policies against crime will need to adjust.

The purpose of the 2004 organised crime situation report therefore is:

- to point at new and changing threats and the main issues of concern;
- to help policy makers in Europe make more informed decisions on anti-crime policies.

While key elements of previous situation reports, such as the environmental scan and the analysis of crime markets, have been kept, a more topical approach has been chosen for this year's report.

---

1. See for example Recommendation No. R (86) 8 on crime policy in Europe in a time of change. Already in 1973, the 8th Conference of European Ministers of Justice dealt with the question of economic crime in the broader sense.

2. The Committee of Experts on Criminal Law and Criminological Aspects of Organised Crime, PC-CO (1997-2000). From 2000 to the end of 2003, the work of this committee was continued by a group of specialists, the PC-S-CO. The committee also drafted Recommendation Rec(2001)11 of the Committee of Ministers to member states concerning guiding principles on the fight against organised crime, adopted on 19 September 2001. The committee, and subsequently the group of specialists, furthermore prepared a series of Best Practice Surveys on countermeasures against organised crime.

Following chapters on the framework of organised crime (Chapter 1) and the overall organised crime situation (Chapter 2), the special topic of this year's report is cybercrime.

Computer networks are turning the world into a global information society in which any kind of information is available to Internet users almost anywhere and in which electronic commerce may soon exceed hundreds of billions of euros. However, this process is accompanied by an increasing dependency on such networks and a growing vulnerability to criminal intrusion and misuse. Networks facilitate illegal access to information, attacks on private or public computer systems, distribution of illegal content as well as cyber-laundering and possibly cyberterrorism.

Cybercrime thus poses new challenges to criminal justice and international co-operation.

In November 2001, the Convention on Cybercrime (ETS No. 185) of the Council of Europe was opened for signature. It entered into force on 1 July 2004. Its implementation will help parties cope with these challenges. The convention is complemented by the Additional Protocol to the Convention on Cybercrime, concerning the criminalisation of acts of a racist and xenophobic nature committed through computer systems (ETS No. 189) of January 2003.

The chapter on cybercrime in this report contains an analysis of the phenomenon, its actual and possible impact, and links to organised crime and terrorism.

The final concluding chapter provides a threat assessment based on the analysis of the organised crime situation and cybercrime.

As in previous years, a questionnaire was sent to member states in March 2004. The situation report is based to a large extent on the replies to the questionnaire[1] as well as other literature, including situation reports and threat analyses which are now made available annually by an increasing number of member states.

---

1. Replies were received from: Andorra, Armenia, Austria, Belgium, Bulgaria, Croatia, Cyprus, the Czech Republic, Denmark, Estonia, Finland, Germany, Georgia, Greece, Iceland, Italy, Latvia, Lithuania, Malta, Moldova, the Netherlands, Norway, Poland, Portugal, Romania, Serbia and Montenegro, Slovakia, Slovenia, Spain, Sweden, Switzerland, "the former Yugoslav Republic of Macedonia", Turkey, Ukraine and the United Kingdom.

Chapters 1 (Organised crime in Europe: the framework) and 2 (The organised crime situation) have been prepared by the Department of Crime Problems (Directorate General of Legal Affairs) of the Council of Europe.[1] The topical chapter on cybercrime was written by Professor Dr Ulrich Sieber supported by his collaborators at the Max Planck Institute for Foreign and International Criminal Law in Freiburg and at the University of Munich, Germany.

The concept of organised crime

The United Nations Convention on Transnational Organized Crime (UNTOC) can be considered the most important attempt to date to arrive at a globally agreed upon concept of organised crime. It entered into force in September 2003. By July 2004 it had been signed by all forty-five member states of the Council of Europe and ratified by twenty-seven of them as well as the European Community. It is thus also highly relevant for Europe.

The UNTOC applies to serious crime, corruption, money laundering and obstruction of justice provided that the offence is transnational in nature and involves an organised criminal group as defined in the convention. According to Article 2:

> (a) "Organized criminal group" shall mean a structured group of three or more persons, existing for a period of time and acting in concert with the aim of committing one or more crimes or offences established in accordance with this Convention, in order to obtain, directly or indirectly, a financial or other material benefit;
>
> (b) "Serious crime" shall mean conduct constituting an offence punishable by maximum deprivation of liberty of at least four years or a more serious penalty;
>
> (c) "Structured group" shall mean a group that is not randomly formed for the immediate commission of an offence and that does not need to have formally defined roles for its members, continuity of its membership or a developed structure.

---

1. Michael Levi (United Kingdom), Toon Van der Heijden (Netherlands) and Tom Vander Beken (Belgium) – all of them former members of the PC-S-CO – provided feedback on drafts of this report.

The Council of Europe – in its "Guiding principles on the fight against organised crime" – adopted a similar definition of "organised crime group" without limiting the scope to transnational offences.[1]

The replies to the 2004 questionnaire show that an increasing number of European countries foresee definitions of organised crime or of organised crime groups in their criminal legislation.[2]

Nevertheless – as stated already in the 2002 situation report – organised crime remains an ambiguous concept:

- It is a concept with a history which keeps changing over time.[3] It is a social construction reflecting forms of crime perceived to be particularly dangerous by society at a given point in time and influenced by different political and institutional interests.

- Organised crime does not take place in a vacuum but in an ever changing environment. It is a dynamic process adapting to new

---

1. According to Recommendation Rec(2001)11 of the Committee of Ministers to member states concerning guiding principles on the fight against organised crime (adopted by the Committee of Ministers on 19 September 2001 at the 765th meeting of the Ministers' Deputies), for the purposes of this recommendation:
– "'organised crime group' shall mean a structured group of three or more persons, existing for a period of time and acting in concert with the aim of committing one or more serious crimes, in order to obtain, directly or indirectly, a financial or material benefit;
– 'serious crime' shall mean conduct constituting an offence punishable by a maximum deprivation of liberty of at least four years or a more serious penalty;".
See also the EU definition of 1998 of a criminal organisation: "1. A criminal organisation means a structured association, established over a period of time, of two or more persons, acting in a concerted manner with a view to committing offences which are punishable by deprivation of liberty or a detention order of a maximum of at least four years or a more serious penalty, whether such offences are an end in themselves or a means of obtaining material benefits and, where appropriate, of improperly influencing the operation public authorities" (Article 1). (Joint action 98/733/JHA of 21 December 1998 adopted by the European Council on the basis of Article K.3 of the Treaty on European Union, on making it a criminal offence to participate in a criminal organisation in the Member States of the European Union.)
2. Such as Belgium, Croatia, Cyprus, Lithuania, Moldova, Romania, Serbia (Serbia and Montenegro), Slovakia, Slovenia, Turkey and Ukraine. In Italy, a distinction is made between "criminal associations" and "Mafia-type associations".
3. See Von Lampe 2001.

opportunities for crime, to resources and skills available to potential criminals as well as to law enforcement and other control efforts.[1] It may take different forms in different societies.

- The idea of organised crime as a clearly distinct form of crime may be misleading. It may be more appropriate to think of a continuum where some forms of serious crime are more organised than others.[2]

- The distinction between organised crime and economic crime seems to pose particular difficulties. Economic crime, like organised crime, has a serious impact on society as a whole. There are strong correlations between economic and organised crime, and both share certain characteristics.[3]

- Similarly, rather than thinking in terms of a dichotomy between organised crime on one side and the state and society on the other, organised crime is shaped by the social, economic and political context in which it is operating, with complex – more often symbiotic and clientelistic than confrontational – relationships between organised crime groups, state and society.

- With the paradigm shifting from hierarchical, "bureaucratic" organised crime groups with well-developed structures to loose and fluid networks, it becomes extremely difficult to identify "structures" and thus organised crime in the conventional sense.

- The occasional linkage or even amalgamation of the concepts of organised crime and of terrorism adds further ambiguities, sometimes generating a misleading connection between terrorism and particular methods by which it is financed or conducted.

Reporting on organised crime thus remains difficult. In order to facilitate this task and promote uniform reporting, the Council of Europe – in the questionnaire on the organised crime situation – asked member states to apply the following criteria when defining crime or criminal groups as "organised crime":[4]

---

1. See Levi 2002.
2. See Levi 2002.
3. See the Explanatory Memorandum to Recommendation Rec(2001)11.
4. Also used by the European Union (Doc 6204/2/97 Enfopol 35 Rev 2) for its annual organised crime reports.

Mandatory criteria:

1. Collaboration of three or more people
2. For a prolonged or indefinite period of time
3. Suspected or convicted of committing serious criminal offences
4. With the objective of pursuing profit and/or power

Optional criteria:

5. Having a specific task or role for each participant
6. Using some form of internal discipline and control
7. Using violence or other means suitable for intimidation
8. Exerting influence on politics, the media, public administration, law enforcement, the administration of justice or the economy by corruption or any other means
9. Using commercial or business-like structures
10. Engaged in money laundering
11. Operating on an international level.

In addition to the minimum characteristics (the "mandatory criteria" 1 to 4), at least two of the "optional criteria" need to be applicable to qualify a criminal group or crime as organised crime.

Through this approach, "organised crime" may not only include traditional criminal groups but also legal entities or professionals engaged in serious forms of organisational or economic crime.

Any analysis of the organised crime situation will need to:

- take into account the specific context and changes in the environment ("environmental scan");
- focus on the main crime markets.

This needs to be complemented by an assessment of the:

- characteristics of organised crime groups and networks, and in particular of their structure;
- *modi operandi* of such groups, including the relationship between illegal and legal structures of society.

Environmental scan

The "environmental scan" was introduced in the 2001 and 2002 reports on the organised crime situation. It consists of the gathering and processing of information about the external environment of organised crime in order to identify major trends affecting it and allowing analyses to define potential changes resulting from these trends. This process contributes to a proactive focus and makes the relationship between the trends identified and the entity more transparent.

PEST analyses help structure the external environment by dividing it into political, economic, social and technological domains.[1]

Politics and governance

The nature of the state and political institutions appear to be critical determinants for organised crime.

General themes, in terms of politics and governance, are the diffusion of power and the changing role of the state. These changes are caused by globalisation, deregulation and market liberalisation, an ever stronger role for transnational corporations delegation of responsibilities "upwards" to supranational and international organisations, and "downwards" to local and regional authorities as well as to non-state actors. This raises questions as to the capacity of national public authorities to control crime.

At the same time, the international framework for the control of organised crime and other forms of serious crime is being reinforced, in particular in the wake of 11 September 2001. For example:

- The current work of the Council of Europe on a new treaty updating the Convention on the Laundering, Search, Seizure and Confiscation of the Proceeds from Crime, and of the European Commission on framework decisions on freezing orders and confiscation of proceeds are a reflection of a renewed focus on criminal money.

- The EU Convention on Mutual Assistance in Criminal Matters of 2000, and the Council of Europe's Second Additional Protocol to the Convention on Mutual Legal Assistance in Criminal Matters provide a range of new tools against transnational organised crime, although they still require broad ratification.

---

1. See Black et al. 2001. Such PEST analyses may appear speculative, but they provide useful insights.

- The United Nations Convention on Transnational Organized Crime entered into force in September 2003.

- The recommendations of the Financial Action Task Force (FATF) have been revised.

- The United Nations Convention against Corruption opened for signature in December 2003. The convention also contains protocols on trafficking in human beings, smuggling of persons and manufacturing and trafficking in firearms.

- The Council of Europe's Convention on Cybercrime entered into force on 1 July 2004.
-
- The preparation of a European convention against trafficking in human beings is underway.

A crucial development in 2004 has been the enlargement of the European Union by ten new member states on 1 May. There have been concerns that open borders would lead to more crime within the "old" European Union. Others argued that security within Europe will be enhanced through better co-operation against and the adoption of the *acquis* by the new members. It is unlikely, however, that enlargement will have an immediate effect on the organised crime situation. Most of the provisions of the Schengen Agreement are not yet in force, which means that border controls will remain in place for individuals for some time; the same is true for restrictions on labour migration.

Corruption remains a priority concern in Europe and a major factor facilitating organised crime. A survey carried out in October 2003 in twenty-eight EU member, accession and candidate countries showed that respondents were particularly concerned about corruption and fraud.[1] Asymmetries within Europe are also obvious with regard to corruption: in 2004, Transparency International's Corruption Perception Index listed seven Council of Europe member states among the ten least corrupt countries worldwide, while a number of others ranked rather low. Several European countries are considered major bribe payers.

---

1. See the Eurobarometer survey at http://europa.eu.int/comm/public_opinion

Research[1] shows significant statistical correlations between governance indicators and indicators of human development for European countries. This means that human development (income, education, health) go hand in hand with accountability, political stability, effectiveness of public administration, rule of law and control of corruption. And, the better the performance in terms of governance, the less a country is affected by organised crime.[2]

Economy

Research suggests that legal and illegal markets operate following similar principles, in that legal and illegal economic activities are both subjected to the dynamics of supply and demand and display similar business-like behaviour when considering lucrative opportunities.

The process of economic globalisation thus alters the conditions not only for legal but also for illegal activities:

- Asymmetries. Globalisation may further multiply asymmetries which are believed to be criminogenic. According to the Human Development Index of the United Nations Development Programme, Europe accounts for fifteen of the world's twenty most developed nations. However, there are a number of Council of Europe member states with only a medium level of human development. At the same time, while asymmetries within Europe are substantial, they are even larger between Europe and other parts of the world, including some in the immediate neighbourhood.

- Transnational organised crime. When the term organised crime appeared in Chicago in the 1930s it was about criminals pursing crime as a business in a given city or territory which they sought to keep under their control, often in relation to the supply of a prohibited drug, in this instance alcohol. In present times, as legitimate business globalises, so does crime. Now, transnational organised crime is able to exploit business opportunities worldwide to increase profits and – caused by weak controls – at reduced risk. Managers of organised crime groups and networks are separated from the location of crime, and thus virtually invisible.

---

1. See Kaufmann et al. 2003.
2. Van Dijk 2003, and Van der Heijden and Landman 2004.

Table 1: Asymmetries in human development in Europe[1]

Country	Population (millions) 2003	Gross nat. income/ capita (US$) 2003	Human devel. rank 2004	Corruption Perception Index rank 2004	Recorded criminal offences 2000	Convictions 2000	Prison population 2004
					Per 100 000 inhabitants in 2000		
Albania	*****3.4	1 740	65	108	149	117	105
Andorra	0.07						90
Armenia	3.2	3 770	82	82	360	203	92
Austria	8.1	26 720	14	13	6 891	512	100
Azerbaijan	8.2	810	91	140	*73	*197	198
Belgium	10.4	25 820	6	17	**8 558	1 446	88
Bosnia and Herzegovina	****3.8	1 540	66	82			67
Bulgaria	7.8	2 130	56	54	1 779	388	127
Croatia	4.4	5 350	48	67	1 597	403	68
Cyprus	0.8		30	36	575	**126	50
Czech Republic	10.2	6 740	32	51	3 811	615	182
Denmark	5.4	33 750	17	3	9 447	**767	70
Estonia	1.4	4 960	36	31	4 038	717	330
Finland	5.2	27 020	13	1	10 262	3 351	69
France	59.6	24 770	16	22	6 405	957	91
Georgia	4.3	830	97	133	269	173	165
Germany	82.5	25 250	19	15	7 616	1 071	96
Greece	10.6	13 720	24	49	3 482		83
Hungary	10.1	6 330	38	42	4 445	1 034	165
Iceland	0.29		7	3		*719	40
Ireland	4.0	26 960	10	17	1 928	193	85
Italy	****56.3	21 560	21	42	**4 123	**484	100
Latvia	2.3	4 070	50	57	2 087	528	339
Liechtenstein	0.03						53
Lithuania	3.5	4 490	41	44	2 275	571	234
Luxembourg	0.4		15	13	5 216		111
Malta	0.4		31	25	4 345		72
Moldova	3.6	590	113	114	864	360	297
Monaco	0.03						39
Netherlands	16.2	26 310	5	10	8 215	658	123
Norway	4.5	43 350	1	8	3 278	1 427	65
Poland	38.2	5 270	37	67	3 278	577	209
Portugal	10.4	12 130	26	27	3 616	534	128

1. Sources:
UNDP 2003 for human development ranking (based on education, life expectancy and gross domestic product in purchasing power parities per capita);
World Bank 2005 for gross national income per capita;
Transparency International Corruption Perception Index 2004 for corruption;
International Centre for Prision studies for prison population 2004
(http://www.kcl.ac.uk/depsta/rel/icps/worldbrief/europe_records.php?code=165)
WODC 2003 with data on crime for 2000 unless indicated otherwise:
*UNODC 2002   **in 1999   ***data for England and Wales only;
Council of Europe 2003 with population data for 2003 unless indicated otherwise:

****in 2002   *****in 2000.

Country	Population (millions) 2003	Gross nat. income/ capita (US$) 2003	Human devel. rank 2004	Corruption Perception Index rank 2004	Recorded criminal offences 2000	Convictions 2000	Prison population 2004
Romania	21.8	2 310	69	87	1 578	338	180
Russian Federation	143.1	2 610	57	90	2 022	811	532
San Marino	0.03						0
Serbia and Montenegro	****10.7	1 910		97			92/ 108
Slovakia	5.4	4 920	42	57	1 642	399	164
Slovenia	2.0	11 830	27	31	3 614	358	59
Spain	40.7	16 990	20	22	2 308	*254	139
Sweden	8.9	28 840	2	6	13 693	1 338	75
Switzerland	7.3	39 880	11	7	3 732	**971	72
"The former Yugoslav Republic of Macedonia"	****2.0	1 980	60	97	*976	*366	78
Turkey	69.6	2 790	88	77	712	*1 512	95
Ukraine	48.0	970	70	122	1 126	470	415
United Kingdom	59.3	28 350	12	11	*** 9 817	*** 2 684	*** 140

- "Traditional" crime markets. As globalisation facilitates the expansion of international trade in almost any sector, so does it facilitate transnational operations of criminal organisations in classical crime markets, such as trafficking in drugs, arms, vehicles, cigarettes and others. Considering asymmetries in human development and push and pull factors for migration, it may seem logical that human beings are a particularly valuable commodity to be smuggled, trafficked and exploited.

- Organised economic crime. While traditional crime markets remain important, globalisation offers new opportunities in terms of fraud, financial crime and other forms of economic crime which are believed to be many times more profitable and at the same time less risky. For many eastern European countries, tax fraud, capital flight and crimes committed in the process of privatisation appear to be of greater relevance than traditional organised crime. The distinction between, on the one hand, legal enterprises employing illegal means for business, committing economic crimes or making use of crime proceeds and, on the other hand, organised crime groups created for the purpose of committing crimes but managed like business enterprises and investing proceeds in the legal economy may becomes less clear. Considering the increasing power of transnational corporations in the context of economic globalisation, organised economic crime raises additional questions with regard to governance.

Sociocultural tendencies

It is often argued that organised crime is facilitated by particular cultural factors and the existence of subcultures with little attachment to mainstream social groups. Organised crime can have a cultural basis in that criminal networks function as an alternative social system or that bonding mechanisms are based on trust, ethnicity or family ties. Ethnic networks are believed to play a significant role in the development of transnational organised crime, especially where immigrant groups have not been fully integrated in their new society. Events in Iraq and continued violence in the near East may further contribute to asymmetries based on cultural, religious and ethnic identity. On the other hand, however, reports by member states suggest that the explanatory value of ethnicity loses its significance over time with more and more organised crime groups and networks showing a multi-ethnic composition. With regard to economic crime, it would appear that organised criminals are predominantly nationals of the country in which the crime is committed (although they may target victims in other countries, thus making the crime a transnational one). Ethnic relationships may not necessarily fulfil the requirements of an environment calling for flexible, adaptable and international networks

Technology and science

The development of information and communication technologies (ICT) and the expansion of the Internet not only change the ways societies communicate but also how societies organise themselves. This creates opportunities for organised crime in that it provides criminals with new tools to commit old types of crime as well as with tools and markets for new types of crime.[1] ICT may also have an impact on the structure of criminal organisations and the management of criminal enterprises. It has been argued that societies and economies built around ICT follow a networking logic rather than one of clear hierarchies.[2] If – as has been stated earlier – organised crime groups are shaped by their environment, one may assume that this logic will increasingly apply to organised crime as network-based organisations.

Given the relevance of ICT for European societies, the potential impact of cybercrime and the many open questions regarding the relationship between organised crime and cybercrime, this year's situation report contains a specific chapter dedicated to the topic of cybercrime.

---

1. See Europol 2002.
2. See Castells 2003, p. 21.

Chapter 2 – The organised crime situation

Knowledge of organised crime depends on controls. Only those criminal activities which are investigated or analysed from an organised crime angle become visible as such. The understanding of the phenomenon thus depends to a large extent on law enforcement priorities and on what a society considers to be particular threats at a given moment in time. Considering the diversity of the forty-six countries which are members of the Council of Europe, organised crime in Europe takes many forms and involves a large variety of criminal activities. However, there are three crime markets which are common to most countries in Europe:

- fraud and other forms of economic crime;
- drug production and trafficking;
- people as commodity in the form of smuggling of persons and trafficking in human beings.

Drug trafficking has been a quasi-synonym for organised crime in Europe for some decades. In contrast, the general perception of smuggling of persons and trafficking in human beings as key problems of organised crime is a relatively recent development. Reporting, now also by countries of central and eastern Europe, of fraud and other forms of economic crime as one of the main markets of organised crime in terms of volume and economic impact is a new trend.

Money laundering is a key issue in Europe and gains in importance as organised crime groups and networks make more and more use of legal commercial structures and as the boundaries between legal and illegal structures – between the upper- and the underworld – become increasingly blurred.

Some other markets and criminal activities – that is, smuggling in cigarettes and other commodities, and trafficking in arms – are mentioned in this report. Many more remain important in different member states, but have not been elaborated in this particular report: these include stolen vehicles, smuggling in cultural property, counterfeiting or extortion and racketeering.[1]

---

1. See the country summaries below.

The sub-chapter on organised crime groups and networks reveals certain difficulties in the identification of organised crime groups. As "organising for crime" may take many different forms, network analyses and – with proceeds as the common denominator of organised crime – analyses of money flows may help overcome conceptual problems, provided that they are collected systematically.

Modi operandi continue to include the use of violence and intimidation. However, the use of influence, including corruption, and the use of legal professionals and commercial structures point at the importance of symbiotic relationships between organised crime and parts of the state and society. Most organised criminals are nationals of the country in which the crime is detected. At the same time, many of them are connected to networks in other countries, confirming that even though its effects may be experienced primarily at the local level, organised crime is increasingly transnational in nature.

Crime markets

Economic crime

Economic crime has been of major concern to European societies for decades, but a clear definition still raises certain difficulties. The Council of Europe's recommendation of 1981[1] lists sixteen specific and non-specific offences which are considered economic crimes:[2]

1. cartel offences;
2. fraudulent practices and abuse of economic situation by multinational companies;

---

1. Recommendation No. R (81) 12 on economic crime adopted by the Committee of Ministers on 25 June 1981. Already in 1973, European Ministers of Justice had requested the Council of Europe to analyse the question of economic crime and to develop an appropriate definition of offences. Fraud, including fiscal fraud, and in particular "problems connected with international companies" were believed to cause the greatest damage to European societies. Given the importance of economic crime and that the situation has evolved since 1981 it may be worthwhile considering a review and update of Recommendation No. R (81) 12.
2. The non-specific offences nos. 3, 4, 9 and 12 to 16 are only to be considered economic crime "when they caused or risked causing substantial loss, presuppose special business knowledge on the part of the offenders, and were committed by businessmen in the exercise of their profession or functions".

3. fraudulent procurement or abuse of state or international organisations' grants;

4. computer crime (e.g. theft of data, violation of secrets, manipulation of computerised data);

5. bogus firms;

6. faking of company balance sheets and book-keeping offences;

7. fraud concerning economic situation and corporate capital of companies;

8. violation by a company of standards of security and health concerning employees;

9. fraud to the detriment of creditors (e.g. bankruptcy, violation of intellectual and industrial property rights);

10. consumer fraud (in particular falsification of and misleading statements on goods, offences against public health, abuse of consumers' weakness or inexperience);

11. unfair competition (including bribery of an employee of a competing company) and misleading advertising;

12. fiscal offences and evasion of social costs by enterprises;

13. customs offences (e.g. evasion of customs duties, breach of quota restrictions);

14. offences concerning money and currency regulations;

15. stock exchange and bank offences (e.g. fraudulent stock exchange manipulation and abuse of the public's inexperience);

16. offences against the environment.

The recommendation is based on the assumption that economic crime has adverse impact beyond individual victims and the material damage in that: (a) it affects a large number of persons, society and the state in general; (b) it damages the functioning of the national or international economy; and (c) it causes a loss of trust and confidence in the economic system.[1]

The drafters of the "Guiding principles on the fight against organised crime" pointed at the "strong correlation between organised crime and economic crime, in particular corruption, money laundering and fraud".[2] However, a distinction between organised crime and economic crime poses certain problems.

---

1. More than twenty years later, similar assumptions are still used in the reporting on economic crime. See, for example, Germany's situation report on economic crime (Bundeskriminalamt (BKA) 2003a).

2. See paragraph 28 of the Explanatory Memorandum to Recommendation Rec(2001) 11.

Reconceptualising organised crime as enterprise crime,[1] the "new mafias" appear less involved in predatory crimes such as theft, kidnapping, contract killing or extortion, but rather act like "regular" businessmen investing in the legal economy, exploiting business opportunities and analysing cost, benefits and risks.[2]

The starting points of organised crime and economic crime may be different: a priori, legal enterprises are created for legal business but may turn to fraud and other illegal practices in legal markets, use corruption and create cartels and monopolies or become involved in criminal markets, while on the other hand, criminal enterprises are created for the purpose of committing crimes even if they invest in the legal economy. In practice, however, economic and organised crimes share characteristics, and the boundaries are rather blurred. It has been argued that both rely on similar illegal know-how and values, use similar techniques, are performed by organised structures, and thrive on collusion; and that a division between organised crime and economic crime would seem artificial in particular in post-communist countries.[3] In the modern knowledge economy, hierarchy and inflexibility work neither for legal nor illegal businesses and despite the power and scale of multinationals, most criminal and legitimate firms operate in looser networks.

In any event, the turnover of economic crime is believed to dwarf the cost and damage of ordinary crime.

The acceleration of economic globalisation since the 1980s – based on the integration of global financial markets and a free-market strategy (fiscal austerity, privatisation, market liberalisation and reduction of trade barriers) – and the end of the East-West conflict multiplied the opportunities for economic crime in Europe. In European "states in transition" the opportunities are related to privatisation, the exploitation and export of raw materials, and emerging financial and banking sectors, accompanied by capital flight, tax evasion, corruption, money laundering and organised crime.[4]

---

1. And despite the view of some authorities that "protection racketeering" and conflict brokerage services constitute the essential characteristics of "mafia".

2. See Nelken 2002 and Cartier-Bresson 1997. According to the BKA reports on economic crime (BKA 2003a) and organised crime (BKA 2003), with €796 million, organised crime made the largest profits through economic and financial crime, that is, primarily through credit fraud, investment fraud, fraud related to commodity futures trading, etc.

3. Nelken 2002, quoting Ruggiero.

4. See Stiglitz 2002 on "Mafia capitalism".

Following the multi-billion dollar financial fraud and misconduct schemes of Enron, WorldCom and Tyco International, the Parmalat scandal at the end of 2003 showed that economic crime of this magnitude is also possible in Europe.

An increasing number of European countries report different forms of economic crime in their assessment of the organised crime situation. These include:

- VAT fraud. Large-scale VAT fraud has been reported by several EU member states (such as Belgium, Poland, Portugal, United Kingdom) and includes "registered and unregistered evader fraud" in cash-based businesses, "thief fraud" by setting up bogus company registrations to steal VAT, and in particular missing trader intra-community (MITC) fraud, that is, VAT carousels.

- Public procurement. Public contracts are a major market for criminal organisations in many countries. Not only fraud and corruption, but also cartel formation, intimidation and violence may be used to monopolise access to public contracts (as reported by Italy for all Mafia-type associations).

- Privatisation. In several countries of the former Soviet Union but also in South-Eastern Europe, the power of organised crime groups and networks is based on assets acquired during the privatisation process (primarily in the 1990s, but continuing today) under unclear legal conditions and reportedly with the involvement of senior political leaders and state officials.

- Counterfeiting of legal products. Counterfeiting has become a highly organised business managed by international entrepreneurs and a very profitable form of organised crime. Some 85 million products were intercepted in the European Union in 2002.[1]

- Investment fraud. Fraud schemes involving non-existing companies and fictitious commodities and services are common in many European countries.

- Fraud against the European Union's financial interest. In 2002, identified fraud related to "traditional own resources" amounted to

---

1. See Union des Fabricants 2004.

€324 million, fraud related to agricultural expenditure to about €198 million and fraud related to structural measures to €614 million. A considerable increase is noted in all areas compared to 2001, but in particular in structural measures (+ 290%).

- A study on organised environmental crime showed only 122 cases for the period from 1992 to 2003 in EU member states but suggests that this field has been underreported. Some 73% of the cases researched showed involvement of corporations or corporate-like structures.[1]

Although difficulties in reporting remain – some countries include all fraud and major economic crime cases in their assessment of the organised crime situation and others none – the following general statements are possible:

- Economic crime accounts for a large number of cases detected. Estonia recorded 2 129 fraud and major economic crime cases in 2003 (compared to 1 080 cases of drug trafficking, that is, the second largest category). Moldova recorded 2 892 such cases (compared to 2 377 cases of drug trafficking). In Serbia (Serbia and Montenegro), 492 (or 61%) of all organised crime cases recorded were related to fraud and major economic crime. In the Russian Federation, more than 370 000 cases of economic crime – including fraud, embezzlement of state funds, counterfeiting, smuggling, tax evasion, illegal entrepreneurship, and others – were recorded in 2002 with an economic damage of almost 40 billion roubles.

- A substantial number of organised crime groups and networks are involved in economic crime. In Belgium, 124 criminal organisations (that is, 24% of the criminal organisations identified in 2003) had financial and economic crime as their main activity (41 of them in excise and VAT fraud and another 40 in various forms of swindling). Similarly in Bulgaria (25%), the Netherlands (26%) and Slovakia (26%), compared to 13.5% in Germany and 6% in Lithuania. In Finland, 8% of offences involving members of organised crime groups and networks were believed to be related to crimes against the economy. In Sweden, economic crime – ranging from tax fraud to investment fraud – is considered the most important market next to drugs.

---

1. Management summary of the study "Organised environmental crime in the 15 EU Member States" prepared by BfU for the European Commission in 2004.

- The proceeds and the material damage of economic crime cases appear to exceed those of other forms of crime. Surveys estimate the economic cost of fraud in the United Kingdom at £14 billion annually.[1] In Germany, 1.3% of all offences were economic crimes in 2003. However, this small share of offences was responsible for 57% (or €6.8 billion) of all material damage.[2] Economic crimes accounted for 13.5% of the offences committed by organised crime groups and networks, but for 54% (€280 million) of the material damage and 35% (€164 million) of the profits generated by organised crime, mostly through credit, investment and public procurement fraud.

- With the growth in economic crime, links to organised crime are increasing. In Belgium, 70% of the criminal organisations identified in 2003 used commercial structures in one or more sectors (such as import-export, transport and the catering industry, construction, services and banking). Similar figures have been reported from the Netherlands. In Germany, the use of legal commercial or business-like structures in connection with a criminal offence is a key indicator of the working definition of organised crime.

- In some European countries it is believed that economic crime constitutes a major threat to the economy and society. In Germany, it is considered a "structural crime" distorting market mechanisms and undermining trust and confidence in the economic and legal system. In Norway, economic crime is seen to increase in complexity and organisation, becoming more and more transnational in nature, and thus a priority issue. In contrast, in Switzerland it is assumed that the damage of economic crime will continue to amount to between 2% and 4% of GDP but that is "does not constitute a threat to the economic, social and political integrity of the country".[3] Although the absolute sums lost through economic crime may be lower in some central and east European countries, the social damage may be greater because the domestic and international public may have less confidence in the economic and political systems.

---

1. Including cigarette smuggling, which in the present report is dealt with in a separate chapter.

2. BKA 2004.

3. Bundesamt für Polizei 2004, p. 43.

Trafficking in drugs

The international drug control system is based on three United Nations conventions[1] which restrict the use of several hundred psychoactive substances to medical and scientific use. Abuse of these substances – primarily of opiates (including heroin), cannabis, cocaine and crack cocaine, and amphetamine-type stimulants (ATS, including ecstasy, amphetamines and other synthetic stimulants) – is a major global issue. It is believed that currently 185 million people worldwide (or 3% of the global population) use drugs, of which 79% cannabis, 20% ATS, 7% cocaine, 5% heroin and 3% other opiates.[2] Most drug users live in developing countries.

Almost all of the heroin consumed in Europe is based on opium from Afghanistan. The Balkan route continues to be the main channel for trafficking of heroin to Europe. However, as the Russian Federation and other countries in eastern Europe become major markets themselves, the Silk Route from Afghanistan via central Asia becomes more significant. Ethnic Albanian criminal groups are reportedly responsible for a large part of the wholesale distribution of heroin in Europe.

Cocaine is produced from coca leaves cultivated in Bolivia, Colombia and Peru and primarily destined for the United States and other American countries. A significant share is trafficked to Europe as reflected in European seizures, which in 2002 accounted for 13% of global seizures. Spain and the Netherlands are considered the most important entry points for cocaine.

Cannabis production is spread over 142 countries around the world. Although Morocco is the main supplier for European markets, domestic production is believed to satisfy a considerable share of demand. Albania and the Netherlands appear to be the main producers within Europe.

In terms of ATS, the main producers of methamphetamines are countries in Southeast Asia and the USA and Mexico. The main producers for amphetamines and ecstasy are located in Europe with the Netherlands as the largest supplier followed by Poland, and to a lesser extent Belgium, the Baltic states, the United Kingdom and Germany. Dutch organised crime groups and

---

1. The Single Convention on Narcotic Drugs (1961), the Convention on Psychotropic Substances (1971) and the Convention against Illicit Traffic in Narcotic Drugs and Psychotropic Substances (1988).
2. Obviously, this includes poly-drug use. Data according to UNODC 2004, p. 8. While 3% use substances under international control, 30% of the world's population uses tobacco.

networks play a major role in the trafficking of ecstasy to European markets and beyond.

Recent reports and data suggest the following trends and issues:

- Considering purchasing power and numbers of drug users – not only in western but now also in central and eastern Europe – Europe is probably the most profitable market globally:

    – within the European Union (EU 15), between 1 and 1.5 million people are believed to be problem drug users, including 0.6 to 0.9 million drug injectors.[1] Surveys suggest that in the new EU member states, drug use has reached similar levels;[2]
    – with regard to heroin, the Russian Federation with between 3 and 4 million drug users, of whom more than 1 million are heroin users, appears to have become the largest European market for heroin. The prevalence rate of 2.1%[3] is among the highest in the world. The Russian Federation also has one of the highest HIV/Aids rates related to intravenous drug use in the world.[4] Prevalence rates are also very high in Latvia (1.7%) and Estonia (1.2%);
    – with regard to cocaine, Spain (2.6%) has the highest prevalence rate in the world, closely followed by Ireland (2.4%) and the United Kingdom (2.1%);[5]
    – rates in terms of cannabis use in Europe are highest in the Czech Republic (10.9%) and the United Kingdom (10.6%);
    – Amphetamine use in Europe is highest in Ireland (1.6%), the United Kingdom (1.6%) and Denmark (1.3%), while ecstasy use in Ireland (3.4%), the Czech Republic (2.5%) and the United Kingdom (2.0%) is among the highest in the world.

- Drug trafficking is considered one of the most important activities of organised crime groups and networks in Europe, and the primary problem – at least in terms of numbers of cases recorded – in the following countries: Albania, Bulgaria, the Czech Republic, Estonia, Finland, Germany, the Netherlands, Portugal, Romania, Slovakia,

---

1. See EMCDDA 2003. "Problem drug use" is defined as "injecting drug use or long duration/regular use of opiates, cocaine and/or amphetamines".
2. See EMCDDA 2003a.
3. Abuse as a percentage of population aged 15-64 (see UNODC 2004, pp. 389 *et seq.*)
4. UNODC 2004, p. 15.
5. Compared to the United States with 2.5%.

Switzerland, "the former Yugoslav Republic of Macedonia", Turkey and the United Kingdom.

- Seizure figures[1] confirm assumptions on drug markets, major trafficking routes and the role of organised crime groups and networks:

    - the United Kingdom (3 929 kg), Italy (2585 kg), Turkey (2 558 kg), the Netherlands (1 122 kg), the Russian Federation (842 kg) and Bulgaria (535 kg) show the highest seizures of heroin in 2002;
    - Spain (17 618 kg) made the largest seizures of cocaine by far, followed by the Netherlands (7 968 kg), Italy (4 049 kg), France (3 660 kg) and Belgium (3 589 kg) in 2002. In 2003, seizures of cocaine more than doubled in the Netherlands (17 500 kg);[2]
    - the United Kingdom (1 716 kg), followed by Belgium (500 kg), the Netherlands (481 kg), Germany (362 kg) and Sweden (350 kg) seized most ATS (including ecstasy) in 2002.

- Increasing numbers of seizures in many central and eastern European countries, in particular of heroin (for example, in Bulgaria, Hungary, Poland and Romania), but also of ATS (for example, Bulgaria and Poland) and to a lesser extent of cocaine (Poland seized 401 kg in 2003), confirm that these countries have become important drug markets.

- Afghanistan remains the largest producer of opium (4 200 metric tonnes or 87% of global production in 2004).[3] Opium poppy cultivation is spreading to new areas within Afghanistan. Obviously, post-Taliban drug control efforts by the international community have failed. This has a considerable impact on Europe, not only in terms of availability of heroin but also in terms of security and stability as well as the credibility of the international community with regard to the reconstruction of Afghanistan.

---

1. Based on UNODC 2004 for the year 2002.

2. "Report on Dutch investigations into organised crime 2003".

3. UNODC 2004b: Afghanistan opium survey 2004. Production in 2004 had increased by 17% when compared to 2003 (3 600 metric tonnes).

Trafficking in human beings

Trafficking in human beings as an issue of human rights and of organised crime has moved higher on the agenda of governments in many countries of Europe – reflected among other things in the ratification of the "trafficking protocol" to the Palermo Convention[1] by twenty-six European countries as at July 2004 and the drafting of a convention against trafficking by the Council of Europe – and higher on the list of law enforcement priorities, as reflected in a number of country reports.

According to Article 3, paragraph a, of the protocol:

> Trafficking in persons shall mean the recruitment, transportation, transfer, harbouring or receipt of persons, by means of the threat or use of force or other forms of coercion, of abduction, of fraud, of deception, of the abuse of power or of a position of vulnerability or of the giving or receiving of payments or benefits to achieve the consent of a person having control over another person, for the purpose of exploitation. Exploitation shall include, as a minimum, the exploitation of the prostitution of others or other forms of sexual exploitation, forced labour or services, slavery or practices similar to slavery, servitude or the removal of organs.

In contrast to the concept of smuggling of migrants with its focus on illegal border crossings, trafficking in human beings is about the violation of the rights of the individual through exploitation. Thus, it is less an issue of migration policies than of the protection of victims and their human rights, and of the punishment of the traffickers and their associates.

The concept of trafficking in human beings implies a strong role of criminal organisations. It includes the threat or use of force, coercion, fraud, deception or other means; it includes several distinct but interrelated acts, and the exploitation is not a one-time event but is carried out over a certain period of time. Organised crime groups and networks exploit market opportunities for sexual services and cheap labour, on the one hand, and the vulnerable situation of women and children in many countries, on the other. Furthermore, they can count on high profits and a relatively low risk of control and sanctions.

---

1. Protocol to Prevent, Suppress and Punish Trafficking in Persons, Especially Women and Children, supplementing the United Nations Convention against Transnational Organized Crime, adopted by Resolution A/RES/55/25 of 15 November 2000 at the Fifty-Fifth Session of the General Assembly of the United Nations.

Although there are many forms of exploitation – according to reports received – in Europe, most victims of trafficking are women and girls who are exploited for sexual purposes. As Europeans spend billions of euro per year on prostitution and other commercial sexual services, trafficking in human beings is a highly profitable business. The market for commercial sexual services is considered a major force driving trafficking. It is therefore no coincidence that the large majority of victims are found in the prostitution sector, and the share of migrant sex workers appears to be ever increasing.

Typically:

- Women respond to job advertisements for babysitters, models, hairdressers, dancers, waitresses, or are encouraged or recruited by friends or relatives.[1]
- Transport and papers are arranged by organised crime groups and networks.
- Identity documents are taken away on arrival and women are confronted with a large debt owed to traffickers which is to be repaid through prostitution.
- Violence may be used to coerce women into prostitution. There are numerous reports of women kept in isolation or beaten or raped in order to "break" them.
- Victims are resold or exchanged between criminal groups and countries in order to ensure the availability of "fresh meat" on the market.

In a number of countries, prostitution or the "red light milieu" serve as an entry point for organised crime groups and networks in a given area. A report on the Russian Federation illustrates this point. "A few pimps can move in with control of a few women and establish a territory, or a manager can pressure a few independent pimps into paying protection fees and collect money from all pimps operating in an area."[2] In this way, individual pimps or smaller criminal organisations are linked to larger organisations through extortion. That is, they have to pay protection money in order to continue their business. This applies to domestic trafficking as well as international trafficking by Russian organisations. Domestic trafficking involves girls (often minors) from rural areas being recruited for the sex industry in urban centres. In order to facilitate international trafficking,

---

1. According to research in Serbia, 64% of recruiters are acquaintances (Nicolic-Ristanovic et al. 2004).

2. IOM 2002, p. 15.

Russian criminals set up fake businesses in destination countries and then issue letters of invitation.

Another expanding market is that of virtual sex. Internet service providers turn increasingly to pornography counting on millions of customers to subscribe to adult websites. New information and communication technologies in turn "facilitate the sexual exploitation of women and children because they enable people to easily buy, sell and exchange millions of images and videos of sexual exploitation of women and children". Reportedly, Budapest serves as a centre for the production of pornography using women trafficked from other countries of central and eastern Europe.[1]

Reports suggest the following trends and issues:

- Trafficking in human beings has become an important market for organised crime groups and networks in many countries, such as in Albania, Belgium, Bulgaria, Croatia, the Czech Republic, Finland, Germany, Italy, Latvia, Lithuania, Moldova, Norway, Romania, Slovakia, Switzerland, "the former Yugoslav Republic of Macedonia", Turkey and Ukraine.[2] For example, in 2003:

    - in Belgium, it is a primary activity of 11% of organised crime groups and networks;
    - in Bulgaria, 50 groups involving 221 suspects were detected. Organised crime groups and networks control prostitution in major cities. Bulgaria also serves as transit country for victims from Ukraine, the Russian Federation, Romania and Moldova;
    - in Germany, sixty-one cases of trafficking were recorded;
    - with regard to Italy, recent research estimates the annual number of victims at up to 5 280, with annual profits from the sale and sexual exploitation of women ranging from €380 million to €950 million;[3]

---

1. Hughes, 2002, p. 131.

2. According to the replies to the questionnaire received from member states. The same may be true for other countries which did not submit their reports. Sweden, on the other hand, noted that not a single case of trafficking in human beings or smuggling of persons in relation to organised crime was recorded in 2003, the reason being that the "present legislation (…) strongly restricts the possibility of proving this organised crime' (National Criminal Investigation Department 2004, "Organised crime in Sweden 2004", Stockholm).

3. Transcrime 2004, pp. 81 and 82). Data for 1999/2000.

- in Lithuania, twenty cases of trafficking and another twenty-nine cases of procuring for prostitution were investigated in connection with organised crime;
- in Moldova, only 27 cases of trafficking – but 575 cases of smuggling of persons – were detected;
- in Romania, 1 203 cases of trafficking were recorded, involving 384 organised crime groups and networks and 979 suspects (of which 187 were arrested in 2003);
- in Slovakia, with twenty-eight cases, trafficking in human beings accounts for the second largest number of organised crime cases detected after drug trafficking;
- in "the former Yugoslav Republic of Macedonia", forty-two cases of trafficking with seventy-eight offenders were registered;
- in Ukraine, 94 cases of trafficking were identified.

- Most victims are women and girls who are foreign to the country in which they are exploited. By far most of them are from central and eastern European countries. Moldova, Romania, Ukraine, the Russian Federation, Bulgaria and Lithuania are the most often quoted countries of origin. For example:

  - in Kosovo, 48% of the women assisted by the International Organisation for Migration between 2000 and 2003 were from Moldova, 21% from Romania and 14% from Ukraine. Other sources suggest that in addition to Moldova, a large number of victims are from Bulgaria as well as from Kosovo itself;[1]
  - in Serbia as well, most victims are from Romania, Moldova, Ukraine and the Russian Federation;[2]
  - in Germany, 18% of victims in 2002 were from the Russian Federation, 15% from Lithuania, 11% from Bulgaria and 11% from Ukraine.

- Trafficking in South-Eastern Europe remains a crucial issue. This is facilitated by its geographical location between source countries (such as Moldova, Romania and Ukraine) and first destination countries (in particular Greece and Italy) for trafficking to the European Union, by close co-operation between Albanian, Kosovan-Albanian, Serbian and Macedonian criminal networks, and by corruption among local officials. The international presence in Kosovo, with at times 40 000

---

1. See Amnesty International 2004.
2. Nicolic-Ristanovic et al. 2004.

KFOR troops and more than 250 international organisations and NGOs, created considerable demand for sexual services and turned Kosovo into a major destination area for trafficked women. Between 1999 and 2004, the Unmik list of bars and establishments to be "off-limit" by Kfor and Unmik staff for their suspected involvement in trafficking had increased from 18 in late 1999 and 75 in January 2001 to more than 200 by January 2004. It is believed that Kosovans now also account for a large number of the clients.[1]

- Information from different countries and regions within Europe point at strong and violent trafficking organisations. This seems particularly true for Albanian and Kosovan organisations operating in Belgium, France, Italy, the United Kingdom and other countries. On the other hand, it is important to underline that in most countries trafficking is not only an issue of foreign criminals but also of local organised crime groups and networks. In Italy, Albanian groups co-operate with local Mafia-type associations. In Germany, almost 40% of suspected offenders are nationals.

- In addition to violence and intimidation, corruption appears to be widespread as a tool facilitating trafficking. Trafficking in human beings requires passivity or the active co-operation of public officials (ranging from visa officers, immigration officials and embassy staff to customs and border police, police, local officials and others), often the protection of politicians or persons of influence, and private sector professionals (travel agencies, the catering industry and others) at different stages of the trafficking chain. Co-operation or collusion of law enforcement and criminal justice officials and political persons of influence is furthermore required to protect traffickers in the criminal justice chain.[2]

- The transnational element is most relevant with regard to trafficking in human beings. However, in many countries of central and eastern Europe, internal trafficking has become very important as local markets for sexual services expand. In most European countries, victims are often resold more than once within their country of destination.

---

1. See Unmik Trafficking and Prostitution Investigative Unit (TPIU) "End of year report 2003" and Amnesty International 2004.
2. Council of Europe 2002.

- Children account for a considerable share of the victims. In some countries of South-Eastern Europe, 50% of victims or more are reportedly below the age of 18, that is, they are children.[1] Greece is the primary destination of children trafficked from Albania. According to media reports, in summer 2004 children were smuggled to Athens specifically for organised begging during the Olympic games.[2] The regions of the Czech Republic bordering Germany and Austria are an area of destination for children trafficked by organised crime networks from other eastern European countries and serving as prostitutes for clients from Austria, Germany and other western countries.[3] Switzerland reports that children are increasingly trafficked into the country for the purpose of drug trafficking, theft and prostitution as well as illegal adoption. It is believed that organised crime groups and networks make profits from these adoption schemes.[4] In the United Kingdom, over 18 000 individuals are registered as sex offenders. Most child sex offenders act alone. However, there is "extensive criminal networking" to exchange images or gain access to victims. Such networks are hierarchical and secretive and shield their activities.[5]

- In many countries, trafficking in human beings continues to be considered a question of illegal migration. This has implications for victims (who are denied protection and support), and on law enforcement (where deportation may be preferred to long-term investigations of organised crime). This may explain why, throughout Europe, there are few investigations into organised crime in connection with trafficking in human beings.

---

1. Save the Children 2004.

2. *Süddeutsche Zeitung*, 30 June 2004.

3. See Bell and Pickar 2003.

4. Bundesamt für Polizei 2004.

5. National Criminal Intelligence Service (NCIS) 2003.

Smuggling of persons

Considerable increases in the smuggling of persons and in trafficking in human beings are reflections of globalisation. Both smuggling and trafficking have become major global businesses of organised crime groups and networks.

Demographic trends in Europe are such that the population in the forty-six member states of the Council of Europe is still growing, but at a lower pace, in an uneven manner and with an aging population. In all countries, with the exception of Turkey, fertility is below replacement level. Some fourteen countries show negative natural growth rates, which is only partly compensated by international migration. At least ten countries, including Iceland, Georgia, Armenia, Moldova, Ukraine and a few others have negative migration rates, whereas in twenty-five countries, the number of immigrants exceeds those of emigrants, including San Marino, Cyprus, Portugal, Switzerland, Luxembourg, Spain, Liechtenstein, Belgium, Sweden and Germany.[1]

According to the International Organisation for Migration, of the 130 million international migrants globally, some 20 to 40 million are irregular migrants, and at any time about 4 million irregular migrants are on the move. Europe is an attractive destination. Some 300 000 to 450 000 irregular migrants are believed to enter the well-off countries of western Europe annually. At the same time, requests for asylum in 2003 reached the lowest level for 20 years, and in 2003 had decreased again by 20% compared to 2002.[2]

The Protocol to the United Nations Convention on Transnational Organized Crime defines smuggling of persons as:

> (…) the procurement, in order to obtain directly or indirectly, a financial or other material benefit, of the illegal entry of a person in to a State Party of which the person is not a national or permanent resident.[3]

---

1. See Council of Europe 2003.

2. UNHCR data for EU 25, Bulgaria, Liechtenstein, Romania and Switzerland (quoted in *Die Tageszeitung*, 25 August 2004).

3. Article 3 of the Protocol against the Smuggling of Migrants by Land, Sea and Air, supplementing the United Nations Convention against Transnational Organized Crime. By July 2004, the Smuggling Protocol had been ratified by twenty-one European countries.

In Europe, smuggling of persons – as one expression of illegal migration – is a politically highly charged issue and has been on top of the European Union's agenda for some time, among other things in connection with EU enlargement, free movement of people and access to labour markets, or xenophobia and racism.

With regard to smuggling of persons and organised crime the following trends and issues are to be noted:

- An increasing number of European countries report on organised crime in connection with smuggling of persons. These reports suggest a strong role of organised crime groups and networks with growing sophistication in the means used for the smuggling of persons, as well as co-operation of different local criminal groups along the smuggling routes. For example:

  - Bulgaria remains a transit country for illegal migration from Turkey to Greece and Italy via Serbia and Montenegro, and to Hungary via Romania. Smugglers sometimes provide migrants with Bulgarian identity documents. Some fifteen organised crime groups with sixty-three suspects were recorded in 2003;
  - in Croatia, smuggling of persons – with 157 cases in 2003 (involving 4 organised crime groups and networks and 156 suspects) – represents the category with the largest number of organised crime related cases;
  - in the Czech Republic, smuggling of persons is considered one of the most profitable markets of organised crime groups and networks;
  - in Germany, 61 cases with 1 321 suspects were reported in 2003;
  - in Italy, recent research suggests that smuggling operations are mainly carried out by foreign organisations based on ethnicity (Albanian, Chinese and Turkish hierarchical groups or networks of Serbian/Croatian or Romanian criminals) with Italian criminals in a supporting role;[1]
  - Moldova recorded 575 cases of smuggling related to organised crime in 2003, including 25 organised crime groups and networks and 825 suspects;
  - in Slovenia too, smuggling of persons is the category with the largest number of organised crime related cases: 165 cases with 16 organised crime groups and networks and 644 suspects in

---

1. Transcrime 2004, pp. 191 *et seq.*

2003. However, it also believed that more effective border controls led to a continued decrease over the past four years;

– Switzerland is an important transit and destination country. Smuggling organisations are becoming increasingly professional, in particular in the forgery of travel documents, and diversify to other types of crime such as trafficking in drugs, arms and human beings;

– Turkey is a major source and transit country for irregular migrants bound for western Europe, as well as a destination country for people from Moldova, Romania, the Russian Federation and Ukraine who come to Turkey to work there illegally. Reports suggest that in 2003 security forces in Turkey apprehended more than 56 000 irregular migrants,[1] 28% of them from Pakistan, 10% from Turkey, 9% from Somalia, 9% from Iraq and 8% from Afghanistan;

– in the United Kingdom, "organised immigration crime" is considered one of the main threats of organised crime. Language and the presence of ethnic communities contribute to making the UK a particularly attractive destination. It is believed that most illegal migration "takes the form of a multi-stage journey, with migrants being passed from criminal to criminal along a chain of territorially-restricted criminal networks".[2]

■ According to Interpol, the following routes are of particular relevance for Europe:[3]

– from Asian countries through the central Asian republics to the Russian Federation, and from there via Ukraine, Slovakia and the Czech Republic to western Europe;

– from Asian countries via Iran and Turkey along the "classical" Balkan route to western Europe;

– from sub-Saharan Africa via northern Africa and the Strait of Gibraltar to Spain or to Italy.

Increasingly vessels are used to smuggle persons to Europe, often at high risk to their lives. Several hundred people die every year

---

1. A considerable decrease compared to 83 000 in 2002, and 92 000 in 2001. See www.byegm.gov.tr/yayinlarimiz/newspot/2004/mar-apr/n8.htm

2. NCIS 2003.

3. www.interpol.org

between northern Africa and southern Europe on their journey across the Mediterranean Sea.[1]

- While the protocols to the United Nations Convention on Transnational Organized Crime make a distinction between trafficking in human beings and smuggling of persons – trafficking in human beings is not limited to illegal border crossing or entry but involves continued exploitation – in some European countries, however, no difference is made, and reports mix up smuggling and trafficking. This may be due to the "economics" of law enforcement – smuggled persons are illegal immigrants who can be deported, while trafficked persons are victims requiring protection – but also to the fact that in reality, smuggling may only turn into trafficking in the course of the operation. For example, smuggled persons may be exploited in the form of forced labour or prostitution to repay debts to smugglers, though this may not be apparent to them or the enforcement agencies at an earlier stage.

- The fight against smuggling of persons may have unintended negative consequence from a human rights point of view. As legal entry to the European Union becomes more difficult and border controls more tight, migrants increasingly rely on smuggling organisations to arrange their transport. This is not only true for "economic migrants" but also for refugees. It has been argued that from the 1980s – and in particular after the end of the cold war – the question of asylum for political refugees has first been turned into a problem of immigration control, and that more recently the sealing off of the outer borders of the European Union and initiatives like the Smuggling Protocol of the United Nations, by leaving no legal routes open, led to a criminalisation of refugees, pushing them into the hands of smugglers:[2]

Recent research has made two things clear:
- The vast majority of asylum seekers who reach Europe have required the assistance of a "human smuggler" at some stage of their journey.
- The effect of blanket enforcement measures has been to push asylum seekers from using safer forms of "deceptive" migration (e.g. using a regular air flight on a forged travel document) to "clandestine" means

---

1. It is believed that more than 3 000 people were killed between 1995 and 2003 when trying to reach Spain; and more than 400 in 2003 when trying to reach Sicily. In August 2004, twenty-eight drowned before reaching Sicily.
2. Morrison 2001.

which are both more expensive and hazardous to the women, children and men involved (e.g. being locked in the back of a lorry).

Smuggling of tobacco and other commodities

Smuggling of commodities involves the illegal transport of such commodities across borders in order to evade taxes on these goods. Organised crime exploits the differential taxes of highly taxed goods such as cigarettes, alcohol and petroleum. According to reports received, in most European countries, smuggling is a market of organised crime – albeit, a limited one.[1] Exceptions include Sweden (reporting high levels of alcohol and cigarette smuggling) and Serbia (a large range of legal and counterfeited goods).

However, there is one area of which a number of countries have expressed concern, namely the smuggling of cigarettes.

Europe plays a major role in world tobacco markets. Council of Europe member states account for some 30% of the world's cigarette production, 60% of global exports and more than 50% of global imports. It is estimated that some 25% of cigarettes produced globally or more than 210 billion cigarettes (the difference between reported exports and imports) go to the black market. Of these about one third are believed to be smuggled into and within Council of Europe member states.

Recent information suggests the following:

- Principal departure and smuggling routes include:[2]

    - Southeast Asia: China is an important country of departure or transhipment with the principal destinations being the United Kingdom, Belgium and Germany. Transit countries for cigarettes from Southeast Asia include, in particular, the United Arab Emirates. Turkey has also emerged as a major transit country;
    - Baltic routes: cigarettes are exported from the United Kingdom, the Netherlands and Germany to central and eastern

1. No recent information has been received with regard to the smuggling of petroleum products, metals (such as nickel, copper and cobalt) and other natural resources, which in the 1990s – purchased locally at subsidised prices and then smuggled abroad and sold at world market prices – contributed to the "criminalisation of economies" in several countries of the former Soviet Union.
2. See Regional Intelligence Liaison Office for Western Europe (RILO) 2001.

Europe, but instead of being delivered at their final destinations they are smuggled back to western Europe;

– eastern Europe via central European countries: interceptions in Germany and Poland show the Russian Federation, but also Moldova and Romania, as countries of origin;

– South-Eastern Europe: Greece appears to be one of the major countries of departure for smuggled cigarettes in Europe, while Italy is a key destination and transit country.

The United Kingdom (more than 2 600 metric tonnes), Italy (502 metric tonnes seized in 2002), Germany (461 metric tonnes), Belgium (345 metric tonnes) and Spain (245 metric tonnes) account for the largest seizures in the European Union.[1] In Sweden, seizures in 2003 amounted to more than 74 million cigarettes (compared to 27 million in 2002). Smuggled cigarettes are most often concealed behind legal freight.

- Tobacco smuggling, on the one hand, is a question of tax evasion. Revenues from the taxation of cigarettes are important to many governments. Losses in national tax revenues have been estimated at €16 billion globally. Criminal organisations take advantage of the in-transit system, which allows for the temporary suspension of taxes and duties in order to facilitate international trade. Smuggling organisations use intermediary companies to place orders for manufactured tobacco products which are then shipped to warehouses. In Europe, the main warehousing facilities for transit cigarettes are presently located in Hamburg, Antwerp and Rotterdam. Other important locations include Salonika (Greece) or tax-free zones in Switzerland. The purchasing company subsequently gives instructions for the cigarettes to be transported to other countries outside the European Union. "The multiple transactions carried out before illegal shipments reach their final destination have the sole purpose of concealing the true purchaser, whose role is to supply the smuggling organisations."[2] Cigarettes are then provided with new papers and channelled to the local black market or smuggled back into the EU. The fact that in many countries tobacco smuggling is primarily considered an issue of tax evasion hampers effective international co-operation, as countries are reluctant to enforce each others' revenue codes, that is, to co-operate on tax matters.

---

1. Council of the European Union 2003.
2. Ibid.

- Tobacco smuggling undermines public health policies. European countries are among those with the highest smoking prevalence in the world, with disturbingly high figures already for 12- to 14-year-old teenagers.[1] About 1.2 of the globally 4.2 million premature smoking-related deaths annually are Europeans. Price levels for cigarettes seem to be the most critical factor preventing or supporting smoking, in particular among young people. The availability of cheap, smuggled cigarettes and pressure from the tobacco industry on governments to reduce taxes seriously undermines prevention policies.

- Tobacco smuggling is a question of organised crime and bad governance. Organised crime networks exploit opportunities and weak control structures, and use fraud, corruption and sometimes violence to smuggle legally produced as well as counterfeited cigarettes. The law enforcement response is weak in many countries; reportedly sometimes organised crime groups and networks act in collusion with corrupt public authorities. Criminal groups also operate in the organisation of the black market once cigarettes arrive in the country of destination.[2] The assumption that tobacco smuggling is less determined by tax levels than by organised crime groups and networks and weak controls helps explain why several high-tax countries show low levels of smuggling while many low-price countries report high levels of smuggling.[3] The share of black market cigarettes in western Europe is much lower than in central and eastern European countries. Moreover, it is not the cheap brands that are smuggled but expensive ones such as "West", "Marlboro" or "Winston".

- Though in recent times, under public and legal pressure, some multinational tobacco companies have become more active in combating smuggling of their own licit products as well as counterfeits, some reportedly collaborate in the smuggling of tobacco. Four multinational tobacco companies control more than 40% of the world market. Since the early 1990s, multinational cigarette companies have massively increased their manufacturing capacity in developing countries and eastern Europe, either alone or through joint ventures.

---

1. See WHO Regional Office for Europe 2004.
2. A case study on the illegal cigarette market in Germany shows the patterns of co-operation and power structures of organised crime (including clear-cut horizontal and vertical differentiation, use of violence and efforts to establish exclusive control over the street market) (Von Lampe 2001).
3. Joosens and Raw 1998, p. 67.

41

Even in countries with state-owned companies, they have acquired strong positions on local markets.

A critical stage in the organised smuggling of cigarettes is the interface between the legal and illegal settings, that is, from the moment when untaxed cigarettes are ordered and procured to the moment when they are provided with false papers or moved to the black market. And it is here that multinational tobacco companies allegedly collude with organised criminals using the transit trade, sometimes with the knowledge or involvement of public authorities.

Subject to any reputational or other damage they may suffer from media publicity or law enforcement action, it is the multinational tobacco companies which benefit most from the smuggling in cigarettes:[1]

–   smuggling stimulates demand in that it offers cigarettes at reduced prices to customers while manufacturers make the same profit per cigarette. Indeed, companies may be pressurised to collaborate with the smuggling of cigarettes to maintain their presence in the market, so a vicious circle is maintained;
–   smuggling serves as a market entry strategy in that it makes internationally known brands available at low prices to image-conscious young customers in low-income countries;
–   the fact of smuggling is used by cigarette manufactures to lobby for tax reductions, arguing that high taxes on cigarettes are the main reason for smuggling.

In 2002, the European Community sued American tobacco companies for colluding with criminal organisations resulting in an annual loss in taxes and customs duties for the European Union of billions of euros. Charges included money laundering offences, corruption and trade with terrorist groups and state sponsors of terrorism.[2]

---

1. Joosens and Raw 1998.
2. From the EU appeal of 10 July 2002. See also press release of 31 October 2002. In July 2004, Philip Morris International announced that it had reached a deal with the European Commission under which it would pay a billion dollars to the EC and take measures to control smuggling. In exchange, the EC would drop the US court case (www.ash.org.uk/html/press/040709.html).

Trafficking in arms

The adoption of the Protocol on the Illicit Manufacturing and Traffic in Firearms supplementing the Palermo Convention underlined that there are links between organised crime and the trafficking in arms. While this protocol is limited to portable barrelled weapons, the OSCE in 2000 adopted a broader approach by focusing on small arms and light weapons (SALW), which were defined as follows:

> Small arms and light weapons are man-portable weapons made or modified to military specifications for use as lethal instruments of war. Small arms are broadly categorized as those weapons intended for use by individual members of armed or security forces. They include revolvers and self-loading pistols; rifles and carbines; sub-machine guns; assault rifles; and light machine guns. Light weapons are broadly categorized as those weapons intended for use by several members of armed or security forces serving as a crew. They include heavy machine guns; hand-held under-barrel and mounted grenade launchers; portable anti-aircraft guns; portable anti-tank guns; recoilless rifles; portable launchers of anti-tank missile and rocket systems; portable launchers of anti-aircraft missile systems; and mortars of calibres less than 100 mm.[1]

Global legal trade in SALW has been estimated at US$4 billion in 2000, and illicit traffic at about US$1 billion. More than 1 100 companies in 98 countries are involved in small arms production. The USA and the Russian Federation produce 70% of global firearms, and another thirty countries are considered significant producers. These include eighteen countries of central and eastern Europe. In 2000, the European Union accounted for 43% of documented exports while other European countries had a share of 12%.[2]

In addition to newly produced weapons, a major problem in Europe is the large stocks of surplus weapons which became redundant after the cold war. Securing and disposing of huge stockpiles of surplus arms posed – and in some countries still poses – major challenges to governments. In the 1990s, millions of these weapons were stolen, sold and exported – legally and illegally – to state and non-state actors within Europe and other parts of the world.[3]

---

1. OSCE document on "Small arms and light weapons" (adopted at the 308th Plenary Meeting of the OSCE Forum for Security Co-operation on 24 November 2000).
2. Small Arms Survey 2003.
3. Bonn International Center for Conversion 2004, p. 130.

In particular, the concerns are that:

- trafficking in SALW fuels conflict within Europe, in particular in South-Eastern Europe and the Caucasus region;
- European countries export SALW to crisis regions outside Europe, thus exacerbating conflicts and human rights violations;
- trafficking in SALW contributes to crime and violence within European societies.

While efforts have been made to control exports,[1] the problem is the enforcement of restrictions. There seems to be little control of arms brokers, and there are few prosecutions.

According to surveys by Transparency International, after construction and public works, the arms and defence sector is the one where corruption is most likely to occur. This includes corruption of senior officials to obtain export permits, forgery of end-user certificates, transport across borders and the laundering of the proceeds.

Europe's recent history has seen examples of the links between trafficking in arms and organised crime, and to some extent also terrorism:[2]

- Russian and Italian criminal organisations were operating in the midst of the Yugoslav conflicts;
- between October 1992 and March 1994, Belgian, Italian and Russian criminals co-operated to ship over 13 000 tonnes of arms and ammunition to Croatia and Bosnia in violation of the UN arms embargo;
- Russian organised crime groups and networks in co-operation with Belgian arms dealers shipped 200 tonnes of weapons to Sierra Leone in 1999 and 2000, in violation of UN embargoes;
- ETA and the Real IRA as well as other terrorist movements are believed to obtain their weapons from the areas of the former Yugoslavia;
- in several parts of South-Eastern Europe, the general availability of illegal arms has led to a "gun culture". In "the former Yugoslav Republic of Macedonia", the spread of illegal arms fuelled the conflict in 2001. Arms were mainly smuggled in from Albania and Kosovo, but also by Bulgarian and Macedonian traffickers from Bulgaria.[3]

---

1. See for example the Code of Conduct on Arms Exports adopted by EU members in 1998.

2. See Davis et al. 2001.

3. Matveeva, A. et al. 2003, p. 35.

Arms trafficking as an issue of organised crime appears to be underreported. Replies to the 2004 questionnaire, but also organised crime situation reports prepared in different countries include only limited data on this question:

- in Lithuania, 72 cases related to arms and explosives were investigated by the Organised Crime Investigation Service in 2003;
- in Slovenia, 148 criminal offences related to weapons and explosives were noted, of which 6 were related to organised crime;
- in "the former Yugoslav Republic of Macedonia", voluntary disarmament and action against trafficking in arms has moved high on the agenda. In 2003, 213 criminal offences related to "unlawful making, possession and trafficking in arms and explosives", committed by 238 offenders, were detected.

Money laundering

While there may be ambiguities about the concept of organised crime and while the assessment of crime markets presented in this report may be selective, there is a common denominator of all organised crime and of most other forms of serious crime, and that is the pursuit of profit. Proceeds from crime may be consumed by criminals or hidden away. However, in order to prevent them from being traced by law enforcement and in order to permit their investment in other business, crime proceeds need to be laundered in a way that they become indistinguishable from legitimate money. The efforts made by launderers depend on the intensity of controls.

Initially aimed at the proceeds of drug-related crime,[1] the adoption of the Strasbourg convention in 1990,[2] and subsequently of the recommendations of the Financial Action Task Force, led to the establishment of anti-money laundering systems aimed at the proceeds of all crimes or at least of all serious crimes in European countries. These systems are primarily set up to detect suspicious transactions which may be related to money laundering.

The past two to three years have seen a large increase in the reporting of suspicious transactions throughout Europe. This does not necessarily mean a dramatic increase in money laundering activities, as it may be due to:

---

1. United Nations Convention Against Illicit Traffic in Narcotic Drugs and Psychotropic Substances (1988).
2. Council of Europe Convention on the Laundering, Search, Seizure and Confiscation of the Proceeds from Crime of 1990 (ETS No. 141)

- a renewed interest in anti-money laundering measures after 11 September 2001 with an additional focus on terrorist financing and greater sensitivity of law enforcement and financial institutions, which have invested substantial sums in compliance procedures;
- an enlarged list of entities required to report their suspicions;
- improved anti-money laundering systems in many countries of Europe, with more active financial intelligence units (FIU).

For example, the Committee for Financial Monitoring of the Russian Federation received more than 370 000 suspicious transaction and mandatory control reports in 2002, that is, in its first year of operations, and the State Department for Financial Monitoring of Ukraine which became operational in 2003, received over 240 000 reports during the first 6 months of 2004.[1] These two, only recently established financial intelligence units, alone account for a considerable share of all suspicious transaction reports received by European FIUs. In the Netherlands, some 177 000 suspicious transaction reports were submitted to the Unusual Transactions Disclosure Office (MOT), of which 37 748 were considered suspicious and referred to the prosecution.[2]

Since most investigations of organised crime are drug related, it can be expected that most laundering is detected in connection with drugs. However, as economic crime gains in importance, fraud and embezzlement make up a large part of money laundering investigations, at least in countries with an all-crimes approach. For example:

- in Belgium in 2003, serious and organised tax fraud, bribery, stock exchange crimes, financial fraud and fraudulent bankruptcy accounted for 33% of the 783 case files transmitted to the prosecution by the CTIF-CFI (the Belgian financial intelligence unit) against 19% for drug trafficking, 17% for trafficking in other goods and 11% for trafficking in human beings. Economic crime has gained in importance when compared to the past ten years where on average it accounted for 18% of the files transmitted;[3]
- in Romania, in 2002 and 2003, more than 80% of the money laundering cases investigated were related to embezzlement and tax evasion,

---

1. These transactions do not necessarily have a criminal background or are related to organised crime. Establishing a link between an unusual or suspicious transaction and a specific crime remains a difficult task.

2. More specifically to the Office for the Provision of Police Support to the National Prosecutor for the Disclosure of Suspicious Transactions (BLOM).

3. CTIF-CFI "Annual report 2003".

and only 8% to organised crime such as drug trafficking or trafficking in human beings;

- in Cyprus, from among ninety-one cases prosecuted, eighty-seven were related to fraud and four to drug trafficking as predicate offences;
- in the Russian Federation, fraud (30%), illegal entrepreneurship (20%), misappropriation of funds and embezzlement (15%) accounted for two thirds of the investigations into money laundering in 2002.

Though it represents a somewhat artificial demarcation – and much laundering amounts to little more than hiding cash – money laundering methods are usually described using a three-stage model:

- placement – the ways in which direct proceeds from crime are channelled into the financial systems, typically in the form of cash payments;
- layering – the circulation of funds through a succession of financial transactions to erase any connection of the placed capital to its criminal origin, typically through money transfers or cheques;
- integration – the investment of originally criminal proceeds into legal and economic flows, typically into real estate, business capital or valuable objects.

The importance of cash – in particular at the placement stage – has been underlined in the United Kingdom[1] and a number of other reports. Laundering methods include the acquisition of property and assets, the use of legitimate and quasi-legitimate businesses with a high turnover of cash (including restaurants, nightclubs, taxi firms, car sales and repair companies, etc.), bureaux de change and other money transmission agents, as well as correspondent banking for cross-jurisdictional transactions. Financial products – including insurance policies and share portfolios – may be bought for almost immediate resale. In the Netherlands, an increasing number of suspicious transactions are reported in connection with the Cash Deposit System through which money can be deposited in a beneficiary's account using a machine.[2]

Back-to-back loans to suspected offenders against the security of funds deposited in foreign or domestic accounts, purchase of real estate – sometimes registered in corporate names in corporate secrecy jurisdictions – and building materials, and the purchase of valuable commodities,

---

1. NCIS 2003.
2. "Report on Dutch investigations into organised crime 2003".

especially diamonds and other lightweight, transportable "products" are common.

Furthermore, launderers may make use of different value transfer systems such as Hawala/Hundi, currency exchange networks, Fei chien, door-to-door and other Asian varieties, invoice manipulation schemes, in-kind fund transfers, trade diversion schemes, courier services and physical transfer methods, including smuggling, gift and money transfer services overseas via special vouchers and Internet websites, Internet-based payments/transfers (including Internet auctions), stored value, such as pre-paid telephone cards and "chits", security transfers, such as brokerage accounts, or debit and credit cards used by multiple individuals.

The Financial Action Task Force – in its 2003-04 typologies exercise – pointed at the following issues, although not all of these are relevant to organised crime:[1]

- wire transfers as a fast and efficient way of moving funds which can also be used for terrorist financing;
- the misuse of non-profit organisations as "a potentially serious terrorist financing problem";
- the exploitation of vulnerabilities in the insurance sector – facilitated by inconsistent regulations – for the integration of crime proceeds;
- the involvement of politically exposed persons with current or past prominent public functions in financial crime, in particular corruption, who "conceal their illicit assets through networks of shell companies and off-shore banks";
- the role of gatekeepers, that is, specialised professionals, legal or financial experts, who facilitate money laundering operations.

Europe is a major stakeholder in global money laundering as a source and destination of criminal proceeds and, through its financial markets, as an actor in different stages of the money laundering process.[2] This is reflected

---

1. FATF 2004.

2. In 1998, in connection with (finally inconclusive) discussions within the FATF on a possible quantification of global money laundering flows, one of the models ranked countries in terms of their attractiveness to money laundering (see Walker 1998). The top ten of this list included seven European countries: 1. Luxembourg, 2. United States, 3. Switzerland, 4. Cayman Islands, 5. Austria, 6. Netherlands, 7. Liechtenstein, 8. Vatican City, 9. United Kingdom, 10. Singapore. According to the same model, 46.3% of the laundered money originated in the United States, followed by Italy (5.3%) and the Russian Federation (5.2%). The United States (with 18.9%) was also the

among other things in the increasing number of investigations, prosecutions and convictions for money laundering in a number of European countries.[1] Most member states confirm that the investment of criminal proceeds in legal businesses has become a regular part of the *modus operandi* of organised crime groups and networks, though only rarely as a bridgehead to integration in the upperworld.

Organised crime groups and networks

Organised crime cases and groups

According to Europol, in 2002 some 4 000 organised crime groups with up to 40 000 members operated in the countries of the European Union:[2]

- The most influential of these groups were indigenous, many of them with links to groups from other EU countries.

- Among organised crime groups form outside the EU, ethnic Albanian organised crime groups – primarily involved in drug trafficking and trafficking in human beings – constituted the main threat, in particular for their extreme use of violence and for the fact that they have "graduated" from criminal service providers to taking control of crime markets.

- Russian organised crime groups – focusing on financial crime and money laundering, as well as extortion of fellow nationals and illegal immigration – remain powerful because of their efficient hierarchical structure and division of labour, the large amounts of financial resources at their disposal for investment in legal businesses and their tight internal discipline, often enforced with violence.

---

main destination of laundered money, but six European countries figured among the top ten as well, namely the Russian Federation, Italy, Romania, Vatican City, Luxembourg and France.

1. The effectiveness of anti-money laundering systems is being reviewed under the current evaluation cycle of the Council of Europe MONEYVAL mechanism.

2. This refers to the EU 15. See Europol 2003.

Table 2: Number of organised crime (OC) cases and groups

Member state	OC cases recorded	OC cases investigated/ prosecuted	OC groups	Suspects/ offenders
Albania		1 014		920
Andorra	27	25	20	130
Armenia	32	33	6	27
Austria	66			
Azerbaijan				
Belgium		292	296	2 158
Bosnia and Herzegovina				
Bulgaria			260	1 360
Croatia	938		25	
Cyprus	0	0	0	0
Czech Republic	1 138	1 067		659
Denmark				
Estonia			7	
Finland	2 329		30	850
France				
Georgia	1402	847	621	2 118
Germany			637	13 098
Greece	157	157	157	889
Hungary				
Iceland				
Ireland				
Italy				16 314
Latvia		435	27	
Liechtenstein				
Lithuania	1 600	1 140	54	
Luxembourg				
Malta	0	0	0	0
Moldova	8	8	20	105
Netherlands		221		1 878
Norway				
Poland		756	522	6 134
Portugal	56	56	56	1 015
Romania	4 963		1062	3 898
Russian Federation				
San Marino				
Serbia	810	455	126	1 250
And Montenegro	1 295			
Slovakia	81		23	427
Slovenia	391	341	65	1 018
Spain			542	4 250
Sweden			98	
Switzerland				
"The former Yugoslav Republic of Macedonia"		222		271
Turkey	1 521	1 471	1 448	6 911
Ukraine	6 159	841	634	2 707
United Kingdom				

- Other groups operating in the EU include Turkish (drugs and arms trafficking, money laundering and protection rackets), Nigerian (trafficking in human beings, drug trafficking and fraud), Moroccan (cannabis trafficking and other smuggling activities), Colombian (cocaine trafficking), Chinese (illegal migration), Vietnamese (criminal service providers in general, illegal migration and commodity smuggling).

- In 2002, organised crime groups from the accession and candidate countries included Polish groups (strong role in Germany, involved in vehicle crime and commodity smuggling), groups from the Baltic states (commodity smuggling and counterfeiting), in particular Lithuanian groups (trafficking in human beings, drug trafficking, extortion, kidnapping and counterfeiting), and Romanian (financial crime, robberies and trafficking in human beings), and Bulgarian groups (counterfeiting of the euro and credit cards, vehicle crime and trafficking in human beings).

Replies to the Council of Europe 2004 questionnaire reflect great difficulties in the identification of organised crime groups and thus in the reporting of organised crime. Data show considerable variance between countries, ranging from none to more than 1 000 organised crime groups. Some countries, while reporting a large number of organised crime cases, have been unable to provide data on organised crime groups. Others suggest that if the criteria for the identification of organised crime groups are applied in a broad manner, almost any crime may be considered organised crime. Common law countries, in particular, may not have a separate "organised crime offence" and therefore difficulty in classifying behaviour under such headings. The table above is thus a rather tentative one.

The structure of organised crime groups and networks

The prevailing concept has been, for some time,[1] one of organised crime groups as ethnically homogeneous, formally and hierarchically structured, multi-functional bureaucratic criminal organisations which confront society.

Examples include:

- family-type organisations, such as the Cosa Nostra in Sicily which consists of some 180 groups with 6 000 members;

---

1. See Von Lampe 2001.

- groups in the countries of the former Soviet Union with a clear division of tasks ("vor v zakone" ("thief in law"), "papka" ("fathers"), "starchina" ("senior officers"), "obstchak" ("joint fund holders"), brigade leaders, fighters, financiers and network personnel) and where membership fees ("krysha" ("the roof")) are paid to the "obstchak";

- British "firm"-type organisations with permanent members, distinct roles and clear chains of command.

The above concept is in question. Replies to the 2004 questionnaire show an important shift in reporting. While in 2001 and 2002, central and eastern European countries suggested that most groups were hierarchically organised, such groups now appear to be the exception. Only in Lithuania are most groups reportedly organised in that way, and in Slovakia about half of the organised crime groups show a clear hierarchical structure. In Italy, even the Cosa Nostra appears to be decentralising, at least with regard to predatory crimes. In the United Kingdom, the traditional "firm" now seems to be the exception.

Moreover, ethnicity is less useful as a criteria for the identification of organised crime groups, as in many countries organised crime groups are said to have a multi-ethnic composition, and in most countries, the large majority of criminals are nationals of the country in which crimes are committed.

The notion of clearly defined hierarchical organisations seems to be increasingly replaced by one of criminal networks, consisting of individual or small cells of criminals, as well as legal structures (most often legal commercial structures) and professionals (such as lawyers, accountants, financial services experts and public notaries – not always appreciating the criminal purposes) which are more or less loosely affiliated and co-operate in varying compositions for particular criminal enterprises:

- Some networks may be directed by a core group of organisers, others may assemble according to needs and opportunities.[1]

- They may range from very small associations to large transnational networks.

---

1. See Williams 2001.

- Some may be fluid and amorphous, with very loose membership and chains of command, while others may be more structured and stable, some may focus on a single purpose or product while others may be involved in a broad range of activities.
- Some individuals or cells or some of the activities of the network may be perfectly legal while others may be criminal.

In short, criminal networks may function and adjust to market conditions and opportunities like business enterprises.

This does not necessarily imply that hierarchical, well-structured organised crime groups are not relevant anymore. As in the business world, some types of activities require better structured organisations than others. And as stated by Europol, "powerful hierarchical groups continue to occupy key positions in OC within the EU".[1]

Nevertheless, the analytical approach to organised crime may need to be adjusted. Often, money or other crime proceeds are the only common denominator of different individuals, cells or groups, legal or illegal structures which organise for crime. Network analyses – such as those used by financial intelligence units to link suspicious financial transactions to criminal offences – may not only allow identification of a broader range of criminal enterprises but also a better understanding of the links between criminal and legal structures of society. [2]

Modi operandi

The relationship between organised crime groups and networks and society is one of the most critical issues with regard to organised crime. The question is whether it is one of confrontation, that is, organised crime versus society, or whether it is of a rather symbiotic nature. An assessment of the *modi operandi* of organised crime groups and networks provides some insights in this respect.

---

1. Europol 2003, p. 5.

2. As underlined in Best Practice Survey 7 (prepared by the PC-S-CO of the Council of Europe) on the effectiveness of provisions criminalising membership in criminal organisations, it may be useful for countries to have in place in the general or special part of their criminal legislation, in addition to the legal framework on membership and setting up of criminal organisations, provisions allowing them to deal with weaker forms of organised crime (criminal associations, aggravating circumstance in case of multiplicity of offendership, etc.).

Use of violence and intimidation

The use of violence is widely used by organised crime groups and networks to enforce discipline within their group or against competing groups. Ethnic Albanian groups are reported to be among the most violent ones in this respect. Bulgaria also experienced organised crime related violence in 2004. In a restaurant in Sofia, the suspected head of an organised crime group and five of his bodyguards were executed in July 2004, most likely by other criminals. There are few European countries in which violence between crime groups and networks is absent.

In most countries witnesses against organised crime are believed to be at risk, in particular if they are collaborators of justice, that is, (former) criminals themselves. Hence the increasing number of witness protection programmes in Europe.

Intimidation and violence against victims are an intrinsic part of specific offences, such as robbery, extortion and racketeering, as well as trafficking in human beings.

In most European countries, organised crime groups and networks avoid open confrontation with public authorities. However, there are exceptions.

For example:

- In Italy, intimidation and violence against state bodies are used by the Camorra,[1] the 'Ndrangheta, the Sacra Corona Unita and other groups in Puglia, but less now by the Cosa Nostra which – following the experience of the 1990s – appears to seek a form of accommodation with the state.

- In Albania, the use of violence by organised criminals against officials is reflected in the large number of law enforcement officials killed in recent years.

- In Lithuania violence and intimidation are not only used to enforce discipline within organised crime groups but frequently against law enforcement officers and witnesses.

- In Serbia, after years of, allegedly, symbiotic relationships, 2003 saw open confrontation reflected in particular in the assassination of late

---

1. In 2004, conflicts among Camorra-gangs in Naples cost more than 100 lives.

Prime Minister Zoran Djindjic and murders or attempted murders of other senior state officials.

Corruption and use of influence

The use of influence on not only the public administration, politicians, the criminal justice system and the media but also on private sector representatives is a primary tool of organised crime groups and networks. This may take the form of corruption – not only in the sense of bribery, but also in the form of trading in influence – and other forms based on patron-client relationships, nepotism, favouritism, family ties, ethnic relationships, relations to persons in powerful positions or "politically exposed persons". Financing of individual politicians, of political parties and electoral campaigns may play an important part in this respect.

Such use of influence – symbiotic relationships based on mutual interest – are more sustainable and reliable than the use of violence and intimidation.

Increasingly, organised crime groups and networks use corruption in a professional manner by hiring legal and business experts as intermediaries or brokers or by planting associates in relevant political or administrative positions.

Corrupt officials may tolerate or participate in criminal activities or protect criminals from law enforcement, or – in the case of senior officials – sponsor organised crime groups and networks. In some countries in transition, corruption appears to have permeated most structures of public life, including law enforcement and criminal justice systems. Low salaries, unemployment, insecurity and poverty, and often the example set by senior officials, make public officials vulnerable targets and reliable partners of organised crime groups and networks.

In more affluent countries, corruption is widely used in connection with organised crime, but plays a less central role. Opportunistic approaches prevail, that is, corruption is used to facilitate a crime if the opportunity arises or if vulnerable officials can be targeted.

With the expansion of economic crime, corruption as a primary tool of organised crime is likely to gain in importance also in these countries, not only with regard to public-private corruption, but also in relation to corruption in the private sector.

While there is a general perception – as reported by most countries – of close links between corruption and organised crime, hard data and precise analyses are limited:

- In Belgium, 17.4% of the 292 organised crime related cases analysed in 2003 involved corruption.

- In Germany, already in 2002, a specific analysis of links between organised crime cases and corruption since 1992 was carried out. Results were that 125 of 476 cases investigated provided indications of the use of influence on politics, media, public administration, justice and economy, either abroad (61 cases) or in Germany (64 cases). Organised crime groups and networks involved in drugs used corruption to seek information on ongoing investigations by police and justice. Those involved in property crime, in particular vehicle theft, sought information on car registration and related investigations, groups involved in trafficking in human beings and prostitution had corruptive relations with immigration and registry offices, and those involved in smuggling of cigarettes bribed customs and border police. Organised crime groups and networks with foreign members frequently had corrupt relationships in the home countries of their members. About 50% of the cases concerned the public administration, 18% the justice system and 16% politicians (mainly abroad).

- With regard to the Netherlands, 50 out of 109 groups analysed in 2003, and for which relevant information is available, used corruptive practices either in the Netherlands or abroad. This included corrupt officials of the Inland Revenue Service, official interpreters leaking information to criminals, but also corruption in the private sector, such as a director of a company or airline officials.

- In the United Kingdom about one quarter of serious and organised criminals are reported to use corruption, although the actual figure may be higher. Criminals may prefer corruption to intimidation or violence in particular if they are interested in longer term relationships. Violence brings publicity and though this may generate a reputational benefit for the practitioners of violence, it also generates law enforcement and political responses that are hard to control.

Shielding practices

Shielding practices have become an important *modus operandi* of organised crime groups and networks to protect themselves from law enforcement and maintain their position on the criminal market against competitors.

The most common shielding practices are aimed at protecting communication between criminals; they include the use of several means of communication and frequent variation of these means, coded oral and written messages and data encryption.

Defensive shielding against public authorities may include counter-surveillance, bribery, strategic networking, buying information or telephone tapping of investigative authorities.[1]

Offensive approaches appear not to be widespread but may include active tracking of civil servants, pressure on civil servants or their families, creating conditions for blackmail and others.

Shielding practices are a major reason for the duration and complexity of investigations into organised crime. An important tool to shield criminal activities is the use of legal commercial structures.

Use of commercial structures

Almost all countries report the use of legal commercial structures by organised crime groups and networks, in that they either collaborate with one or more insiders or in that they own or invest in legal structures, thus blending legal and illegal activities, or that they set up shell companies.

The use of commercial structures serves different purposes:

- as a cover or shield for illegal activities;
- to provide logistical support and other services for criminal activities;
- to facilitate money laundering;
- to interface with public authorities and other legal structures of society;
- to participate in public procurement;
- to diversify business interests;
- to control or monopolise markets.

---

1. See report by the Netherlands.

Sectors such as real estate, car dealers, the catering industry, construction and works, nightlife, gambling and the sex industry, security firms, transport and import/export companies are still preferred by organised crime groups and networks, since they are either cash-intensive or related to the criminal activities carried out by such groups. For example, in Belgium, 208 out of 292 organised crime groups and networks used commercial structures in one or more sectors in 2003, in particular import/export (15%), transport (9%), catering industry (7%) and real estate (7%).

However, as organised crime groups and networks become more sophisticated and professional, any sector may be used, ranging from investment in shares in foreign companies, the creation of, or participation in, financial holdings or investments in the oil industry to interests in, or ownership of, banks. Organised crime groups and networks may provide loans or invest in a company with the purpose of making a subsequent take-over, sometimes without informing others about changes in ownership.

The increasing use of legal commercial structures by organised crime groups and networks throughout Europe points to an important trend, namely intensifying links between the underworld and the upperworld, with the boundaries of organised crime groups and networks becoming increasingly blurred. However, this is not to argue that organised criminals wish to somehow gain control over the levers of power in society: such ambitions and conduct are actually rare, especially in western Europe.

Transnational operations

The traditional concept of organised crime as shaped in the United States in the 1930s implied the control by organised crime groups of a certain territory. It can be assumed that in the age of globalisation, territorial control is less relevant than the global exploitation of opportunities for criminal profits.

According to Article 3, paragraph 2, of the United Nations Convention on Transnational Organized Crime, an offence is "transnational in nature" if:

(a) It is committed in more than one State;
(b) It is committed in one State but a substantial part of its preparation, planning, direction or control takes place in another State;
(c) It is committed in one State but involves an organized criminal group that engages in criminal activities in more than one State; or
(d) It is committed in one State but has substantial effects in another State.

Reports by member states suggest the involvement of a large variety of nationalities in organised crime. At the same time, the majority of suspects are from the country where the offences are committed. For example:

- In Belgium in 2003, more than seventy different nationalities were identified in organised crime groups and networks. Some 38% of the suspects were Belgian. The main non-Belgian nationalities mentioned were Dutch, Italian, Moroccan, Albanian, Turkish, Romanian, French, Nigerian and Russian.

- In the Czech Republic, 547 out of 659 criminals prosecuted in 2003 were Czech nationals while foreigners were primarily from the Russian Federation, Slovakia, Vietnam, Ukraine, the former Yugoslavia and Moldova.

- In Finland, 92% of suspects were Finnish, while the foreigners were mainly Russians and Estonians.

- In Germany, most organised criminals are German (in particular with regard to economic crime and cocaine trafficking), while suspects from Turkey, Lithuania, Nigeria and Serbia and Montenegro dominate the heroin market, Polish and Lithuanian the stolen vehicle market, and, in addition to German, Ukrainian, Turkish, Vietnamese, Lithuanian and Moldavian groups play a strong role in smuggling of persons and trafficking in human beings. Russian and Vietnamese criminals dominate violent crimes.

- In Italy, groups from eastern Europe, Latin America, Africa and Asia operate in addition to the Italian Mafia-type associations. The 'Ndrangheta, in particular, operates internationally and has concluded agreements with foreign groups.

- In the Netherlands in 2003, 68% of suspects were Dutch nationals (however, only half of them were of Dutch ethnic origin). In terms of other nationalities and ethnic groups, Turkey, Albania, Netherlands Antilles, Surinam, Morocco, China, Colombia and Germany have been mentioned most often in connection with organised crime investigations. About half of the organised crime groups and networks had a multi-ethnic composition.

- In Poland in 2002, 80% of organised crime groups and networks identified consisted of Polish members, while the others had a multinational or foreign ethnic ("Russian-speaking") composition.

These reports seem to support the argument that organised crime consists of networks whereby individuals or smaller groups are involved in particular transactions in a given country, though they may make use of individuals and groups elsewhere.

Use of information and communication technologies[1]

Information and communication technologies are gaining in importance not only to facilitate communication among members of organised crime groups and networks and shielding through encryption, but also as tools to commit "old forms" of crime more efficiently as well as to move into new fields of crime.

An hypothesis in this connection is that as societies around the world gradually turn into "network societies", organised crime groups will even more take on the form of criminal networks.

Country summaries[2]

Albania

Primary activities of organised crime are related to trafficking in human beings and illicit drugs which accounted for almost 60% of the 1 024 proceedings against organised crime, illicit traffic and corruption in 2003. Most of the remainder was related to illegal activities by state employees and public officials, including corruption. In addition, 1 418 offences recorded were related to counterfeiting of documents.

Data do not reflect the involvement of organised crime groups and networks. Only 4 proceedings with 5 defendants were initiated against criminal gangs.

Measures against trafficking in human beings and illegal migration seem to show effect: while in 2002 more than 2 500 persons were intercepted, their number dropped to less than 60 in 2003.

---

1. For more on this topic see the chapter on cybercrime.
2. Based on replies to the questionnaire and reports provided by member states.

Andorra

Organised crime is of limited scale. Most offences are not committed and reported in Andorra but abroad. Primary markets in 2003 were money laundering (12 cases submitted to justice), smuggling – in particular of cigarettes – (6 cases), fraud and economic crime (5 cases recorded and 3 submitted to justice) and drug trafficking (4 cases – usually petty trafficking but 2 major cases in 2003)

About 20 organised crime groups and networks have been reported. Those involved in drug trafficking, money laundering and tobacco smuggling appear to be more hierarchically organised than those involved in economic crime. Criminals are from Andorra, Spain, Portugal, France and – in the case of economic crime – also from Romania. Violence and corruption are rarely used by these groups when operating within Andorra. All cases of organised crime are transnational in nature. Shielding measures (coded communications and counter-surveillance) are used in particular by groups involved in economic crime and money laundering.

No major changes or new trends or threats have been observed in comparison to previous years.

Armenia

Thirty-three organised crime-related cases were prosecuted in 2003 involving Six organised crime groups and networks and 27 suspects. One case was related to smuggling of goods while the others were to theft and robbery.

Austria

Organised theft and burglary, traffic in stolen vehicles, production and distribution of amphetamine-type substances, trafficking in human beings and money laundering were considered the main markets in 2003.

In 2003, a total of 66 organised crime cases were recorded of which 47 were clarified. Criminal groups from different countries – and in particular from South-Eastern Europe – operate in Austria. With some 700 night-clubs and 3 500 registered prostitutes, and an unknown number of clandestine prostitutes, the sex industry is a major market of organised crime. Women are mostly procured by foreign organisations, while employment is organised by Austrians. Russian organised crime appears not be active in Austria, but is using the country as a retreat, including the purchase of property.

Belgium

As primary activity of organised crime groups and networks: crime against goods 31% (in particular theft, trafficking in stolen vehicles, fencing, falsification of documents), financial and economic crime 24% (excise and VAT fraud, swindle), drugs 15%, money laundering 11%, trafficking in human beings and smuggling of persons 11%. Financial investigations into 159 cases suggest proceeds of €2.14 billion.

There were some 292 investigations into organised crime in 2003, involving 296 organised crime groups and networks with 2 158 suspects/offenders. Some 38% are Belgian nationals. Ethnic-based groups include Albanians, Estonians and Lithuanians. There are 68 groups who have contacts with groups abroad, mainly in the Netherlands, Germany, Italy and the United Kingdom. Some 60% used violence and intimidation, primarily within criminal circles. Some 71% used commercial structures (primarily import/export, transport and the catering industry)

Bulgaria

Drugs (in particular heroin trafficking along the Balkan route and amphetamine-type substances not only for international but also local consumers) and economic crime (smuggling of cigarettes and counterfeiting of CDs, videotapes and other goods) are the main markets in Bulgaria. In addition, smuggling of persons and trafficking in human beings have gained in importance.

In 2003, 260 organised crime groups and networks with 1 360 members (1 121 of them Bulgarians) were identified. The structures of these groups seems to have changed from hierarchical ones to enterprise structures with fluctuating membership and structure. Newly established groups are more likely to use violence and intimidation. Corruption is widely resorted to. Proceeds from crime are increasingly invested into the legal economy. Extensive co-operation with Serbian and Turkish criminals (for drug trafficking) and Austrian, German, French and Dutch criminals (for trafficking in human beings) has been reported.

Drug trafficking will continue to pose a major challenge, in particular with regard to synthetic drugs. Bulgaria will continue to be used for smuggling and trafficking in goods and people.

Croatia

Smuggling of persons and trafficking in human beings, economic crime (smuggling of goods, counterfeiting money and securities) and trafficking in drugs, weapons and stolen motor vehicles are the main markets.

Organised crime groups and networks emerged in the early 1990s taking advantage of the war situation in South-Eastern Europe. Criminals during those times acquired considerable wealth which they are now investing in the legal economy or new criminal activities. It is believed that the number of organised crime groups and networks in Croatia is rather limited and that these groups are relatively small with flexible structures and strong relations to criminals in other countries of the region. They mainly consist of persons from the former Yugoslavia.

Cyprus

No cases of organised crime have been recorded. Information available points at illegal drugs, prostitution, extortion and gambling as possible organised crime markets.

With regard to money laundering, 106 reports of suspicious transactions were submitted to the financial intelligence unit and 246 requests for information have been received from abroad. However, there is no evidence that these are related to organised crime.

Trafficking in human beings is considered a future threat against which preventive measures are being taken.

Czech Republic

Illegal migration, trafficking in human beings, drugs and arms, smuggling and fraud are considered the main markets. This is partially reflected in statistics on drug trafficking (398 persons prosecuted in 2003), fraud and embezzlement (138) and illegal border crossing (40) and trafficking in women (5). Material damage is estimated at more than CZK76 million, of which almost 50% (CZK37 million) is through fraud and embezzlement.

A significant share of organised crime groups and networks is based on ethnicity, but there are also many with multinational compositions. In 2003, foreign perpetrators came from a variety of countries, for example Russian Federation, Slovakia, Vietnam, Ukraine, the former Yugoslavia and

Moldova. However, most offenders are Czech nationals (547 Czechs prosecuted in 2003 against 112 foreigners).

Future threats include, in particular, increasing migration, including the involvement of migrants in criminal activities. Ethnicity will be of less relevance in the future. More Czech citizens will be involved in organised crime. As a EU member, the Czech Republic will be more attractive to organised crime. Corruptive relationships between criminal and official structures may expand.

Denmark

The main markets are drug trafficking, credit card crimes (counterfeiting), trafficking in human beings from central and eastern Europe (primarily Latvia) and Thailand, and smuggling of high taxed goods. The markets of organised crime in Denmark are considered to be of relatively modest size.

Danish nationals and ethnic Danes were involved in a range of activities. The biker (outlawed motorcycle gangs) and street gangs (typically groups of young men of immigrant origin) attracted the particular attention of law enforcement agencies. Criminals from different EU countries, often in association with Danes, were involved in economic and financial crime. Latvians were involved in trafficking in human beings, while Lithuanian gangs were smuggling cigarettes and involved in large-scale thefts and burglaries. Serbs and Albanians have been trafficking in heroin but also committed other crimes. There is no indication of undue influence exercised by organised crime groups and networks on the public administration, political circles or law enforcement agencies. Increasingly, organised crime is based on "flexible network co-operation".

Internationalisation, globalisation, network organisation of criminals, and the use of information and communication technologies will shape organised crime in the coming years.

Estonia

Fraud and other major economic crime (1 446 prosecutions in 2003), drug trafficking (716) extortion (136), prostitution, vehicle theft and smuggling of legal goods, including alcohol and tobacco (26), are the main crime markets.

Some 7 major organised crime groups have been identified, some of them active in car theft, blackmail, drugs and prostitution, whilst others are also involved in drug trafficking, abduction, money laundering and economic crimes. Violence is not used that often, but some of these groups may resort to intimidation. International connections are primarily with criminals in the Russian Federation and to a more limited extent with Spain. Organised crime groups and networks invest more and more in legal business, in particular real estate.

With Estonia in the EU, it is expected that organised crime will use Estonia as a transit point between the Russian Federation and the EU for drug trafficking and the smuggling of persons. Economic crime will play a more important role in the future.

Finland

Illegal drugs (by Finnish in co-operation with Estonian and Russian groups), illegal sex business (by Estonian and Russian groups), property crime (including vehicle theft by Russian groups) and economic crime (by Finish and foreign groups) constitute the main markets for organised crime. In 2003, members of organised crime groups and networks were suspected of having been involved on 2 329 occasions, of which 389 relate to drug trafficking, 454 to property crimes and 459 to other trafficking.

In 2003, some 850 persons were under operational monitoring by law enforcement authorities for their involvement in organised crime. Of these, 8% were foreigners (mainly Estonians and Russians). About 30 organised crime groups and networks are active in Finland. They are heavily armed, but open violence is rarely applied. Shielding activities such as using cash transfers, coded language and avoiding mobile phones are frequently used. Proceeds are invested in new crimes, luxury goods or transferred abroad.

The future will see:
- more disciplined and violent criminal organisations in Finland;
- an increase in the activities of Estonian and Russian organised crime groups and networks in Finland and their expansion in the field of economic crime.

Georgia

Fraud and major economic crime (189 cases recorded in 2003), followed by counterfeiting of commercial products (150 cases), smuggling of legal goods (48 cases) and racketeering and extortion (48 cases) seem to be the primary markets. Some 19 cases of drug trafficking were recorded.

Organised crime is considered one type of "group crime". In total, 1 402 cases of crimes committed by groups were recorded in 2003 involving 621 "group crime" related groups and 2 118 offenders. Some 737 cases were prosecuted, leading to the conviction of 1 772 persons.

Germany

Primary markets are drug trafficking, in particular of heroin and cocaine (212 cases related to organised crime recorded, equivalent to 33.3%), property offences, in particular trafficking in stolen vehicles (14%), and economic crime, including fraud in connection with investments, stock markets, bankruptcies, insurances, credit cards, unfair competition and public tenders (85 cases, 13.5%).

Other markets include smuggling of persons (64 cases), trafficking in human beings (61), tax and customs offences, in particular tobacco smuggling (56 cases), counterfeiting, VAT fraud, racketeering and other forms of violent crime. In addition, 143 cases of money laundering were investigated. Economic crimes accounted for only 13.5% of the offences committed by organised crime groups and networks, but for 54% (€280 million) of the material damage and 35% (€164 million) of the profits generated by organised crime

In total, 637 organised crime groups and networks were identified involving 13 098 suspects. With regard to drugs, German criminals play a leading role in cocaine trafficking, while the heroin market is dominated by nationals from Turkey, Lithuania, Nigeria, and Serbia and Montenegro. Polish and Lithuanian organised crime groups and networks play a strong role in the trafficking of stolen vehicles. Economic crime is mostly carried out by German organised crime groups and networks (60%). Smuggling of persons involves German (25%) but also Ukrainian, Turkish, Vietnamese and Moldavian groups. Trafficking in human beings is mostly committed by Germans, followed by Turkish, Bulgarian and Lithuanian groups. Russian and Vietnamese criminals dominate violent crimes.

An analysis in 2002 of organised crime cases and their links to corruption showed that in Germany such links are rather weak and only used in a few cases, such as public procurement.

No major changes are expected in the near future.

Greece

Drug trafficking (30 cases, 118 convictions), trafficking in human beings (18 cases, 49 convictions), forgery (14 cases, 77 convictions), smuggling in cigarettes (6 cases, 26 convictions) and fraud (6 cases, 31 convictions) are the main markets. Some 753 suspicious transaction reports led to 20 convictions for money laundering.

In 2003 a total of 157 cases of organised crime were prosecuted involving 889 suspects and leading to 551 convictions. The structure of criminal organisations lacks consistency and hierarchy. Criminal organisations involved in trafficking in human beings (Albanian, Romanian, Bulgarian, Georgian, Ukrainian and Lithuanian) and smuggling of persons (Turkish, Pakistani, Iraqi and Chinese) use violence and intimidation against their victims. Greek criminal organisations resort to extortion and kidnappings and use violence against businessmen and partners. Organised crime groups may use corruption to obtain identity papers for smuggled persons.

Iceland

Drug trafficking, violation of customs laws, violations of the fisheries management act (fraudulent transfer and accounting of fishery quotas) and VAT fraud are the main criminal activities committed in an organised way.

The majority of offenders are Icelandic citizens. Some 500 people are believed to be involved in drugs offences of which 10% in an organised manner and with drugs purchased in the Netherlands, Denmark and Spain. Violence and intimidation are sometimes used to collect debts. Foreign criminal organisations do not yet have a foothold in Iceland.

Organised crime in Iceland is still at a modest stage, but it may gain in importance by making use of new technologies and shielding practices. Danish outlawed motorcycle gangs repeatedly tried to move to Iceland but so far, it would seem, without success.

Italy

Mafia-type associations are involved in different markets:

- Cosa Nostra (Sicily): financial and economic crime and territorial control by main families, and predatory crimes through local groups;
- Camorra (Naples and the surrounding area): drug trafficking, gambling, intermediation in labour world, and offences and intimi-

67

dation against the public administration, administration of justice, persons and property. Profits through "ecomafia", control of public construction contracts and fraud related to EU finances;

- 'Ndrangheta (Calabria): drug trafficking (national and international), extortion and infiltration of public contracts (through protection money), and money laundering;
- mafia-type associations in Puglia (for example, Sacra Corona Unita): trafficking in human beings, cigarettes, drugs, arms, environmental crime, extortion and control of public contracts. Intimidation and offences against the public administration.

Mafia-type associations are organisations that resort to intimidation ("omertà"), aim at control and affect the functioning of the local economy and public administration. They include:

- Cosa Nostra (Sicily): central management of finances and relations with politics and legal economic structures by big families. Major economic and financial crimes are carried out by new criminals who report directly to the leaders of the organisation. Predatory crimes (extortion, prostitution and drug trafficking) are left to local groups;
- Camorra (Naples);
- 'Ndrangheta (Calabria): very dynamic; operates beyond Calabria, also internationally; agreements with other, foreign groups;
- mafia-type associations in Puglia.

In addition, a range of other Mafia- and non-Mafia-type organisations operates in Italy, coming from eastern Europe, Latin America, Africa and Asia.

In 2003:

- 10 456 individuals were reported for involvement in criminal associations;
- 3 177 for Mafia-type associations;
- 2 681 for association involved in drug trafficking.

While the Cosa Nostra seems to seek coexistence with the state, avoiding violence and confrontation, experiences difficult relationships between detained bosses and members at liberty and is forced to reorganise, it appears to be succeeded by the very dynamic and versatile 'Ndrangheta of Calabria, which also operates internationally. In terms of influencing the public administration, intimidating the criminal justice system and distorting the local economy, the Mafia in Puglia stands out.

Latvia

Trafficking in human beings, drug trafficking and vehicle theft together with a range of economic crimes (unlawful use of payments, smuggling of legal goods and violation of tax laws) are the main markets.

In 2003, 435 cases were investigated and 27 organised crime groups and networks were detected. Groups are believed to work in a given territory and specialise in certain crimes. Of these groups, 6 were trafficking in human beings. Cases related to drug trafficking in 2003 increased considerably compared to 2002.

Trafficking in human beings, smuggling of persons, drug trafficking and car theft with increasing internationalisation will remain the main threats.

Lithuania

In 2003, the Organised Crime Investigation Service of the police investigated more than 1 600 crimes. The largest numbers were related to car theft (309), drugs (294), robberies (201), residential burglary (196) and extortion (143). These as well as trafficking in human beings and various forms of economic crime constitute the main markets.

In 2003, some 10 higher-level and 44 lower-level organised crime groups with 1 200 individuals were identified. Most of them were Lithuanian citizens. Groups are mostly hierarchically structured and based on the territorial principle. Higher-level organised crime groups are more involved in economic crime and protect themselves through shielding measures. Violence and intimidation are not only used to enforce discipline within the group but also against investigating law enforcement officers and witnesses. Corruption is an important part of the *modus operandi*. Proceeds are invested in real estate and restaurants, and also transport and a range of other sectors. Lithuanian groups increasingly maintain relations with groups in other countries, in particular in the Russian Federation, Germany and Belarus.

Organised crime groups adjust rapidly to changing circumstances. They avoid open confrontation and invest more into the legal economy. Threats become more subtle.

Organised crime groups will become more specialised and enhance their transnational contacts. They will seek to extend their influence on public authorities.

Malta

Malta does not have organised crime groups in the sense of the definition. Criminals team up for a particular crime and disband subsequently.

Moldova

Major fraud and economic crime (2 892 offences recorded in 2003) and drug trafficking and production (2 377 cases) followed by smuggling of persons (575 cases) and legal goods (243 cases) are the main markets. In addition, 23 cases of trafficking in human beings were recorded.

The large number of offences recorded contrasts with the small number of organised groups identified (only 20 groups with 105 suspects identified in 2003).

Poverty and the socio-political situation will continue to favour organised crime.

Netherlands

In 2003, 221 investigations were analysed involving 1 878 suspects. Major markets, in terms of principal or subsidiary activities of organised crime groups and networks investigated, were:

- drug trafficking (146 investigations);
- money laundering (119);
- fraud (57);
- smuggling of persons (16);
- trafficking in human beings (14);
- vehicle theft (23);
- counterfeiting and falsification of documents, currencies or goods (50);
- burglary and robbery (22);
- extortion (12).

A broad diversity of criminal organisations are found, often best described as "project-based criminal organising".

Some 221 investigations involved 1 878 suspects, of which 911 were believed to be key members. Some 68% of suspects were Dutch. Others frequently mentioned include Turkish, Antillean, Surinamese, Moroccan and Albanian nationals. Some 101 groups used commercial structures, in particular in the transport, real estate and import/export sectors.

Lawyers, accountants, public notaries and others were used as third-party professionals. Intimidation and violence against persons outside criminal circles were known to be used in 58 cases, within criminal circles in 68 cases, and within the same group in 80 cases. Use of several means and frequent variations of the means of communication and coded oral messages were the primary techniques for shielding. Some 22.6% of criminal groups were known to use corruptive contacts.

The main trends in 2003:

- a considerable increase in investigations related to cocaine trafficking; at the same time a decrease in heroin trafficking;
- an increased share of Dutch nationals involved in organised crime, including drug trafficking;
- a stronger role of Chinese criminals in various sectors;
- continued production and export of ecstasy and amphetamines;
- suspects from South-Eastern Europe continue to be involved in the most violent forms of organised crime;
- a larger number of fraud-related investigations.

Norway

Economic crime, drug trafficking (136 cases with large quantities) and trafficking in human beings (73 cases) are the main markets.

Organised crime groups and networks are multi-criminal, multinational and multi-ethnic; they consist of flexible and transnational networks. Criminal motorcycle gangs show more hierarchical structures and are dominated by Norwegians. They specialise in drug trafficking and economic crime, using intimidation and violence to enforce discipline.

Groups from the Baltic states, in particular Lithuania, are also more hierarchical and involved in drugs, the smuggling of persons and trafficking in human beings, as well as robbery, theft and trafficking in stolen vehicles.

Organised crime groups and networks are becoming more professional and transnational. Crimes are more serious and brutal. It is believed that organised crime will increase in quantity and quality.

Illegal migration, trafficking in human beings, and financial and economic crime will be the main markets.

Poland

In 2002, with 140 out of 765 cases, economic crime, smuggling and counter-feiting represented the largest number of criminal proceedings initiated by the Central Bureau of Investigations (CBI). Some 151 groups were primarily involved in this field, including fraud, counterfeiting of money, forgery of documents, smuggling of alcohol, tobacco and fuel and VAT fraud.

Some 178 groups were prosecuted for predatory criminal activities such as extortion (52 cases), homicide (43), highway robbery (29) and vehicle theft (24). Some 133 groups engaged primarily in the production of synthetic drugs, and trafficking and sale of all types of drugs in 2002. In addition, in 2003, 550 investigations into suspicious transactions related to money laundering were carried out, and 63 cases were forwarded to the prosecution service in the first half of 2003.

In 2002, the CBI identified 522 organised criminal groups operating in Poland. Some 417 (80%) of them were composed of Polish nationals, 96 had an international or ethnic composition, and 9 were considered Russian-speaking groups.

In total, they had 6 134 members, of which 790 were considered group leaders. Drug-related crimes continue to increase. More than 47 000 cases were recorded in 2003 (compared to 36 000 in 2002, and 29 000 in 2001).

Portugal

By far the largest number of organised crime cases in 2003 were drug related (35 out of 56 cases, and organised crime groups and networks) involving 50% of the suspects (507 out of 1 015). This was followed by economic crime (8 cases), including VAT fraud, credit card fraud and smuggling in alcohol and tobacco.

Some 56 organised crime groups and networks were identified in 2003. Although the majority of groups consist of Portuguese nationals, increasingly groups diversify in terms of nationalities and activities. With regard to drug trafficking, criminals use Portugal as an entry point to the European Union. Several cases of economic crime in 2003 involved forgery of employment contracts, forgery of commercial documents, and cheque and credit card fraud. Some cases were accompanied by money laundering activities. Violence is used against Asian immigrants in connection with extortion and protection rackets. False employment contracts are used in connection with illegal migration.

A decrease in organised crime related to eastern European criminals was observed in 2003, probably due to law enforcement action against such groups. A lower number of organised crime cases was recorded in 2003 as compared to previous years.

Major present and future threats include:

- increased illegal migration and related offences is expected;
- drug trafficking will stabilise, although trafficking routes and *modi operandi* will diversify;
- in terms of economic and financial crime, modern technologies will open up new markets and the state will be the primary victim.

Romania

Drug trafficking (3 454 organised crime related cases recorded in 2003), trafficking in human beings (1 203 cases) and illegal migration (626 cases) constitute the main markets. Counterfeiting of currency, credit cards and traveller's cheques as well as other forms of economic crime are also of concern.

In total, 4 963 organised crime related cases were recorded in 2003 committed by 1 062 organised crime groups and networks (744 of which were dismantled) and 3 898 suspects. Some 809 persons were arrested, of whom 248 were foreigners.

Organised crime groups and networks mostly take the form of networks or cells with less than 10 members. Some 35% of groups have connections with other European countries. Most of them use violence and intimidation within their groups. Proceeds are consumed by group members and only 10% of proceeds are believed to be invested in real estate, nightclubs, the sex industry, trade, hotels or restaurants.

The number of organised crime related cases recorded in 2003 was 31% higher than in 2002 (due in part to more efficient law enforcement). Trafficking stolen vehicles decreased considerably.

Economic crime as well as cybercrime will deserve special attention. Drug trafficking, trafficking in human beings and illegal migration are likely to remain major challenges.

Serbia and Montenegro

In Serbia and Montenegro, fraud and major economic crime (492 cases recorded in 2003 in Serbia and 627 in Montenegro), smuggling of legal goods (206 cases in Serbia, none in Montenegro), extortion and racketeering (80 and 20 cases respectively) and drug trafficking (52 and 295 cases respectively) are the main markets. The distribution of pirate CDs and other counterfeited products, in particular from Kosovo, is another important issue (although this is not a criminal offence in Montenegro). Trafficking in human beings has been high on the agenda, in particular in Montenegro, but few cases have been recorded and prosecuted. Kosovo is a major market and source of organised crime, in particular in terms of drug trafficking, trafficking in human beings and trafficking in counterfeited products.

In Serbia, 810 cases involving 126 organised crime groups and networks and 1 250 suspects were recorded in 2003 (leading to 371 convictions). Several organised crime groups were eliminated in Serbia in 2003 in the course of Operation Saber: among others, the 'Zemun clan' with about 45 members (former members of the Special Operations Unit) involved in kidnapping, extortion, and trafficking in drugs and arms, as well as murder to create a crime monopoly and those of political leaders and senior government officials. Their leaders Spasojevic Dusan and Lukovic Mile were killed in a police encounter in March 2003. Milorad Ulemek Legija was arrested in June 2004. A number of other groups are involved in murder, kidnapping, extortion and racketeering, drug trafficking and trafficking in human beings.

In Montenegro, more than 1 200 cases were recorded. The issue of trafficking in human beings was high on the agenda in 2003, with one particular case highlighting shortcomings in the handling of trafficking cases by the criminal justice system, in particular the prosecution service, and pointing at possible collusion of traffickers with high-ranking officials

2003 marked a year of open confrontation between organised crime and state structures, reflected in particular in the assassination of late Serbian Prime Minister Djindjic in March. The murders of other high officials were carried out or planned. This resulted in Operation Saber against organised crime and the arrest and killing of certain suspected key leaders of organised crime groups and networks in 2003 and 2004.

Economic crime – in particular in connection with privatisation and believed to involve organised crime groups and networks having relations with high officials – will remain a key issue. Kosovo will remain a major source of organised crime related to trafficking in human beings, drugs and counter-feited products.

Slovakia

Drug trafficking (32 of 81 organised crime related cases recorded in 2003), trafficking in human beings (28 cases), economic crime (21 cases) and racketeering/extortion (16 cases) are the main markets.

In 2003 (January to November), 23 criminal groups were identified, of which 11 are considered organised crime groups in the sense that they have a hierarchical structure with a division of labour. Of these groups, 3 include foreigners, among them ethnic Albanians involved in drug trafficking. Groups do not specialise, but are involved in a variety of violent and non-violent (including economic) crimes.

Slovakia will continue to be used as a transit country for the smuggling of persons. Such operations are increasingly organised. The same is true for trafficking in human beings (including also Slovakian victims).

Slovenia

Drug trafficking (137 cases recorded in 2003), counterfeiting of money, smuggling of persons (165), arms and explosives, and blackmail and extortion are the main markets. The total damage of organised crime groups and networks is estimated at SIT777 million.

Some 65 organised crime groups and networks have been identified in Slovenia, some of them with hierarchical structures, and others which are more loosely organised. Leaders of these groups are mostly Slovenians while members also come from other countries of the former Yugoslavia. Corruption may be used to bribe local police officers in cases involving the smuggling of persons. Almost all criminal groups use legal commercial structures (tourist industry and restaurants) for shielding.

Drug trafficking will continue and the influx of synthetic drugs is likely to increase. With Slovenia having joined the EU and being an outer border, problems related to illegal migration will increase.

Spain

Almost half of all cases of organised crime in 2003 were related to drug trafficking (249 of the 542 cases), followed by trafficking in human beings (74 cases), illegal immigration (49 cases), extortion (43 cases) and forgery (43 cases). Money laundering (116 cases) is an integral part of the operations of those groups involved in drugs and trafficking in human beings.

Groups average 18 members, about half of them Spaniards in association with individuals from a range of other countries. Of the 542 groups identified in 2003, 73 meet all the criteria of organised crime groups, including transnational operations. Some 63% of the groups were new, while the remaining 37% seem to have a more permanent structure and to be more specialised. Some of the latter are of Bulgarian origin. Romanian criminal organisations show the largest increase. Information and communication technologies as well as shielding practices are increasingly made use of. Use of violence within criminal organisations slightly increased in 2003. Corruption somewhat decreased but is still resorted to in many sectors.

In 2003, law enforcement broke up 65% of the known criminal organisations. Nevertheless organised crime continues to evolve rapidly. Drug trafficking (cocaine, hashish and synthetic drugs) will continue to pose a major threat. Networks organising illegal migration are expanding. Eastern European organised crime involved in a diverse range of crime markets and making use of ICT will be most difficult to dismantle.

Sweden

Economic crime – including in particular tax fraud related to shell companies, black labour, intra EU trade, import of vehicles and investment fraud – and drugs crimes are the main markets. Smuggling of alcohol and tobacco remains at high levels.

A total of 98 organised crime groups or networks are believed to be involved in organised crime in Sweden. Most of them have a stable core of 1 to 4 members and are otherwise flexible in terms of their membership. Some 14 of the groups – including outlawed motorcycle gangs and some groups involved in drug trafficking and extortion – are more hierarchically organised. Networks are usually held together by some members with a strong criminal background as well as the need for efficiency.

Use of commercial structures is widely used to shield illicit activities. Links to the Baltic and other EU countries are the most common transnational links.

Switzerland

Trafficking in drugs, trafficking in human beings, smuggling of persons and money laundering are the main markets. Cybercrime and child pornography on the Internet have gained in importance.

Ethnic Albanian groups are particularly active in drug trafficking and trafficking in human beings. They consist mostly of flexible, opportunistic networks based on family ties. Legal businesses in the red light area are used for shielding. Serbian criminals are increasingly involved in these markets as well.

Criminal groups from the former Soviet Union use Switzerland for the laundering of proceeds (reportedly, 15.4% of all Russian capital abroad is in Swiss banks), and are also involved in trafficking in arms and of stolen art objects. Furthermore, they appear to use Switzerland for meetings with other criminal groups in order to devise crime strategies and plan offences. These groups are characterised by their flexibility and network structures. West African (predominantly Nigerian) criminal groups are involved in a large range of offences. Ethnic Albanian groups will continue to pose high risks. Serbian groups will gain in importance.

The Swiss financial system will continue to attract criminal money. Switzerland will remain a target for Russian flight capital. Criminal organisations operating in Switzerland infiltrate legal structures in their home countries, in particular those of the former Soviet Union. This hampers law enforcement. In terms of smuggling of persons, tighter measures in the EU (for example, EURODAC) may make Switzerland a more attractive target.

Economic crime does not pose a risk for the integrity of Switzerland.

"The former Yugoslav Republic of Macedonia"

Drug trafficking (306 offences with 412 suspects recorded in 2003), trafficking in arms (213 offences and 238 suspects recorded), and counterfeiting of money (144 offences and 139 suspects) are the main markets. Increasing attention is also paid to trafficking in human beings (82 offences and 129 suspects recorded in 2003, as against 49 cases and 72 suspects in 2002).

Criminal organisations tend to be ethnically homogeneous and operate internationally. Groups involved in drug trafficking, illegal migration and trafficking in human beings may also have foreign leaders. Violence is used in connection with extortion rackets as well as against victims of trafficking in human beings. Corruption is a major problem as shown in the course of an increasing number of investigations in 2003.

Trafficking in human beings, arms and drugs will continue to increase and pose security problems for the country and the region.

Turkey

More than two thirds of all organised crime cases identified are related to drug trafficking. Other markets include, in particular, trafficking in human beings (sexual exploitation of women), trafficking in fuel, fraud, counterfeiting, extortion, robbery, kidnapping and other forms of violent crime.

In 2003, more than 1 500 organised crime related cases with almost 7 000 suspects were recorded. Some 1 448 criminal networks were identified showing different characteristics in different parts of Turkey. For example, tribal networks are found in Diyarbakir, while the "godfather" culture is prevalent in Istanbul. In Erzurum, networks trafficking in women often involve foreign women as leaders who are married to Turkish men. Violence and corruption are widespread. Many groups have international links, in particular those involved in drug trafficking. Legal commercial structures are used to shield criminal activities. Proceeds are often invested in real estate.

The main threats in the future appear to be:

- links between drug-related organised crime and terrorism;
- increasing drug use among young people and drug trafficking in tourist areas;
- investment of crime money in tourism real estate;
- corruption in public procurement and the adjudication of justice.

Ukraine

The market is divided into general organised crime markets (in particular, drug trafficking, trafficking in human beings, counterfeiting of products, racketeering and extortion) and economic crime which is related to privatisation, fuel and energy sectors, agriculture, metallurgy and raw material industries. Some 37 organised crime groups and networks were involved in money laundering.

Some 634 organised crime groups and networks with 2 707 suspects have been identified, of which the majority (70%) are involved in general crime markets and have a life span of less than one year.

Organised crime related murder, banditry and racketeering is decreasing while economic crime gains in importance.

United Kingdom

Drug trafficking represents the main threat from organised crime. Others include, in particular, organised immigration crime and fraud (the cost of which is estimated at £14 billion annually).

Loosely organised criminal networks appear to be more prevalent than hierarchical groups in the UK. Over half of the groups identified are involved in smuggling and trafficking of goods and persons. Legitimate or quasi-legitimate businesses are widely used.

Organised immigration crime will continue to pose a major threat. Organised criminals are likely to exploit the opportunities of information and communication technologies.

Chapter 3 – The threat of cybercrime[1]

Introduction: background and aims of the analysis

New risks to the information society

The use of computer systems and computer networks is of great benefit to society. However, they also create new vulnerabilities. These vulnerabilities are primarily due to the fact that today's information society processes most of its important economic and social transactions by means of computer systems and is therefore highly dependent on the efficiency and security of modern information technology.

In addition, in the age of the Internet and other electronic communication systems, these intangible values can be attacked not only by perpetrators within victimised companies but by external perpetrators as well. The fact that telecommunication systems play a significant role in such attacks means that companies can even be attacked from abroad. Moreover, the technical software applications necessary for the flexible administration of these systems are so complex that security cannot be guaranteed, especially if the systems must be accessible to numerous users via telecommunication facilities.

Thus, technological developments have created a society that is extremely dependent on computer systems and especially vulnerable to all kinds of computer-based attacks:

- In the business community, most financial transactions are carried out by computer systems and therefore depend on a secure technological

1. The author of this chapter on "The threat of cybercrime" is Professor Dr Ulrich Sieber, Director of the Max Planck Institute for Foreign and International Criminal Law in Freiburg (Germany). He would like to thank the following collaborators at the Max Planck Institute in Freiburg and at the University of Munich for their kind help: Phillip Brunst, Marc Engelhart, Nadine Groeseling, René Kieselmann, Jörg Knupfer, Johanna Rinceanu and Emily Silverman. Special thanks are due to Alexander Seger of the Council of Europe for his co-operation.

Feedback on this chapter is welcome and should be sent to Professor Dr Ulrich Sieber, Max Planck Institute for Foreign and International Criminal Law, Guenterstalstr. 73, 79100 Freiburg, Germany, U.Sieber@iuscrim.mpg.de infrastructure. In addition, computer data represent not only money but also stocks, shares, and other monetary instruments. The resulting dependency on safe information technology can also be seen, for example, in the context of electronic commerce, which requires secure systems for the transfer of money and for the exchange of legally enforceable electronic transactions. However, these systems are especially prone to computer fraud because of the complexity of computer programmes, the negligence of users, bad administration of company intranets, abuses committed by insiders, and attacks by external hackers.

- Many businesses store their most valuable company secrets on electronic systems. These systems can often be accessed both from within the company as well as externally. This presents new opportunities for industrial espionage, especially since modern information technology allows huge amounts of data to be copied secretly in milliseconds. Thus, the advantage of having data that is available all over the world at any time is accompanied by the risk that hackers will circumvent the protections established to prevent illegal access. Successful hacking attacks against the computer systems of the Pentagon, the FBI and Nato units show that an effective protection of computer-stored information cannot yet be guaranteed. A new dimension to the problem has emerged in the last few years with the advent of Wireless Local Area Networks (WLANs) and other forms of wireless communication.

- With the implementation of computer systems in industrial production, for example in the automobile or food industries, a company's entire production frequently relies on the functioning of its data-processing system. Computer system shut-downs regularly paralyse computer-run, computer-optimised production processes. Attacks on production can be carried out by employees within the company. More and more frequently, however, networked companies are subject to external attacks carried out by means of computer viruses, worms, and Trojan Horses. These attacks, which can lead to denial of service (DoS) attacks that may block all Internet communication for days, vividly illustrate the difficulty of protecting networked computer systems.

- International computer networks are not only an essential element of today's economy but also of the public sector and of society in general. Marine, air, and space control systems, electric power supply and nuclear power stations, as well as medical systems depend to a great extent on computer technology. In addition, the entire military sector depends on secure computer systems, particularly with respect to communications, planning, and weapons management. The expert discussion following the blackouts that struck US and Canadian electricity systems in 2003 shows that these systems could be primary targets for cyber terrorists since a single attack could have disastrous results. Attacks on nuclear power stations or military systems via the Internet could obviously lead to even more serious consequences: the effects of such a strike could theoretically outstrip in magnitude those caused by the attacks of 11 September 2001.

- Computers and global networks such as the Internet play an increasing role in a multitude of social interactions. A most important example of this is the education and entertainment of minors. Computer applications in this area lead to new risks of children being confronted with illegal and harmful contents, such as child pornography, glorification of violence, hate speech, and even being enticed to commit suicide, engage in cannibalism, or become involved in dubious cults. Due to the anonymity of the Internet, minors often do not know whether they are contacting another minor or an adult who, after "grooming" a child online, may go on to abuse the minor in the real world.

Aims of this analysis

This general introduction shows that the security of information technology and the prevention of cybercrime are of great importance for today's society. In order to protect society, both the threatening phenomenon itself as well as its extent must be understood. Such knowledge is not only necessary in order to educate computer users and to develop technical measures of protection, which are the most important means for preventing cybercrime, it is also indispensable for creating an effective criminal law system to fight computer-related crime.

With respect to these aims, this chapter analyses the phenomena, the pervasiveness, and the impact of cybercrime:

- The first section provides an overview of the various phenomena of computer-related crime, the structure of the phenomena as well as the latest developments and current trends.[1]

---

1. With respect to these aims, it has not always been possible to establish the authenticity of the case material cited by checking original sources. Reliance solely on

- In order to evaluate the risks of computer-related crime, the second section analyses the links between computer-related crime and organised crime as well as the links between computer-related crime and terrorism.

- The following third section assesses the extent of computer-related crime by looking both at criminal justice statistics and the real world.

- The final fourth section proposes conclusions which may be relevant for the reform of criminal justice systems.

Phenomena of cybercrime

Definition and typology of computer-related crime and cybercrime

Historical development

When the first reports on computer-related crime were published some decades ago, the phenomenon of computer-related crime was considered a new form of criminality.[1] With time, however, it has become clear that this "specific new form of criminality" in fact consists of a wide range of offences committed either with the aid of, or against, computer systems:

- The initial discussion of computer-related crime in the 1960s was primarily concerned with infringements of privacy. Although there were no PCs at this time, police and other agencies were able to store and to access large amounts of data. In this early discussion, issues of

---

cases on file with police and judiciary or reliance on the verification of cases by victims would have been impossible within the time frame foreseen for the preparation of this report. Moreover, limiting the analysis to police and judicial sources would also have made it practically impossible to illustrate new trends in the commission of criminal offences on the Internet, as only a small percentage of crime committed on the Internet is reported to the authorities and, of these, only a small portion end with a conviction. In addition, the length of time necessary for a criminal case to work its way through the judicial system would hinder the goal of presenting a current assessment of the potential threats posed by computer and Internet crime. However, in order to verify the results of this report, a more in-depth analysis based on criminological methods is part of the future research agenda of the Max Planck Institute for Foreign and International Criminal Law.

1. Sieber 1977 and 1980.

civil and public law dominated, and criminal law played only a minor role.

- As computers became more and more popular in all sectors of industry and in the business community, the focus in the 1970s turned to economic crimes such as computer fraud, computer manipulation, sabotage, and espionage as well as to hacking as a predicate offence for all of these crimes. For many years, these offences were considered to be "computer-related crime" or at least its principal manifestation.

- With the growth in the number of businesses using computers and with rising sales of personal computers all over the world, standard software packages became increasingly popular in the 1980s. Soon after the first standardised products were sold, illegal copies appeared. These infringements of intellectual property, first encountered in the area of computer programmes, spread by the end of the century to all types of multimedia content, especially music and movies.

- Due to the rapidly growing number of users connected to computer networks and especially as a result of the development of the World Wide Web, the Internet in the 1990s became attractive for people offering illegal or harmful content such as child pornography, hate speech and illegal gambling.

- At the same time, the surge in civil, governmental, and military services highly dependent on a well-functioning Internet led to new risks of cyberterrorism and cyber war. The development of methods of attacking as well as methods of protecting computer systems has become important with regard to both military research and to the prevention of terrorist activity.

- Today, information technology plays a key role not only in the business community but also in the private, everyday lives of millions of people. As a consequence, computers and networks are increasingly used as tools (for example, communication and planning) for committing – or assisting in the commission of – many "traditional" crimes, such as homicide, drug trafficking, terrorism, and other forms of organised crime. Although these crimes are not specifically computer-related, information technology is used more and more frequently as a tool in their commission, for example, for covert communication, financial transactions and the encryption of key information.

Definition of computer-related crime and cybercrime

Thus, it has become obvious over the years that computer-related crime is not merely one new form of crime but that it comprises a wide variety of new phenomena, including new types of crime as well as traditional crimes committed in connection with computer systems.[1] Before examining these various forms of crime, it is therefore necessary to clarify the scope and definition of computer-related crime and cybercrime and to identify the attributes these offences have in common:

- The common denominator and characteristic features of offences known as computer-related crime (or computer crime) can be found in their relationship to computer systems. The major substantive aspect of this is the relationship between crime and computer data or – as far as content is concerned – computer-stored information. On the basis of this relationship between computer-related crime and computer-stored information, it becomes clear that the question of how to deal with the aforementioned heterogeneous offences cannot be answered without addressing fundamental questions concerning the paradigm shift of the information society, in which intangible objects (especially information) have become more and more important and have created new challenges for traditional legal systems, which were developed mainly on the basis of tangible objects.[2]

- The common denominator and characteristic features of offences known as cybercrime are their relationship to computer networks. This relationship is especially important in the context of the global computer network known as the Internet. Since data in international computer networks can be transferred in both unencrypted and encrypted form around the globe in milliseconds without being subject to any effective control mechanisms by national states, cybercrime is the most "international" type of crime in existence and the most serious challenge to existing criminal justice systems, which are based on the concept of territorial control and which are seriously challenged by the need to exert control over a global cyberspace.

---

1. See Sieber 1986.
2. See Sieber 1992.

Typology and structure of computer-related crime

This analysis shows that meaningful definitions of computer-related crime and cybercrime are possible despite the wide variety within each of the two categories. However, due to the breadth of these definitions, a more precise typology and structure of computer-related crime and cybercrime must be developed. Within the framework of such a structure, it will then be possible to define more precisely the relevant phenomena and subgroups of computer-related crime and cybercrime.

It is obvious that the appropriate structure of the various forms of computer-related crime or cybercrime depends on the aim of the analysis undertaken. Since this report is closely linked to the legal work of the Council of Europe, the following analysis is patterned on the dominating structure provided and required by substantive criminal law differentiating between the relevant protected interests. These various protected interests are also clearly reflected in the Convention on Cybercrime of the Council of Europe and its additional protocol concerning acts of a racist and xenophobic nature. Thus, this section examines:

- offences against the confidentiality, integrity and availability of computer data and systems;
- traditional computer-related offences;
- content-related offences;
- copyright infringement offences and offences to related rights;
- infringement-of-privacy offences.

Offences against the confidentiality, integrity and availability of computer data and systems

Computer hacking and other forms of illegal access

Illegal access to computer systems and data is a basic requirement of many types of computer-related crimes. It can be used for espionage, sabotage, fraud, forgery and many other computer-related crimes. For that reason, the *modi operandi* of illegal access to computer systems are often in the focus of analysis of computer-related crime. The main forms of *modus operandi* for obtaining illegal access to computer systems and data are hacking, interception and the deception of users:

- The term "computer hacking" refers to the penetration of computer systems by technical manipulations perpetrated either solely for the "buzz" of overcoming technical security measures or with the aim of sabotage, espionage or manipulation.[1]

- The term "computer interception" refers to closely related actions that, on occasion, overlap: whereas computer "hacking" involves attacks on stored data, computer "interception" involves attacks on transmitted data or data flows. In particular cases it may be difficult to distinguish between computer hacking and computer interception. However, the differentiation is especially important since a distinction in the legal treatment of the two phenomena is made by the Convention on Cybercrime in Articles 2 and 3.

- Hacking and interception committed by technical means are not the only forms of illegally accessing computer systems and data. Another form of illegal penetration is the deception of users in order to gain illegally and fraudulently access to their systems. These three main types of *modus operandi* of unauthorised procurement of data will be analysed in the following.

Hacking computer systems

Circumventing password protection

"Traditional" forms of hacking in computer networks were developed during the 1980s based, for example, on the insecure use of standard passwords (which often were not changed regularly by computer users). These techniques are based on the fact that, even today, Internet users often do not change the installation passwords of computer systems, use common language words (which are tested by hackers) and frequently use the same passwords for long periods of time and for many different resources.

For that reason, simply changing passwords regularly is not enough: in order to offer a reasonable degree of protection, passwords should not consist simply of a string of letters; rather, a combination of alphabetic, numeric and special characters is necessary. Furthermore, the use of words found in dictionaries should be avoided. Finally, a different password should be used for every resource in order to prevent greater damage in case of a successful hacking incident.

---

1. As a consequence, the term "hacking" will be used in this report not only in the context of cases in which offenders penetrate systems for fun (joyriding) but also in the context of cases in which offenders hack in order to cause damage or to pave the way for further action, such as espionage, fraud or forgery.

In other cases, passwords gained either by breaking into a computer or by intercepting traffic are used and – if necessary – are decrypted. An interesting method of decrypting passwords was used in the KGB case mentioned in more detail below.

> In this case, the passwords involved had been encrypted and stored in password files. The form of one-way encryption enabled anyone to encrypt his password with the assistance of publicly available encryption keys. However, it was not possible to "calculate back" the password being entered. The hackers got around this method, which was regarded as safe, by encrypting an entire dictionary using a publicly available encryption procedure and then comparing the results of their own encryption procedure with the data of the encrypted passwords they hacked. Wherever encrypted passwords in their dictionary matched those in the password files of their victims, they had obtained a valid password.

A popular method of obtaining passwords within universities used to be to intercept the login procedure by means of special interception software.

> This interception of the login procedure involved displaying not the actual login screen but rather a seemingly identical "interception programme" on a user's computer system. When the user entered his login information, the programme would record the password and the user identification. The user would then see a display indicating that he had entered a false password, assume that he had made a typing error, and re-enter his details, this time into the legitimate login screen.

Today, a similar but much more efficient method can be employed by anyone with access to a particular hardware device.

> This device looks like a plug connector and can be installed between the keyboard plug and the main computer. The little device looks like a harmless part of the computer system. However, it logs and stores all passwords inputted in the keyboard and transmitted to the central unit of the computer system.

Using faulty hardware or software implementations

Finally, faulty hardware or software implementation can be exploited to steal login information and other personal data. Furthermore, faulty implementations that cause programmes to malfunction can convince users that they need to acquire additional software.

An example attracted attention in June 2004: pop-up ads originating at certain websites secretly downloaded software onto the user's system. This software recorded the keystrokes of users who visited any of a number of targeted financial websites. The data – especially login information – was then sent to a website in Estonia. This Internet threat affected only users of Microsoft's Internet Explorer, as the covert installation of the keystroke-recording software exploited a security hole in this browser's software.[1]

In September 2004, a means of exploiting a bug in the software that is used for displaying JPG pictures was discovered. The method involves inducing a buffer overflow that can then be used to execute hostile code on the victim's computer. In a worst case scenario, a victim could completely lose control over a computer merely by surfing on a website that contains prepared pictures or by opening a picture attached to an e-mail.[2]

IP and DNS spoofing

Although computer security has since become more sophisticated and the handling of passwords has improved, in recent years new techniques of computer manipulation have developed in the Internet context, such as IP spoofing, DNS spoofing and infiltration of computer networks by malicious web applets. These methods evolved from the use of communication protocols such as the Internet Protocol (IP) and the Hypertext Transfer Protocol (HTTP) used to run web servers.

The technique of IP spoofing is used to gain unauthorised access to computers or networks from outside by pretending to be an authorised and trusted device inside the penetrated network. This is done through modification of IP addresses in data packet headers transmitted to an incoming port of the network's router. Although the fake IP address is known as a valid address inside the network only, in the past routers were often not distinguishing between data transmitted from outside and data from inside the network. Newer routers and so-called "firewalls" offer protection against this kind of attack.[3]

---

1. See Mike Musgrove, "Net attack aimed at banking data", *Washington Post*, 30 June 2004 at E01, available at http://www.washingtonpost.com/ac2/wp-dyn/A16023-2004Jun29 (as of: November 2004).

2. Cf. http://www.bsi.de/av/texte/schwachstelle-jpeg.htm and http://www.heise.de/security/news/meldung/51546 (as of: November 2004).

3. Cf. also McClure et al. 2001, pp. 374 *et seq.*

DNS spoofing is based on the fact that in order to access a server on the Internet, the user contacts a domain name server (DNS). As a rule, the DNS translates the domain name to a machine-readable IP address and passes this information back to the user. In cases of DNS spoofing, however, the user is given the spoofer's IP address rather than the requested address. In other words, in a DNS spoofing attack, the hacker intercepts the communication between user-victim and DNS and sends fake IP addresses to the victim's computer. This can be done by using malicious applets downloaded by the attacked user himself. Once the applet is activated, the user's communication can be re-routed and the transmitted data gathered.[1]

Deceiving computer users

Web spoofing

While IP and DNS spoofing depend on sophisticated technical knowledge, web spoofing attacks use a much simpler approach which is based on the principle of deceiving computer users. It is based on optical illusions.

Hyperlinks on web pages can contain characters that make an address look real, but in fact lead to the wrong website, for example, replacing the letter "o" in the address <www.microsoft.com> with the number "0" would result in the address <www.micr0s0ft.com>. Most users would not suspect any malicious intention. In this example, the hacker could set up a web page asking for the input of sensitive user information, for example, credit card information.

Distribution of false software

Attackers have also found other ways to deceive computer users. A very successful technique for example is the distribution of false software with Trojan Horse routines.

The following is an example from 1998: an e-mail was distributed that seemed to originate from Microsoft and apparently contained in an attachment a "bugfix" software update to remedy a problem with the e-mail programme Outlook 98/Outlook Express. Whenever a recipient of the e-mail installed the programme onto his computer system, copies of all his sent e-mails were diverted to Bulgaria, regardless of where the intended recipients of the e-mails were located.[2]

---

1. Cf. also Viktor Mraz and Klaus Weidner, http://www.heise.de/ct/97/10/286 (as of: November 2004).
2. Cf. Peter H. Lewis, "Melissa and her cousins", *New York Times*, 1 April 1999, p. 1.

Cross site scripting (XSS)

A newer method used to gain access to personal data makes use of a technique called "cross site scripting" (frequently abbreviated XSS). A perpetrator inserts scripting code into a web page (for example, a description on an eBay web page) that is activated when the victim opens the prepared page. The scripting code can be used to steal information stored in cookies or to read user inputs on this page. Favourite targets for XSS attacks are online shops, employee portal pages, and Internet banking sites, since the attacker can use integrated forms on these pages.[1]

> In December 2004, an error based on an XSS vulnerability in the http proxy of the CyberGuard firewall was discovered. It enabled attackers to read cookies stored in the browsers of users on protected networks. This kind of attack was possible because the proxy did not filter URLs for possible script code.[2]

> In early 2004, the security company Symantec reported a vulnerability on its website: according to the website, Symantec Web Security failed to check and parse HTML tags in URLs included in error or block page messages that are displayed to the user if a page is blocked. As a result, an attacker could potentially include malicious scripts in the URL, which the user would execute in the context of the site specified in the URL, in the event that the page is blocked.[3]

Phishing as a new form of social engineering

A method known as "social engineering" has also been used frequently. One example of this method is the use of "trick calls", where the person called is asked to disclose sensitive information.[4]

---

1. See Steffen Gundel, "XSS: cross site scripting", *Gefahr für Benutzerdaten*, Vol. IX, No. 8, 2004, pp. 48-53 and http://httpd.apache.org/info/css-security/ (as of: November 2004).

2. Cf. http://www.heise.de/security/news/meldung/43141 (as of: November 2004).

3. Cf. http://www.sarc.com/avcenter/security/Content/2004.01.13.html (as of: November 2004).

4. An example would be "Have you already received your new password?" This method is still being used. Subscribers to America Online (AOL) have occasionally received e-mail requests from supposed AOL employees stating that due to technical problems they should disclose their password. As a result, AOL and other service providers now warn their subscribers that their personnel will never request a user's password.

Recently, this well-known method has been employed on the Internet in the form of so-called phishing.[1] In these cases the perpetrators send to numerous Internet users e-mails that seem to identify the perpetrator as an employee of a trusted Internet provider or other service institution (for example, a credit institution). The e-mail states that the institution is experiencing technical problems and the user must disclose, add to, or correct his or her user ID and password, personal account information or other sensitive data (such as PINs[2] or TANs[3]). For this purpose, the e-mail contains a link (often using the aforementioned web spoofing technique) to a fraudulent website set up by the perpetrator that is disguised to appear to recipients to be the website of the trusted service provider that seems to have sent the e-mail.[4] If the Internet user inputs the demanded data this procedure allows the perpetrator to access sensitive data that can subsequently be used for fraudulent purposes.

> In Germany in May 2004, for example, Internet users were asked to visit web pages fraudulently attributed to the Volksbank and the Raiffeisenbank and to disclose sensitive information (for example, PINs) as well as unused TANs. Compliant users not only enabled the phisher to access bank statements but – among other things – to carry out fund transfers as well.[5]

> Phishers who advertised a Porsche Cayenne on eBay in July 2004 proceeded similarly. A click on the article description transferred the user automatically to a web page that asked the user to register by re-entering credit card information. Although the URL continued to show the website of eBay, the registration form in fact sent the data to 1eboy.com, a website set up by the phishers.[6]

---

1. Further information at http://www.antiphishing.org (as of: November 2004). See also Frank O'Donnell, "New technology and new methods of conning money from the public", *Scotsman*, 19 August 2004, p. 10. The term "phishing" derives from the words "password" and "fishing".

2. PIN stands for personal identification number.

3. TAN stands for transaction number, a number that can only be used for one transaction.

4. Cf. http://www4.gartner.com/5_about/press_releases/asset_71087_11.jsp (as of: November 2004). See also Jonathan Krim, "Justice Dept. to announce cyber-crime crackdown", *Washington Post*, 25 August 2004, at E05.

5. Cf. http://www.heise.de/newsticker/meldung/47841 (as of: November 2004). See also Constantin Gillies, "Mit der Angel in fremden Bankkonten", *Die Welt*, 31 July 2004, p. 1.

6. See *c't Magazin für Computertechnik*, No. 17, 2004, p. 17.

At approximately the same time, the British Hi-Tech Crime Unit (NHTCU) arrested a group of twelve eastern Europeans who participated in a large-scale phishing scam that targeted the bank accounts of computer users. The police presume that the scam led to the transfer of hundreds of thousands of British pounds to the Russian Federation. According to the English media, the police seized, among other things, computers and passwords from numerous addresses in London and Ramsgate in Kent.[1]

In August 2004, two other well-known German banks, the Postbank and the Deutsche Bank, became the victims of phishing attacks as internationally organised criminal groups roamed the globe seeking new targets. The Post-bank suffered two phishing attacks in less than four weeks. The attack utilised a spoofed e-mail written in German warning customers of a security risk and asking them to enter personal financial data such as credit card numbers, PINs and TANs to resolve the problem.[2]

Phishing attacks are becoming more and more sophisticated. While the first phishing attacks were poorly written and contained grammatical errors that made it relatively easy to identify the mails as "fakes", recent phishing mails are well written and often contain logos and graphics copied from original websites. The higher quality of these more recent attacks makes it easier to convince the user of the message's authenticity. In addition, in the near future, phishers in search of easy access to the confidential information of Internet users may elect to proceed by means of domain hijacking. Because it is possible for attackers to take control of entire domains – eBay.de was in fact hijacked in August 2004 – users of original websites can never be entirely sure that their data will not fall into the wrong hands; indeed, it is unknown whether the hijacking of the eBay.de domain was coupled with a phishing attack.

---

1. Cf. http://www.golem.de/0405/31176.html (as of: November 2004). See also Clare Francis, "Alert over risks of e-banking", *Sunday Times* (London), 22 August 2004, p. 5.
2. Cf.
http://www.computerweekly.com/articles/article.asp?liArticleID=132861&liFlavourID=1&sp=1 bylined by John Blau for IDG news service (as of: November 2004). See also "Betrugsversuche im Internet reissen nicht ab", *General Anzeiger* (Bonn), 24 August 2004, p. 3. See also Bill Goodwin, "Banks look at phishing alert systems", *Computer Weekly*, 27 January 2004, p. 5; Beat Balzli and Jörg Schmidt, "Raubzug im Netz", *Der Spiegel*, 36/2004, 30 August 2004, pp. 78-79; and Florian Eder and Angela Maier "Kunden fallen auf Konto-Netzattacken herein", *Financial Times Deutschland*, 26 August 2004, http://www.ftd.de/ub/fi/1093076510499.html (as of: November 2004).

In other cases, users have been tricked by malicious graphics at the bottom of a web page that seem to show a status bar of the browser and that imitate a secure and encrypted connection with the bank.[1] In the meantime the bank's real web page was displayed in the background, thus creating a perfect illusion that fake window and real website originate from the same site and are trustworthy.

Obtaining data by means of Trojan Horses, especially in connection with viruses and worms

Today, Trojan Horses are frequently employed for accessing and obtaining data. Trojan Horse programmes, often sub-programmes hidden within other larger computer programmes, are capable of collecting and sending data as soon as they are installed into the computer system. They represent a mass phenomenon and are a huge threat to the individual Internet user.[2] Computer experts distinguish between pure Trojan Horses as well as viruses and worms with a Trojan version.

Pure Trojan Horses are often sent piggy-back in e-mail attachments, and, after they are activated (by a click on the e-mail attachment, for example), they establish themselves in the operating system and spy on keystrokes and other sensitive information.

The following example illustrates the use of Trojan Horses: in spring 1998, two hackers made use of Trojan Horse programmes and in so doing demonstrated the vulnerability of the German online service "T-Online", which – up until that point – had been regarded as secure. They made the software "T-Online Power Tools" available for downloading on the Internet, a programme that apparently optimised the existing T-Online access software. However, the programme in fact contained a Trojan Horse that, upon installation, secretly forwarded the access data of the T-Online subscriber to the hackers.[3] The process was successful only when the access passwords of the subscribers were stored on their hard drives (although these passwords were stored in an encrypted format, the algorithms used were simple to decrypt).[4]

---

1. See Holger Bleich and Jürgen Schmidt, "Auf Phishzug", *c't Magazin für Computertechnik*, No. 17, 2004, pp. 178 *et seq.*

2. See also Peter Schüler, "PC spioniert", *c't Magazin für Computertechnik* , No. 15, 2002, pp. 128-30.

3. See http://www.bsi.de/literat/ecomerz/ecom_es.pdf (pp. 12 *et seq.*). (as of: November 2004).

4. Thus, as a general rule, passwords should not be stored on hard drives, but rather should be entered by the user individually on each occasion. The T-Online access software has since been updated to remove this vulnerability; as a result, this form of

95

A new example of a Trojan Horse is Bankhook.A.[1] With the help of this Trojan Horse, which records keystrokes and sends them to other locations, passwords, bank account numbers, credit card numbers, etc., can be acquired. Bankhook.A is programmed to target a limited number of websites offering banking and other financial services. These websites include, in Germany, deutsche-bank.de and sparkasse-banking.de.[2] Bankhook is a software, which is integrated as a so-called "browser helper object" in Internet Explorer. The Trojan Horse propagates via security holes in Microsoft Internet Explorer.

In many cases, Trojan Horses are distributed by viruses and worms. Indeed, the anti-virus software company Sophos counted 959 new viruses and worms used in co-operation with Trojan Horses in May 2004 alone.[3] The following are examples of worms with an "espionage function":

The strategy of the SirCam worm is to send its malicious code via e-mail in attachments with file extensions such as "doc", "zip" or "jpg". SirCam sends not only itself, it also sends files that it finds on the infected machine, favouring files in the "my files" directory. The worm propagates by means of e-mail attachments.[4]

The Nimda worm creates a guest account on compromised computer systems and provides the account with administrator privileges. This allows for the exercise of complete control over the compromised computer system. In addition, all existing drives become susceptible to external access. The worm propagates by means of e-mail attachments via security holes in the Microsoft Internet Information Server (IIS) and via externally accessible drives.[5]

---

sabotage is only possible on computers that have not been updated with the appropriate software.

1. Alias PWSteal.Refest, alias PWS-WebMoney.gen, alias TrojanSpy.Win32.Small.aa.
2. Cf. http://www.spiegel.de/netzwelt/technologie/0,1518,306642,00.html (as of: November 2004).
3. Cf. http://www.spiegel.de/netzwelt/technologie/0,1518,302704,00.html (as of: November 2004); and URL of Sophos: http://www.sophos.com (as of: November 2004).
4. http://www.pctipp.ch/helpdesk/virenticker/archiv/18905.asp (as of: November 2004).
5. http://www.sophos.com/virusinfo/analyses/w32nimdaa.html (as of: November 2004).

The Mimail worm – of which several varieties exist – seeks to collect personal data stored on infected computer systems, such as credit card information, and send them to selected e-mail addresses. The worm propagates via e-mail.[1]

Interception

Besides hacking stored data, interception of data flows is another important method to gain access to computer data by technical means. Such interception can be found especially with respect to telecommunication and telephone technology as well as with respect to wireless LANs.

Interception involving telecommunication and telephone technology

In the field of telecommunication between computers, data can be intercepted, for example, at certain connection points within a telecommunications company or by means of so-called "packet sniffing".[2] As a result, interception can take place from outside a building, as physical access to cables is unnecessary.

Due to developments in the field of telephone and telecommunications technology (such as ISDN), interception of telephone technology not only concern classic telephone systems but also affects answer phones, and voice-mail systems. Since the 1980s, "telephone hackers" or "phreakers"[3] have been able to dial themselves into a telephone company's local phone exchanges and eavesdrop on conversations held in another part of town.[4] Although the introduction of digital transmission stations made penetration by these means much more difficult, the advent of new Internet-based telephone technologies – such as Voice-over-IP (VoIP) – may reawaken hacker interest in the interception of telephone calls.

Today, criminals penetrate the telephone exchanges of telephone companies primarily via normal data lines that serve, in some case, as a means of remote access for technicians. With the convergence of data processing and

---

1. http://www.bsi.de/av/vb/mimailj.htm (as of: November 2004).

2. "Packet sniffing" involves the use of hacker programmes or standard software used to analyse the network traffic (known as a "packet sniffer") in order to gain access to packets of data sent between computers within a network. It is thus possible to filter data according to particular parameters and to acquire knowledge of sensitive data, usually passwords. Cf. Garfinkel and Spafford 1996, pp. 471 *et seq.* and http://netsecurity.about.com/cs/hackertools/a/aa121403.htm (as of: November 2004).

3. The term "phreakers" derives from the expression "phone freak".

4. Cf. *Focus Magazin*, No. 17, 1993, p. 106.

telecommunication as well as with the digitalisation of telecommunication, the line between telephone, fax and e-mail monitoring as well as computer hacking is becoming increasingly blurred.

Car phones, directional radio stations, and satellite connections are particularly easy to attack when uncoded communication is used.[1] Digital networks and digital broadcasting networks as well as the convergence of telephone and computer technology will gradually facilitate new offences in this area in the future.[2]

> An example of telephone wiretapping is a 1992 case in which young Germans penetrated the speech computer of the Barclays Bank in Hamburg. The bank's clients reported to this computer the receipt of their credit cards as well as the corresponding secret personal identification numbers. They also used the speech computer to report lost or stolen cards and when asking for an increase of their credit limits – a transaction for which they had to disclose the appropriate secret number.[3]

> In the US, eavesdropping has, among other things, enabled criminals to determine the numbers of telephone access cards (so-called calling cards), which they then sell. In 1999, two ringleaders in the hacker organisation "Phone Masters" were convicted in the United States for hacking into the computer systems of several large telecommunication companies, illegally obtaining long distance calling card numbers, and selling the stolen numbers.[4]

> Another example of the potential impact of such activities can be found in Germany, where reliable sources refer to the competition between the German company Siemens and a French competitor with respect to a large contract for high-speed train systems in South Korea: French agents were able to intercept the satellite-based fax transmission of the bid made by the German company, thus allowing the French company to undercut the German bid.

---

1. See also http://www.uplink.com.au/lawlibrary/Documents/Docs/Doc122.html (as of: November 2004).

2. Carsten Holm, "Kriminalität – Stundenlang nach Nigeria", *Der Spiegel*, 9 July 2001, pp. 48 *et seq.*

3. "Kennwort 888", *Der Spiegel*, 17 August 1992, pp. 206 *et seq.*

4. See http://www.usdoj.gov/criminal/cybercrime/phonmast.htm (as of: November 2004).

Interception involving Wireless Local Area Networks

A newly emerging trend is the interception of Wireless Local Area Networks (WLANs).[1] By means of a special WLAN adapter – found, for example, in a notebook or a personal digital assistant (PDA) – and so-called "sniffer" software, a hacker in a vehicle or on foot will look for visible WLANs (this is commonly known as WarDriving or WarWalking). Since many WLAN users, including businesses, frequently do not or do not sufficiently secure their wireless networks, hackers often succeed in accessing a wireless network. This, in turn, enables the hacker to gain access to data transmitted via the WLAN or – in some cases – even to use the WLAN to anonymously connect to the Internet.[2]

According to a study conducted in Germany in 2003 by the professional services firm Ernst & Young, 15% of the businesses studied did not encrypt WLAN data traffic at all and 37% of the businesses relied on the encryption process known as Wireless Equivalent Privacy (WEP), a process that is insufficient because it is relatively easy to hack.[3] In the business world, such open WLANs exist in part because employees install and operate so-called access points (that is, reception stations for computer systems that communicate without wires) within the firm's network even though they are not authorised to do so, thereby compromising the entire network security strategy of their employer. In other cases, the comfort of WLANs combined with the ignorance of its users allows attacks even at officially installed access points.

Interception via Bluetooth

The wireless communications of Bluetooth users can also be intercepted.[4] Although public opinion would limit such attacks to a range of some 10

---

1. Cf. Ernst & Young, "Wireless LAN – ein Paradies für Hacker?", http://www.ey.com/global/download.nsf/Germany/WLAN_Studie/$file/WLAN. pdf (as of: November 2004).
2. Cf. Ulrich Clauss, "Der Feind in meinem Netz", Die Welt, 6 July 2004, also available at http://www.welt.de/data/2004/07/06/301250.html?prx=1 (as of: November 2004).
3. Cf. http://www.ey.com/global/download.nsf/Germany/WLAN_Studie/$file/WLAN. pdf, p. 20 (as of: November 2004).
4. Bluetooth is a standard for wireless data communication between electronic devices (for example, PCs, personal digital assistants, cell phones) and is supported by such well-known companies as Ericsson, IBM, Intel, Microsoft, Nokia and Toshiba. An

meters, in fact, recent studies show that attackers can strike from a distance of up to 1.74 kilometres, if appropriate technology is used.[1] Current standard antennas have a range of about 200 metres.[2]

> Bluesnarfing allows hackers to gain access to data stored on a Bluetooth-enabled phone using Bluetooth wireless technology without alerting the phone's user of the connection made to the device. The information that can be accessed in this manner includes the phonebook and associated images, calendar and IMEI (International Mobile Equipment Identity).[3] Theoretically, Bluetooth phones can only be accessed in this way when they are in "discoverable" or "visible" mode. However, tools available on the Internet allow attackers to access these phones even if they are in non-discoverable mode. Attackers can even use the manipulated device to make telephone calls or to surf at the user's expense.[4] In addition, so-called "chaos attacks" have used Bluetooth phones to send text messages and to call pay-per-call telephone numbers.

Cell phones are not the only devices using the Bluetooth standard that are in danger: personal digital assistants (PDAs) and PCs are also vulnerable to abuse.

> The British company Pentest has discovered a security hole in a Bluetooth application. According to Pentest, unauthenticated remote attackers who submit various malformed service requests via Bluetooth can circumvent the software. These attackers have been able to use remote devices for their own ends.[5]

---

advantage of Bluetooth over infra-red techniques is that no direct visual contact between various pieces of equipment is necessary for data exchange. Cf. http://www.bluetooth.com (as of: November 2004).

1. See Dusan Zivadinovic, "Richtfunk-Attacke auf Bluetooth-Handy", *c't Magazin für Computertechnik*, No. 18, 2004, p. 41 and http://www.heise.de/newsticker/meldung/49907 (as of: November 2004).

2. See http://www.heise.de/newsticker/meldung/53700 (as of: November 2004).

3. See Dusan Zivadinovic op. cit.

4. See "Bluetooth-Handies ermöglichen WLAN-Surfen auf fremde Kosten", *c't Magazin für Computertechnik*, No. 14, 2004, p. 45; Cf. http://www.heise.de/newsticker/meldung/48216 (as of: November 2004).

5. See http://www.heise.de/newsticker/meldung/50068 and http://www.pentest.co.uk/documents/ptl-2004-03.html (as of: November 2004).

Damages

As far as the damage caused by computer hacking is concerned, a differentiation is essential: in numerous cases, the penetrated computer is not actually harmed, but merely endangered, and the data found on the computer are neither modified nor otherwise used. However, in these instances, too, the "formal sphere of secrecy" or the integrity of the computer systems concerned is violated. On the other hand, considerable damage can occur in cases where the perpetrators later use their knowledge to commit espionage, sabotage, fraud, or copyright infringements. For that reason, hacking cases comprise a wide spectrum of differing cases.

Hacking cases that cause no tangible damage are those in which hackers simply search for security holes, inform the affected company of the problem, and give the company a deadline within which to alleviate the situation. If the company fails to solve the problem within the stated deadline, the hackers publish their findings on Internet homepages.[1] Publication is not designed to embarrass or to blackmail the affected companies but rather to inform the general public about computer-related security problems.

Examples of hacking include an attack in 2001 on the official website of the White House, where hackers replaced the US Government site with a near-empty black screen containing a reference to a previous break-in.[2] Although this hack caused no large-scale economic damage, the ensuing damage to reputation and to the public confidence is great.

On the other hand, one of the most serious cases of sophisticated "hacking" involved a group of German teenagers in the late 1980s. After accessing various American computer systems, they sold the knowledge obtained in their "data journeys" to the former Soviet Secret Service, the KGB. The incident was discovered because one of the young hackers sought help from the author of this report when he was a professor at the University of Bayreuth, a step that led to a deal with the prosecution authorities: the hacker revealed his knowledge, and the investigation against him was dropped. The case was of particular interest because information on new techniques of computer hacking

---

1. See numerous examples in the bugtraq mailing list

http://www.securityfocus.com/archive/1 and

http://msgs.securepoint.com/bugtraq (as of: November 2004).

2. Cf. http://www.wired.com/news/politics/0,1283,43993,00.html (as of: November 2004).

was disclosed to the prosecution authorities in the course of the proceeding.[1] This case clearly shows the enormous potential damage that may be caused by computer hacking, especially – in this case – if the espionage had continued without being discovered.

Espionage

Risks

As described above, in many cases of hacking, interception, and other forms of illegal access to computer systems, perpetrators not only access and download the hacked data, they also exploit the illegally obtained information. This is especially the case in the field of espionage.

Computer espionage – which only rarely appears in official statistics[2] – introduces dangers above and beyond those posed by traditional economic espionage. Huge quantities of data are stored in extremely small spaces in computer systems. The data carriers used today allow the theft of amounts of data so large that in the old days the data might have had to be transported by truck. Computer-stored data can be copied quickly and easily with the help of modern technology, especially via wired or wireless data telecommunication. Furthermore, it is difficult to detect espionage conducted by these means. As a rule, the information sent blends into the normal data traffic of a large company. In addition, encryption and steganographic techniques can be employed to hamper discovery. Finally, data espionage is benefited by the increasing mobility of persons in possession of data and by the fact that travellers often take their data with them. For example, a laptop can be stolen from a train passenger or can be subject to other forms of attack as described in this report. If the laptop has access to WLAN or Bluetooth applications, the risks are even greater.

Targets

The targets of computer espionage include computer programmes, research and defence data, data of commercial value, as well as client addresses. The

---

1. Cf. for this case Hafner and Markoff 1993, pp. 139 et seq. The successful outcome of this case confirms the effectiveness of granting immunity in certain cases to hackers who agree to co-operate fully with law enforcement agencies, an approach that has been advocated for some time; cf. Sieber 1985, pp. 54 et seq.

2. According to the German Police Crime Statistics (Polizeiliche Kriminalstatistik) for 2000, less than 1% of computer crime cases are attributable to computer espionage. See also Möhrenschlager, in Sieber 1994, pp. 200 et seq.

following are examples of the betrayal of trade secrets and of espionage involving classified weapons information.

In March 1993, General Motors's global purchasing chief, José Ignacio López, and a number of other executives moved from General Motors to Volkswagen. Thereafter, General Motors accused its former employees and Volkswagen of stealing thousands of pages of company documents full of trade secrets. The two automobile mammoths ended up embroiled in both criminal and civil litigation. The civil litigation ended in a settlement in which Volkswagen agreed to pay US$100 million and to buy at least US$1 billion worth of parts from General Motors over seven years.[1]

At regular intervals, the Los Alamos National Laboratory (LANL) – a key centre of nuclear weapons research in the United States and one that is responsible for the storage and maintenance of the country's nuclear weapons arsenal – reports the loss of computer disks containing classified information. It is not clear whether the most recent reported loss, in early July 2004, is due to espionage or to the failure on the part of Los Alamos researchers to comply with security measures; indeed, a month after the report, it was not even clear that any disks were actually missing. In response to the alleged loss, US Secretary of Energy Spencer Abraham ordered a halt in late July 2004 to almost all classified work using such disks and other removable computer data storage devices at all Energy Department laboratories for an unforeseeable period of time. According to a statement from a spokesperson for Los Alamos in mid-August 2004, "low risk" operations at the LANL had resumed and the laboratory was expected to be fully functional by October 2004.[2]

Modi operandi

The *modi operandi* of computer espionage are extremely varied. In some cases, traditional forms of data copying are used, as in the case of José Ignacio López described above. The theft of data carriers, the evaluation of "remaining data", and the absorbing of electromagnetic emissions also

1. Cf. http://zeus.zeit.de/text/archiv/1997/04/lopez.txt.19970117.xml (as of: November 2004); and Robyn Meredith, "VW agrees to pay GM $100 million in espionage suit", *New York Times*, 10 January 1997, at A1.
2. Cf. http://www.stern.de/wissenschaft/forschung/index.html?id=527605&q=los%20ala mos and http://www.heise.de/newsticker/meldung/print/47577 (as of: November 2004); Sandra Blakeslee, "Nuclear lab's missing disks may not exist", *New York Times*, 12 August 2004, at A17; and Kenneth Chang and Sandra Blakeslee, "U.S. halts secret work at more nuclear laboratories", *New York Times*, 24 July 2004, at A11.

occur. In many cases, the hacking described above is used to penetrate systems and subsequently to copy the computer data. More and more frequently, perpetrators are making use of opportunities to deceive users, especially by means of social engineering as well as by exploiting viruses and worms with Trojan components and pure Trojan Horses for the purpose of espionage. The above described interception techniques also play a considerable role and will be increasingly used especially for attacks on WLANs. It is also possible to use ISDN telephones to wiretap rooms where these phones are located.[1]

Perpetrators

Today, not only hackers have recognised that stored data are a potential goldmine but business competitors and state intelligence agencies have come to the same realisation. As a consequence, hacking techniques are more and more used by professional organisations. This development has been facilitated by the fact that perpetrators need not move to another place of residence, and espionage perpetrated by means of the Internet is relatively cheap and low risk. As a consequence, the US National Counterintelligence Centre (NCIC) describes the use of the Internet by secret agents as the most rapidly growing form of industrial espionage.[2]

> An example of this trend to use hacking techniques for industrial espionage was the "Ecole de guerre économique" (School for Economic War) in France, which offered courses in espionage techniques. The Ecole de guerre économique was officially a private institute of a Paris management firm, but it was financed by other consulting firms.[3]

> The "KGB hacking case" mentioned above illustrates the close relationship between hacking and computer espionage. In addition, the Russian intelligence services and the State Security Service of the former German Democratic Republic engaged in widespread telephone surveillance: in the German Democratic Republic the telephone numbers of politicians, members of the secret service, and other important bearers of secrets of the Federal Republic of

---

1. See also http://www.epic.org/privacy/wiretap (as of: November 2004).
2. See Office of the National Counterintelligence Executive, "Annual report to Congress on foreign economic collection and industrial espionage 2003", http://www.nacic.gov/publications/reports_speeches/reports/fecie_all/fecie_2003/fecie_2003.pdf (as of: November 2004).
3. Cf. "Vorbereitung auf den 'Krieg von morgen'", *Frankfurter Allgemeiner Zeitung*, 2 September 1998, at Politik p. 12.

Germany were registered as target numbers, so that the telephone communications of these persons were automatically recorded.[1]

In the 1990s, the US National Security Agency (NSA) was already heavily involved in telephone tapping. Already at that time, according to published reports,[2] the NSA was said to run more than 2 000 installations for bugging telephones worldwide, which can eavesdrop on up to 54 000 telephone conversations at the same time.[3] The largest known global interception network, ECHELON, which was established by the United States, the UK, Canada, Australia and New Zealand in 1948, provides technical support for these actions. A report by Duncan Campbell on the ECHELON intelligence interception network has been the subject of a European Parliament public hearing. His report argues that although ECHELON was conceived for national security purposes, it has also been used for industrial espionage.[4]

Computer sabotage and computer extortion

Risks

Computer sabotage represents a serious problem, especially due to the fact that the economy, the government and frequently individuals are highly dependent on the functioning of modern computer and communication systems.[5] In addition, the above described high concentration of data stored

---

1. See http://www.heise.de/newsticker/meldung/31194

2. See *International Herald Tribune*, 18 July 1980, cited after
http://www.hermetic.ch/crypto/echelon/iht1.htm (as of: November 2004).

3. See Robert García, "'Garbage in, garbage out': criminal discovery, computer reliability, and the constitution", *UCLA Law Review*, 1043, 1055, 1991, and http://www.cbsnews.com/stories/2000/02/24/world/main164465.shtml (as of: November 2004).

4. The European Parliament set up a temporary committee to study the subject. The committee concluded that ECHELON does exist and that the global surveillance system has the ability to eavesdrop on telephone calls, faxes, and e-mail messages but that it is very unlikely that it has been used for industrial espionage. Mr Campbell's report is available at http://www.europarl.eu.int/stoa/publi/pdf/98-14-01-2en_en.pdf; the European Parliament's report is available at http://cryptome.org/echelon-ep.htm (as of: November 2004); and concerning ECHELON and related data interception (Thomson CSF and Brazil) see http://www.geocities.com/Area51/Shuttle/5604/data3.html (as of: November 2004).

5. This dependence leads to the huge total damage amounts quoted by various sources as consequences of computer crashes. Damage resulting from the "I Love

in electronic devices coupled with the dependence of many companies and administrative authorities on data processing makes computer sabotage and extortion particularly dangerous for business and administration. While information has always been an extremely valuable commodity, the increased use of computer networks are not always matched with adequate security measures.

Targets

The targets of computer sabotage are tangible computer facilities (for example, cutting cables) as well as intangible data that contain computer programmes or other valuable information (for example, DoS attacks). Thus, preventive measures should target both hardware (for example, by providing back-up systems) and data (by making regular back-up copies and implementing effective security measures).[1]

Modi operandi

The *modus operandi* of computer sabotage can be causing either physical or logical damage. Whereas causing physical damage was dominating in the early years of computers, today there is a clear preference of perpetrators for more sophisticated forms of logical damage particularly by means of use of viruses and worms.

Traditional forms of physical damage

During the 1970s, the most frequently practised methods of causing physical damage were setting fire to or bombing a building. These techniques were typically applied by "outsiders" not employed or otherwise related to the owners of the damaged facilities.

For "insiders" aiming to affect facilities within the company, mainly in cases of labour and other social conflicts, the following additional techniques of physical destruction were recommended by left-wing European underground magazines: gluing emery paper onto the electronically readable

---

You" virus, for example, has been estimated worldwide at over US$10 million. See, for example, Robert Kilborn and Joshua S. Burek, "News in brief", *Christian Science Monitor*, 14 June 2000, p. 20.

1. For some of these problems and corresponding security measures, see the KPMG Report (2000) entitled "E-commerce and cybercrime: new strategies for managing the risks of exploitation", pp. 11 *et seq.*, available at http://www.kpmg.com (as of: November 2004). Cf. Friederike von Tiesenhausen, "Computer hackers strike at 80% of large businesses", *Financial Times*, 25 February 2004, at National News, p. 6.

parts of cards in order to destroy badge- or card readers; inserting iron-cuttings, paper clips or small pieces of aluminium foil into computer devices in order to cause electrical shorts; pouring coffee, saline solution or caustic cleaning agents into the operator console and other equipment; blowing smoke, hair spray or other gases into sensitive devices; putting a container of hydrochloric acid in front of the air-conditioning's induction pipe or suction fan; causing extreme temperatures by sabotaging the air-conditioning or by heating computer parts with a lit cigarette; interfering with the electric power station; and cutting cables or putting mice under a raised floor where they could gnaw through the insulation of electrical power cords.

Due to the aforementioned convergence of computer and telecommunication systems physical acts of sabotage are also being directed against telephone and other data lines.

> An example of hardware sabotage in the field of data lines can be seen in an attack on the network of Deutsche Telekom in February 1995. In this case, offenders cut seven underground optic fibre cables, thus interrupting approximately 7 000 telephone and data lines around Frankfurt-on-Main airport. In a letter, a group called "Keine Verbindung e.V." claimed responsibility and declared that they had tried to disturb the deportation of persons seeking political asylum in Germany.[1]

Logical damage, especially by means of viruses and worms

Today, the predominant form of computer sabotage is the causing of logical damage, particularly by means of use of viruses and worms. These programmes can be self-written (macro-)code, built into application programmes or introduced into the operating system via the World Wide Web. Programmes can also exploit hardware and software defects ("bugs").

Computer viruses are programmes designed to infect computer resources (for example, files, operating systems, hard drives). Although a virus cannot spread itself intentionally from one computer to another, the user may inadvertently or intentionally spread a virus, either by sending an infected file to another computer electronically or by means of an infected disc. As a consequence, cases involving viruses constitute a considerable share of all computer-related crime cases.[2] The variety of viruses in circulation has

---

1. See "Anschlag auf Telefonnetz rund um den Frankfurter Flughafen", *Frankfurter Allgemeine Zeitung*, 2 February 1995, Politik, p. 1.

2. A recent survey revealed that in 2000, 81% of 176 respondent companies in Germany, Switzerland and Austria admitted to having been the victim of a virus attack in the past; and Gerhard Hunnius, "Sicherheitsstudie 2000 – Hacker und Viren:

increased in recent years. In some cases, newly produced software has been infected with a virus at the time of its issuance.[1]

In recent years, the technical design of these viruses has become more sophisticated, thus enhancing the spreading of viruses and making their prevention more difficult. This development is primarily due to the fact that, in the meantime, so-called "virus kits" are available on the Internet. Virus kits are computer programmes that enable the user to create a virus or a worm by simply clicking the mouse. The user need not even have programming experience, as these computer programmes offer user-friendly interfaces. Persons who make use of virus kits are known commonly as "script kiddies".

Macro viruses in particular are examples of the increasing sophistication of computer viruses. Macro viruses have emerged since 1996 and are based on the fact that standard applications such as word processors and spreadsheets have become more and more sophisticated. For example, these applications now allow the user to add programming codes directly into document files to automate different tasks. This feature – called macro programming – is increasingly being abused to develop new types of viruses. Up to this point, only executable binary files were believed to be proper carriers of malicious virus data. However, by adding the feature of macro development, formerly harmless files (documents, spreadsheets, etc.) can now delete file contents or activate hidden processes simply by being opened. Thus, macro viruses use the application's built-in programme functionality to replicate to other files stored on the computer. Macro viruses are spread through the exchange of infected documents and represent by far the most common type of viruses in circulation.

While viruses only spread in "host programmes", worm programmes are designed to be self-replicating and attack other computer systems independently, without human intervention. Thus, worm programmes can be described as viruses that self-replicate within computer networks and affect a whole multitude of computers. Malicious worms even target mobile devices, and experts expect to see more attempts to exploit mobile devices in

---

die Welt in der Internetfalle?", *Zeitschrift für Kommunikations- und EDV-Sicherheit*, 3 (4), 2000, p. 22. Cf. also Kaspersen, in Sieber 1994, p. 347 (with explanations about the various offences on p. 345).

1. See http://www1.keyboards.de/magazine/m0997/kbcd.htm (as of: November 2004).

the future.[1] The following examples illustrate sabotage committed by means of worms in cases in which the motivation of the perpetrator was – at least in part – to cause damage.

> Already in the early 1990s, a similar network crash occurred in the so-called "Christmas Tree" case. Numerous Internet users received an e-mail containing a simple Christmas greeting together with an attached file. They were asked to open the file if they wanted to see more of the greeting. Upon opening the file the stored programme displayed a Christmas tree on the monitor of the user. Unbeknownst to users, however, the programme was simultaneously accessing their e-mail address books and forwarding the same greeting to all the stored e-mail addresses. The result was a snowball-effect distribution of the e-mail greeting that soon caused many computer systems to crash. The student responsible for the greeting later told police that he was only experimenting and did not actually intend to attach the worm programme.[2]

> Another illustrative example of the possible dangers of worms is the American "Internet worm". In this case, a young computer scientist created an extremely complex virus consisting of several programmes. The virus was injected into a Department of Defence research computer system. Due to a design error, it replicated wildly in a manner similar to a worm, ultimately jamming more than 6 000 computers. Although the virus caused no actual damage to any files, thousands of employee hours were needed to locate and erase it.[3]

> In May 2000, thousands of Microsoft Outlook e-mail users throughout the world received an e-mail entitled "I Love You" that included an attachment. Many users were intrigued and promptly opened the attachment, which was in fact a worm programme. The worm infiltrated the user's Microsoft Outlook e-mail address book and forwarded copies of itself to everyone listed therein, causing millions of computer systems to crash within a few hours and resulting in losses to businesses and governments estimated at some US$10 billion.[4]

---

1. See "Symantec Internet security threat report", Vol. VI,
http://enterprisesecurity.symantec.com/content.cfm?articleid=1539 (as of:
November 2004).

2. Cf. Claas Wolter and Holger Pinnow, "WWWeihnachten im World Wide Web",
Berliner Morgenpost, 24 December 2000.

3. http://www.swiss.ai.mit.edu/6805/articles/morris-worm.html (as of:
November 2004).

4. See *Investor's Business Daily*, 17 May 2000, p. 9. According to the results of a study
by the Hamburg consulting firm Media Transfer AG, the "I Love You" virus led to

Causing logical damage, especially by means of faulty hardware or software implementation

An additional problem is the abuse of faulty hardware or software implementation (so-called "bugs") to crash computer programmes or computer systems.

> In 1997, this strategy was employed to cause computers running on certain versions of the Intel Pentium chip to crash while executing programmes containing special machine code commands. The result of this error is that the system may "freeze" and would have to be turned off and rebooted to return to normal operation.[1]

> A similar phenomenon is the "ping of death", which occurs when a simple and customised programme based on the common ping utility[2] sends certain data to Windows 95 systems and causes them to halt due to a conceptional error in Windows's TCP/IP software implementation.

Normally, these kinds of attack do not cause permanent damage to the system; rather, a system reset typically cures the problem. Unsaved data, however, is usually irreparably lost. The manufacturers of the affected devices or software usually develop so-called "bug fixes", "patches" or "workarounds" to prevent such forced crashes. Nevertheless, the rapid development of technologies leads to a situation where potential offenders will always be at least one step ahead.

Denial of service attacks

A more recent phenomenon has been the use of denial of service (DoS) attacks. Such programmes paralyse computer networks by bombarding them with meaningless requests for information, thereby degrading or

---

21% of all computers at the workplace in Germany crashing or experiencing disruption. See http://www.chip.de (as of: July 2001). Cf. Maney and Zuckerman, "FBI hunts 'love bug' source", *USA Today*, 5 May 2000, p. 1A.

1. A bug was found in Intel Pentium processors and was discussed widely on the Internet. The "Pentium F0" bug could crash Pentium MMX and "classic" Pentium (non–MMX) computers; cf. http://www.dgl.com/dglinfo/1997/dg971108.html and http://support.intel.com/support/processors/pentium/ppiie (as of: November 2004).

2. The "ping" programme is used to determine whether an Internet host is reachable via the Internet. For additional details, see http://en.wikipedia.org/wiki/Ping (as of: November 2004).

denying service to legitimate users. A distributed denial of service attack (DDoS) occurs when numerous computers are "hacked", loaded with the appropriate software to carry out a DoS attack and programmed to simultaneously bombard a particular computer network. The "bots" (short for robots) that are installed on remote computers can be co-ordinated and sometimes even updated with newer software versions, allowing attacks against new-found vulnerabilities. In the first half of 2004, the number of monitored bots rose from less than 2 000 to more than 30 000.[1] The effects of DDoS attacks are illustrated by the following cases:

> In February 2000, a 16-year-old Canadian hacker nicknamed "Mafiaboy" wreaked havoc on the Internet by launching DDoS attacks on major Internet websites, including CNN, Yahoo, eBay, Amazon, Dell and Outlawnet. His attacks flooded the sites with traffic and left them inaccessible for hours.[2]

> The Blaster worm (also known as the Lovesan worm), dating from 2003, is an example of the use of worms to cause a DDoS. The worm propagated via the Internet as well as other networks and caused uncontrollable computer crashes. Computer systems infected by the Blaster worm carried out a DDoS attack against a Microsoft server. It exploited a vulnerability in Windows NT/2000/XP and Windows Server 2003 systems.

> In 2004, the Sasser worm also exploited a vulnerability in the operating systems of Microsoft Windows XP and Windows 2000. It caused programmes on infected computers to start over and over, thus blocking the computer. The worm propagated by automatically jumping from an infected to an uninfected computer as soon as the machines established a connection via the Internet.

Unsolicited e-mails

Damage to computer systems is also caused by unsolicited e-mails. This generally occurs by one of three methods: "mail bombing", "spamming", or e-mails generated by viruses or worms.

In the case of mail bombing, specific e-mail accounts are bombarded with large numbers of unsolicited, automatically generated e-mails, usually with no content of any value. In many cases, this tactic has led to system failure. The sole purpose of mail-bombing attacks is to occupy the attacked system

---

1. See "Symantec Internet security report", Vol. VI, http://enterprisesecurity.symantec.com/content.cfm?articleid=1539 (as of: November 2004).

2. See http://www.wired.com/news/politics/0,1283,38011,00.html (as of: November 2004).

with the processing of inquiries. Mail data – and in many cases servers as well – become unusable.

Spamming is the unsolicited mass-mailing of commercial or broadcast messages as personal e-mails. Generally, the interest of the sender of such commercial e-mail is having the recipient read the e-mail (and, in some cases, having the recipient place an order as a result). Given that there are numerous spammers sending numerous spams, individual recipients receive large amounts of this kind of unsolicited mail. Thus, spam can have the same effect as mail bombing: mail boxes are filled to the overflowing, important e-mails are lost in the congestion and valuable work time is wasted.

This effect can also be used on purpose, for example, as a means of carrying out DoS attacks. In these cases, spam can no longer be seen as a mere annoyance. Instead it has to be treated as a serious security concern. For example, Trojans, viruses and phishing attempts spread widely by means of spam.[1]

The Mimail.B downloader used spam to propagate the Mimail.P worm. The latter in turn used a phishing attack to entice users to install the payload onto their systems. Once installed, users were confronted with false PayPal dialogue boxes that could intercept information and send it on to the original attackers.[2]

In some cases, "botnets" (bots installed on remote computers that can be used for malicious purposes) that were established by viruses or for DDoS attacks are rented to spammers who use the bots to spread their e-mails. In other cases, the bots are used to change the default homepage of the remote computers. This lead to an increase in the number of requests for the website and, in turn, to higher prices for advertisements.[3]

---

1. Verisign sees spam even as the primary vehicle for net crimes, such as advance fee fraud, phishing fraud and work-at-home carding schemes. See "Internet security intelligence briefing", 11/04,
http://www.verisign.com/Resources/Intelligence_and_Control_Services_White_Pa pers/page_005574.html (as of: November 2004).
2. See "Symantec Internet security threat report", Vol. VI,
http://enterprisesecurity.symantec.com/content.cfm?articleid=1539 (as of: November 2004).
3. See Jürgen Schmidt, "Jagd auf Surfer", *c't Magazin für Computertechnik*, No. 17, 2004, p. 172.

However, spam cannot be classified generally as an act of sabotage. On the one hand, there are no relevant international legal regulations.[1] On the other, in many situations it is not easy to distinguish between (illegal) spam and (legitimate) e-mail (for example, in cases of desired advertisement, advertisement in the context of existing business relationships, or mass protest e-mails that can have a "spam effect" on the recipient but that are legitimate from the perspective of the individual senders).

The use of viruses and worms sent in e-mail attachments is also frequent. When the attachment is opened, the programme searches for e-mail addresses stored on the infected computer system (especially in address books). If addresses are found, the bug automatically sends them e-mails that include the malicious attachment. In order to hide the origin of these e-mails, the sender address is generally manipulated or an address found on the infected computer is used as the sender address. The Sober.H worm, which sends e-mails containing xenophobic texts, is based on this principle.

Sabotage of telephone and other data lines

In addition to the physical acts described above, the sabotage of telephone and other data lines can be achieved by means of worms. This can also include mobile communication, as was seen in the case of the first mobile phone virus, dating from June 2004.

> In this case, a worm named Cabir infected mobile telephones and other de-
> vices that used the Symbian operating system, a system employed, for
> example, by all Nokia mobile telephones.[2] The worm spread from mobile
> phone to mobile phone by exploiting a security hole in the Bluetooth interface.
> As a result, the mobile telephones that support Bluetooth, had Bluetooth
> switched on and were in discoverable mode were at risk.

Extortion with respect to computer sabotage

Computer sabotage is not only used to cause victims financial damage. It is also used to blackmail the victims, threatening them with harm if they fail to satisfy the attacker's demands. The above described dependence of the information society on computer systems makes these cases of computer

---

1. But see the US Canspam Act, which requires that commercial e-mail be identified as an advertisement and include the sender's valid physical postal address. See http://www.ftc.gov/bcp/conline/pubs/buspubs/canspam.htm (as of: November 2004).

2. Cf. http://news.bbc.co.uk/go/pr/fr/-/1/hi/technology/3809855.stm (as of: November 2004).

extortion a dangerous form of attack. The following cases illustrate the difficult situation of victims in these incidents.

> In 2000, two men from Kazakhstan hacked into the computer system of the financial information company Bloomberg and sent an e-mail to the founder and chief executive, Michael Bloomberg, informing him that they had detailed knowledge of his company's computer systems, including passwords of senior company employees. They proposed that Bloomberg pay them for highlighting the security breach. The company informed the FBI, and a sting operation was organised with Mr Bloomberg arranging to meet the two hackers in person in London. On their meeting, London police arrested the two hackers.[1]

> Another example of computer extortion is the case of an American scientist who distributed more than 20 000 floppy disks that supposedly contained information about the Aids virus but instead encrypted the user's hard disk when the user opened the stored files. By means of an announcement on the screen, users were asked to transfer an amount of at least $189 to a bank account in Panama in order to obtain the code for decoding their hard disk.[2]

> Similar situations for the victim occur with respect to the threat to disseminate confidential data. In a number of cases, banks were blackmailed by the threat to publish customer data (including data of customers who had presumably committed tax fraud offences).

Computer-related traditional crimes

From a legal standpoint, computer-related crime not only comprises attacks against new computer-specific interests, such as the aforementioned crimes against the confidentiality, integrity and availability of computer systems, it also includes attacks against traditional interests committed by new, computer-specific means.

In the context of attacks against traditional interests, legal analysis concentrates mostly on phenomena that raise new legal issues, such as computer fraud (which is difficult to address in jurisdictions where the criminal fraud provision requires that the deception be carried out against a person) and

---

1. Cf. John Sullivan, "Two arrested in Bloomberg extortion case", *New York Times*, 15 August 2000, at C2, also available at:
http://www.nytimes.com/library/tech/00/08/biztech/articles/15extortion.html (as of: November 2004).
2. Cf. for this case Kaspersen, in Sieber 1994, pp. 351 *et seq.*

forgery (which in some legal orders requires a tangible document). However, as far as risk analysis and issues of criminal procedure in the computer-related crime context are concerned, other offences such as online enticement or computer-related attacks on life should also be considered.

Since computers can be used to assist most traditional crimes, clearly, it is impossible to examine all of these crimes here. Instead, two selected groups of crimes will be examined in the following section: those that are especially relevant from the perspective of legal analysis (namely, fraud and forgery) and those that pose a dangerous new threat to society (namely, online child enticement and attacks to life).

Computer-related fraud

Historical development

During the era of large mainframe computers, fraud committed by computer manipulations constituted a uniform group of crimes. However, due to the diversification of computer systems in the 1980s and 1990s, the term "computer fraud" currently describes a wide spectrum of offences within the field of economic crime. In particular, the growth in e-commerce has been accompanied by a rise in the incidence of Internet fraud related cases. The relevant offences of computer fraud are therefore as diverse as invoice and bank account manipulations, illegal use of credit cards and other smartcards, misuse of the telephone network, including calling card and mobile telephone fraud, and – more recently – online fraud such as share price manipulation and general online consumer fraud, including fraudulent auctions and pyramid scams.

Classic manipulation cases

Among the "classical" large-scale computer fraud cases, invoice manipulations concerning the payment of bills and salaries of industrial companies as well as the manipulations of account balances and balance sheets at banks were and still are the predominant offences. An additional form of computer fraud involves the manipulation of inventories.

> In Germany, a complex invoice manipulation was committed as early as 1974 by a programmer who carried out salary manipulations worth over €98 679[1] by altering the salary data as well as the bookkeeping and balance sheet programmes of his company. Using a programme written especially for this pur-

---

1. This corresponded to DM193 000.

pose, he entered the salary information of fictitious employees into the data memories containing company salary information and entered his own account as the account to which the fictitious salaries should be transferred. These salary manipulations would normally have been discovered by the company because the computer prepared wage slips, checklists, account summaries, and balance sheets that were carefully checked. In order to prevent discovery by these control print-outs, the offender first altered the salary payments programme to ensure that no pay-slips would be printed for payments to the fictitious employees, thus preventing the payments from appearing in the checklists produced by the computer. By further manipulation of the programme that produced the company's accounting summaries and balance sheets, the perpetrator succeeded in having the fraudulently diverted amounts deducted from the income tax to be paid to the tax office. As a result, the sums did not appear as deficient amounts in the company's accounting summaries and balance sheets.

With respect to balance sheet manipulations, the 1974 case involving the German Herstatt Bank must also be mentioned, in which balances totalling over half a billion euros[1] were manipulated. The *modus operandi* of the crime was the manipulation of the keyboard used to enter bank business.[2]

A typical example of a case involving the manipulation of a bank account balance took place in Japan in 1981, when a bank employee made a false entry of 1.8 billion yen into his account and then withdrew 50 million yen in cash and 80 million yen in cheques at another branch of the same bank.[3]

Online manipulations of computer systems

The connection of computers to international telecommunication networks soon made it possible to commit many of the aforementioned computer manipulations from outside the victimised companies. The first cases of online manipulations became known in the United States during the 1970s. Today, most big companies are connected to the Internet and other computer networks. As a consequence, the Internet is increasingly used to commit online manipulations. Frequently, perpetrators take advantage of insufficient security measures in computer systems, the lack or inadequate use of firewall systems or the inexperience of the system administrators of corporate networks. Moreover, of the growing number of individual users who have only recently begun to use online communication, many lack technical experience.

---

1. This corresponded to DM1 billion.
2. Cf. for the last two cases, Sieber 1977 and 1980, pp. 58 *et seq.* and 61 *et seq.*
3. Cf. for this case, Yamaguchi, in Sieber 1994, p. 307.

Banner and advertisement fraud

In order to bring their products and services to the attention of potential customers, companies often place advertisements for their websites on other popular sites. These advertisements often take the form of banners. Hidden behind the banner is a link that takes the interested user to the advertised site. The cost of an Internet banner advertisement, to be paid to the operator of the page carrying the banner, generally depends upon the frequency with which users click on the link to the advertised page. Fraudsters may increase their advertising fees by installing programmes that automatically click on the banner, thus creating the illusion of heavy traffic on the advertised website. Such actions can lead to significant profits, as the revenue of online advertising agencies is very high. It has been estimated that in 2004 investments in the German online advertising market will reach some €535 million.[1]

Additional offences associated with banner advertisements cannot always, however, be judged by criminal law alone. In the United States, for example, a class action was brought against Bonzi Software for employing deceptive banner advertisements. The company's advertisements made use of so-called fake user interfaces (FUI), in which users are confronted with banners disguised as computer alerts with false error messages such as the following: "Security alert: your computer is broadcasting its IP address. With this address, someone can immediately begin attacking your computer." The lawsuit claimed that FUI was tricking "millions of Internet users into interrupting the work they were performing to respond to the fraudulent system message, only to unexpectedly find both computer and computer user thus hijacked to defendants' commercial website, where defendants attempted to hawk services and software of defendants."[2] Although this particular class action lawsuit (Sammelklage) was settled in 2003,[3] the reaction of other banner ad providers remains to be seen.

Search engine advertisements can also be manipulated. In addition to actual search results, most search engines also offer advertisements. Some search engines integrate these advertisements into the regular search results (usually at a very high position), others (such as Google) display advertise-

---

1. Cf. http://www.bvdw.org/ww/de/7_pub/content9011.cfm (as of: November 2004).

2. Cf. http://msnbc.msn.com/id/3078514 (as of: November 2004).

3. Cf. http://www.lukins.com/bonzi/index.php?pid=settlement (as of: November 2004).

ments separately. The position within these so-called "sponsored links" depends on several factors and differs among search engine providers. Customers usually pay a fixed fee plus a certain amount per click; the fee can be (and usually is) limited to a maximum amount per day. To achieve a higher position within the sponsored links or within regular results (if paid advertisements are included within these), several techniques, such as fraudulent clicks or "click spam" may be used.

> Fraudulent clicks or "click spam" can be defined as any kind of click received from a cost per click (CPC) search engine – or from any other online traffic source that is using the CPC pricing model – that occurs with zero possibility for a conversion to occur, or for a website visit from a legitimate user to occur.[1] As soon as the maximum budget is reached, Google no longer displays the advertisement; as a result, all other advertisements rise up one rank. By clicking a €5 advertisement only ten times a day, the advertising party suffers a loss of €1 500 a month.[2]

Fraudulent auctions and other fraudulent online order services

Other examples of fraud on the Internet include fraudulent auctions, other fraudulent online order services where the purchased goods are never delivered,[3] and the sending of packages that contain nothing but newspaper and stones. Taken together, fraudulent activities connected with online auctions and fraudulent sales on websites comprise up to 50% of the fraud on the Internet.[4]

> The offenders always proceed according to the same plan: certain goods, such as computers, are offered. Potential buyers are asked to pay in advance. However, even after payment is received, the merchandise is never delivered.

> The credulous Internet user faces additional forms of fraud as well: the sale of stolen merchandise. For example, between November 2002 and August 2003, in Germany a 38-year-old employee of a cosmetic company auctioned cos-

---

1. See http://www.alchemistmedia.com/CPC_Click_Fraud.htm (as of: November 2004).
2. See Jo Bager, "Gerangel an der Bande", *c't Magazin für Computertechnik*, No. 13, 2004, pp. 170 *et seq.*
3. Cf. http://www1.ifccfbi.gov/strategy/2002_IFCCReport.pdf (as of: November 2004).
4. Cf. http://www1.ifccfbi.gov/strategy/2002_IFCCReport.pdf (as of: November 2004).

metic products valued at €200 000 without the knowledge of the company's managers.[1]

Another example of online auction fraud arose in March 2001 in the United States when three men who had been part of a bidding ring were arrested and charged with fraud. They were accused of placing "shill" bids in 1 100 auctions between October 1998 and May 2000. The bidders had used more than forty online user IDs or screen names to buoy prices and trick other bidders into believing that the sellers were respected users of eBay. The fraud cost hundreds of art buyers a total of US$450 000.[2]

Another example of the commission of fraud on the Internet can be seen in the offer to ship tax-free cigarettes. This fraud involves websites that refer to a fictitious EU administrative provision – one that supposedly amended Sections 18 and 20 of the German law regulating the taxation of tobacco – and advertise the availability of tax-free cigarettes. Since the legal purchase from a European supplier of tobacco products that have not been taxed in Germany is de facto impossible, Internet users who order and actually receive cigarettes may be guilty of tax evasion.[3]

Other forms of consumer fraud

Internet users are vulnerable to fraud not only when they auction merchandise on the Internet or when they make purchases from Internet shops. Fraudsters also seek to charge Internet users for services that have not been rendered as well as for services for which the user never contracted.

An example of such an Internet fraud scheme was carried out by the firm Hanseatische Abrechnungssysteme (HAS). In 2004, HAS sent bills to some 160 000 people, charging them for their alleged use of pornographic sites on the Internet. According to HAS, a contract came into existence when users closed annoying ad banners created by HAS. Ashamed to be associated with such websites, numerous victims paid their bills.[4]

---

1. Cf. http://www.golem.de/0311/28348.html (as of: November 2004).
2. Cf. Michelle Slatalla, "Online shopper; turning to eBay as a cure for auction fever", *New York Times*, 15 March 2001, at G4.
3. Cf. http://www.computerbetrug.de/diverses/zigaretten.php?p=0|126| (as of: November 2004).
4. Cf. Katja Gerhartz, "Das Geschäft mit der Scham", *Die Welt*, 1 July 2004, Panorama 26 151 also available at http://www.welt.de/data/2004/07/01/298920.html?prx=1 (as of: November 2004); "Warum Internet-Nutzer falsche Rechnungen für Pornoseiten

The following case dating from 2004 is similar: The firm DMM Forderungsmanagement Ltd., allegedly based in Birmingham, billed Internet users €49.90 for call-by-call telephone calls and Internet-by-call connections that the user had not made. The bill included a threat to involve the courts, should the user refuse to pay. Users with legitimate claims were told to call a 01908 number that cost €1.86 per minute, with the charges collected by DMM. Calls to this number were answered by a recorded message.[1]

Fraud in the Internet also concerns share price manipulations, false advertising or pyramid scams (so-called "chain letters").

In 1997, a US federal district court sentenced the publisher of a daily stock newsletter to a prison term for conspiracy to commit securities fraud. The publisher had systematically printed favourable coverage of stock issues in exchange for economic benefits without disclosing this fact in his Internet financial newsletter.[2]

In 2000, two Australians were prosecuted in Melbourne after they sent more than 4 million e-mails and posted bulletin board messages urging investors to buy stock in a particular US company. The value of the stock doubled on the trading day after the e-mails were sent, and the trading volume was more than ten times the previous month's average. The two men pleaded guilty to charges relating to misleading stock information and "interference with, interruption or obstruction of the lawful use of file server computers" operated by numerous companies that had received the messages.[3]

Likewise, in Taiwan, a student was arrested for posting intentionally rumours about two companies on the Internet in order to drop the value of their shares. The posting of rumours on the Internet reportedly caused the stock to drop by 50%. The student subsequently bought a large number of shares.[4]

---

bezahlen". Cf. http://www.computerbetrug.de/news/040704_01.php (as of: November 2004).

1. Cf. http://www.computerbetrug.de/news/040717_01.php (as of: November 2004).
2. *LABnews*, No. 4 September 1997, p. 4 available at
http://europa.eu.int/ISPO/legal/en/news/9709/chapter3.html#1 (as of: November 2004); and United States v. Melcher, Jr., Cr. 97-244-A (AVB) (E.D. Va).
3. Cf. Simon Hayes, "Rentech guilty plea", *Australian*, 13 March 2001, p. 37.
4. See http://globalarchive.ft.com/globalarchive/article.html?id=010315002241 (as of: November 2001).

A case involving chain letters – or pyramid scams – was discovered in 1997: the victims were asked to send a particular sum of money to a company apparently owned by the perpetrator. Large profits were promised but were never paid out.

Illegal uses of ATM cards (or smartcards) and similar forms of payment

Another form of computer fraud can be found in the numerous illegal uses of ATM[1] cards (or smartcards) and similar forms of payment since the late 1980s. Although these offences often only lead to the stealing of small amounts of money in each transaction, statistics indicate that the overall loss caused by such misuse of ATM cards easily surpasses that of classical manipulations and that it now represents the most frequent form of computer-related crime. The protection of these cards – primarily by chip technology – has become more important because of the prevalence of electronic cash and point-of-sales systems. Appropriate security measures are essential since classic credit card crime is now being committed by organised criminals. As far as electronic cash is concerned, law enforcement is confronted by organised criminal groups who not only have access to technical specialists but also to well-organised, international logistical structures.

Currently, offences involving the misuse of bankcards range from the simple use and manipulation of stolen cards with the help of computers to the production of copies of such cards. In addition to ATM cards, other magnetic cards are also being manipulated, for example, phone cards or cards for horse betting.[2]

Perpetrators often obtain the necessary PIN numbers for these cards by trick telephone calls, by preparing (and manipulating) keyboards or by using a false keyboard. Occasionally, cardholders inadvertently help perpetrators by noting their PIN number in an address book as a fictitious telephone number. Should the perpetrator obtain the address book, it is an easy task to determine which numbers are genuine and which are not by using freely available telephone number databases.

An Hungarian case was remarkable for the large amount of damage caused: within the space of only one month, the perpetrator used forged bankcards to make 1583 withdrawals, each time withdrawing the maximum amount of approximately US$250.[3]

---

1. ATM is a commonly used abbreviation for automated teller machine.
2. Cf. Yamaguchi, in Sieber 1994, p. 307.
3. Cf. for this case, Kertész and Pustazai, in Sieber 1994, pp. 251 *et seq.*

A French case from 2000 involving a criminal who cracked the codes on smartcard chips revealed the ease with which such smartcards could be copied. The technology necessary included a code-reading machine that is readily available on the Internet, blank smartcards, and customer details stolen or hacked from e-commerce sites.

Abuse of credit cards

Credit cards, as distinguished from ATM cards, are also subject to multiple forms of abuse on the Internet. A credit card is a bankcard that assures a seller that the person using the card has a satisfactory credit rating and that the card's issuer will see to it that the seller receives payment for the merchandise delivered if the seller follows certain (security-related) rules and procedures. In addition to cases in which fraudsters pay with physical credit cards that belong to other (real) people or simply pay with the credit card number of another person (long lists of such credit card numbers are available for purchase), cases have arisen in which offenders have themselves produced credit cards.

In 2002 there were numerous reports in Germany, primarily from northern Bavaria, of EC[1] card theft in which an attempt was made, following the theft, to discover by fraudulent means the PIN numbers of the stolen cards. The offenders identified themselves on the telephone as police officers, claimed that the stolen EC cards had been turned in at the police station, and stated that the PIN numbers were necessary in order to block the cards in the police computer.[2]

In the case of online orders, it is not necessary to present the credit card. In these cases it is only necessary to input the relevant card information. In this context perpetrators do not only use the credit card information of other persons who are deceived into giving their credit card information to the perpetrators. In addition, perpetrators exploit the fact that the procedure for online payment from time to time does not check immediately whether a particular credit card number really belongs to a particular customer. Rather, in many cases the only check carried out is whether a given credit card number can in fact exist. However, software existed that made it possible to create credit card numbers that can be used to "pay" for goods. It was therefore advisable for sellers to check other customer data to ensure

---

1. EC card means eurocheque card.
2. Cf. http://www.computerbetrug.de/news/021218_01.php (as of: November 2004).

authenticity – for example, residential address – before delivering the goods.[1]

> In 2003, perpetrators used e-mail fraudulently to acquire the personal data of eBay users. The e-mails asked eBay users to re-enter their eBay access data as well as their credit card numbers on certain designated websites. As the faked websites were so well constructed as to appear legitimate, even highly critical users were deceived.[2]

> In 2001, the FBI arrested ninety online fraudsters under Operation Cyber Loss. The perpetrators had between them fraudulently acquired over US$117 million on the Internet from approximately 56 000 Internet users. The director of fraud detection at Amazon.com has stated publicly that the company loses between 1% and 3% of its annual revenues to online fraud.[3]

Identity theft

Perpetrators do not only abuse their victims credit card information but also other personal information and documents. The phenomenon of hacking or illegally obtaining personal information and using this information together with stolen or copied credit cards has become known as "identity theft" and is giving considerable cause for concern in many countries. According to the US Federal Trade Commission, more than 160 000 cases of identity fraud were reported in 2002 alone.[4] Other organisations estimate that these cases could increase to 21 000 stolen identities a month in the United States alone.[5] At the US national level, businesses lose nearly US$48 billion annually to commercial identity theft. Meanwhile, victims lose nearly US$4 billion annually, reflecting identity theft losses averaging US$18 000 per person per annum, with an upper value of over US$200 000.[6]

---

1. Cf. http://www.kso.co.uk/de/tt/ec024.html (as of: November 2001).

2. Cf. http://www.computerbetrug.de/news/030913_01.php (as of: November 2004). See also Holger Schmidt, "Der 'Bankraub per E-Mail' kommt in Mode", *Frankfurter Allgemeine Zeitung*, 23 August 2004, p. 17.

3. Cf. http://www.wired.com/news/ebiz/0,1272,44203,00.html (as of: November 2004). See also Jonathan Lambeth, "Crooks set up worldwide web of deceit", *Daily Telegraph* (London), 2 April 2002, p. 29; and Don Oldenburg, "Getting help on ID theft", *Washington Post*, 7 November 2001, at C12.

4. Cf. http://www.iii.org/individuals/other/insurance/identitytheft (as of: November 2004).

5. Cf. "Internet identity theft: a tragedy for victims", a report published in June 2000 by the Software and Information Industry Association (SIIA).

6. Cf. http://www.identity-theft.us.com/commercial-theft.htm (as of: November 2004).

Using the techniques of hacking, interception or espionage described above, it is fairly easy – especially on the Internet – to gather information such as names and corresponding credit card numbers. Once the suspect has obtained a stolen identity, he or she can defraud many businesses online or via telephone in a very short time, because no visual or other identification is necessary or even possible (foe example, in cases where orders are taken by telephone). The thieves usually act very fast - the frauds often take place within minutes or hours of the thefts. In other cases, the identity thief opens fraudulent bank accounts with the help of the new personal data that was acquired. In one case, over thirty fraudulent accounts were opened in the victim's name.[1]

> In 2000, the well-known golfer Tiger Woods testified in court that someone stole his social security number, and applied for and received numerous credit cards. Goods worth US$17 000 were ordered on the account of Woods, including several television sets and stereos. The perpetrator finally aroused suspicion when he tried to buy a used luxury car in the name of a person with an annual estimated income of more than US$44 million from endorsements alone.[2]

> In another case, the perpetrator constructed a false driving licence using the personal data of the victim and the perpetrator's own picture. The perpetrator then bought a car (in the name of the victim) to drive to the victim's law office in order to steal business cards. Additional crimes were committed with the use of these documents. In the end, it took the victim 500 hours to solve the puzzle, which included a lawsuit against her filed by a rental car company and US$50 000 in unauthorised credit card charges. On the positive side, the victim used the experience to write one of the first books about identity theft.[3]

After an identity has been stolen, additional crimes, such as collection of the goods acquired online by means of a stolen identity, are often committed. A common tactic for this part of the process – which is the part most likely to result in an arrest – is the promotion of "work-at-home" schemes in which individuals are recruited by means of offers of easy, well-paid work. In some cases, recruits are required to receive goods (which were bought with stolen identities) and forward them to the so-called "carding ring" via an interna-

---

1. Cf. "Consumer sues TRW and others over alleged credit data access misuse", *Los Angeles Times*, 24 March 1994, Part D, p. 7.
2. Cf. http://www.identity-theft.us.com/commercial-theft.htm (as of: November 2004).
3. Cf. http://info.insure.com/auto/identitytheft.html (as of: November 2004).

tional shipper ("package reshipper"). In other cases, "money movers" perform similar functions with stolen money. Both package reshippers and money movers are usually unaware of the origin of the goods and money they are asked to handle.[1]

Recently, banks have reacted to this threat: customers are being informed about the dangers of identity theft and in some cases dubious payments are automatically stopped and manually re-checked or customers are required to further identify themselves.[2] Also insurance companies have begun providing reimbursement to crime victims for the cost of restoring their identity and repairing credit reports. Some companies even include this kind of coverage as part of their homeowners insurance policy. On average, policies cost between US$25 and US$50 for US$15 000 to US$25 000 worth of coverage.[3]

Misuse of the traditional telephone networks

The misuse of telephone networks, a field that has experienced considerable qualitative changes in recent years, has also evolved into a "mass crime": in the 1960s, offenders sought only to avoid expenditures for their own phone calls. Since the end of the 1980s, the techniques originally developed by hackers have also been used by "companies" that – with the help of mobile telephones, or by changing their addresses frequently – offer conversations commercially for sale, especially for intercontinental telecommunication.

> The traditional blue boxing, which was developed in the 1960s, is based on the fact that in the old analogue telephone networks, control tones for establishing a link are transmitted through the same line as the information and can therefore be manipulated with the help of a so-called "blue box". By using a charge-fee telephone number (in Germany a 0130 number), an operator of, for example, an American telephone company was called. The conversation was then ended with the help of a "break tone", and the free line was held with the help of a "seize tone". After the input of certain control impulses, the desired number in the United States could be dialled free of charge. However, so-called frequency blockers have limited the utility of the blue boxing technique. It now works for telecommunications between countries only if so-

1. See "Internet security intelligence briefing", 11/04,
http://www.verisign.com/Resources/Intelligence_and_Control_Services_White_Pa pers/page_005574.html (as of: November 2004).
2. Cf. http://www.citibank.com/us/cards/cardserv/advice/abt-id-theft.htm (as of: November 2004).
3. Cf. http://www.iii.org/individuals/other/insurance/identitytheft (as of: November 2004).

called outband signalling is not being used. Systems using outband signalling, such as ISDN, send control information – which can be influenced by the blue boxing process – via a separate, independent network. As a result, the telecommunication partner can no longer influence the net.

As a result of the limited utility of blue boxing, telephone hackers today use other manipulation techniques that allow phone calls to be made at the expense of other network participants. They achieve this goal by breaking into inadequately protected voice-mail systems where they then exploit the direct-dialling functions.[1]

Another widespread form of manipulation involves the trade in foreign calling card numbers. Telephone company insiders sell these numbers after obtaining them from card holders with the help of trick phone calls. The calling card numbers are also "hacked" by invading computers or by eavesdropping on phone calls. Some of the phone calls are carried out at the expense of other users with the help of modified walkie-talkies or home-made devices.[2]

In addition, telephone cards for public phone boxes can be faked or manipulated. These manipulations can easily affect countries where only magnetic strip systems are used. In other countries, such as Germany, the telephone companies use phone cards with integrated chips which are especially secured against "recharging" by hardware design.[3] However, German youths have succeeded in copying these phone cards. They decoded the signals of the cards by using adapter cables and small computers which then simulated the signals with their own "intelligent" cards. The first successful "copying" of a German phone card with an integrated rechargeable chip took place back in 1994.

Mobile telephones have also been manipulated. In April 1998, the "Chaos Computer Club" (CCC) presented a new method for cloning a SIM card – the central element of a mobile phone – produced by the Mannesmann mobile phone operator in Germany. This made it possible for unauthorised third parties to telephone at the expense of the owner of the original SIM card, if the necessary data could be gathered.[4]

---

1. Andrew Martin, "Gang taps voice mail to get message across", *Chicago Tribune*, 16 October 1996, p. 1.
2. See also http://www.securityfocus.com/infocus/1527 (as of: November 2004).
3. The chips are destroyed and therefore cannot be "recharged".
4. Cf. "Zehn Nullen bei Mannesmann", *Sueddeutsche Zeitung*, 27 April 1998.

When examining these phenomena, it was foreseeable that the misuse of weakly protected telephone networks would lead to a new wave of manipulations in the 1990s. In Germany, the "sex telephone" and "party line" – numbers with a 0190 area code – were used in combination with hacked phone cards and other abuses of other persons telephone accounts: 0190 numbers were dialled; however, due to the manipulation no telephone costs accrued to the caller and profits were gained by the collaborating purveyor of the 0190 line. In the following, examples of telephone manipulation are given:

> The first larger inquiries concerning these telephone manipulations in Germany were carried out in 1994 when the flats of sixty suspects were simultaneously searched in nine German regions, leading to the arrest of four persons. Two employees of Deutsche Telekom who were suspected of having collaborated with foreign organised crime groups were arrested. The employee had manipulated Deutsche Telekom's systems so that the costs for calling the 0190 numbers were not charged to anybody. At that time it was estimated that more than 80% of the turnover from all sex-phones resulted from manipulations such as those described above. According to some perpetrators involved in the scam, they obtained monthly commissions of more than €50 000.[1] The total damage for Deutsche Telekom and its affected clients was estimated at more than €51 million[2] for the year 1994 alone.[3]

> In an other example of telephone manipulation, clients of Deutsche Telekom were charged when so-called electronic dialling machines (about the size of a cigarette box and available for €77)[4] were arbitrarily connected to some switches, local telephone exchanges or wires. The electronic dialling machines were dialling 0190 numbers at night-time thus creating profits for the perpetrator's 0190 numbers.

---

1. This corresponds to DM100 000.

2. This corresponds to DM100 million.

3. Cf. *Die Welt*, 19 March 1994, p. 12; "Der Computer telefoniert unentwegt mit sich selbst", *Frankfurter Allgemeine Zeitung*, 13 December 1994, p. 22; and "Telefon-Betrugsaffäre weitet sich aus", *Frankfurter Allgemeine Zeitung*, 6 January 1995, p. 4. H.-P. Canibol and C. Pittscheid, "Telefonsex; Der Gebührenbetrug", *Focus Magazin*, 12 December 1994, pp. 244 *et seq.* German Telekom reacted to these cases with public security measures including individual invoicing, special warning reports if the telephone bill increases dramatically, and the setting up of a centre for network security in Darmstadt.

4. This corresponds to DM150.

A rather new phenomenon is the combination of 0190 numbers with a call-back function: a German telephone company offered a service where users could dial a free 0800 number to order a call-back to any given number. The users did not have to register, and any number for the call-back could be given. The call-back itself was charged at the rate of a 0190 number, and at the beginning of the call the party was only asked whether "the conditions are known"; no information about the costs was offered. This procedure circumvented measures against 0190 numbers, such as complete blocking of certain numbers, as such measures only regulate outgoing connections whereas a call-back is an incoming connection. Also, proving a case against this kind of provider is extremely difficult: according to German telecommunication laws, data concerning toll-free calls may not be saved – thus preventing the victim from proving that no call-back had been ordered.[1]

Abuse of Internet diallers

The abuse of telephone and other telecommunication networks reached a new level with the fraudulent use of diallers. These dialling programmes, which in Germany are available under the 0190 and 0900 prefixes, are actually supposed to help the user establish a pay-per-use connection to the Internet in order to take advantage of certain services. After the user has downloaded and activated the dialler, the dialler (if it is one offered by a serious vendor) disconnects the open connection and establishes a new one – generally one with higher charges. The next time the user seeks to establish a regular connection, the normal channels are used.

Unscrupulous vendors have numerous ways of duping users by means of their dialler programmes. In many cases, the cost of the dialler service is stated unclear or not mentioned at all. In another approach, the user is confronted with a flood of pop-up windows. These windows all pose questions that the user answers in the same way (for example, with a click on the right-most of two buttons). The user's consent to enter into a contract is often exacted in one of the last windows. However, this window, which seems to work in the same way as did previous windows, is in fact different: in this window, the user – who has been conditioned to click on the right-most of the two buttons – would have to click on the left-most button in order to refuse his consent to enter into a contract. As a result, the user (who has clicked the right-most button) either believes that he has refused consent or does not realise that he has made the equivalent of a legally binding statement. Finally, users can also be duped by warnings that specifically

---

1. See Urs Mansmann, "Rückruf-Abzocke", *c't Magazin für Computertechnik*, No. 20, 2002, p. 94.

point out that the download of the dialler is free; what the user is not told is that the use of the dialler is not free.[1]

Users duped by dialler vendors often end up paying high fees to surf the Internet. This is because – unbeknownst to the user – he is no longer using his chosen telephone service but has instead been switched (involuntarily) to the vendor's more expensive service.[2]

> An interesting technique for illegal profits through telephone sex-lines was discovered in Canada and the United States: over 38 000 users were convinced to download a gratis picture viewer of several sex sites. The software enabled the user to view pornographic pictures over the Internet while seemingly not being charged for the service. However, as soon as the user had started the programme, it silently disconnected the users from their local Internet service provider and reconnected them to the website by rerouting the phone call to a telephone sex service in Moldova. As a result, consumers were billed more than US$2 per minute by their long distance providers. After shutting down the picture viewer or web browser, the software kept the modem connected to Moldova, resulting in some long distance telephone calls totalling several thousand dollars.

> A case in Spain against the dialling company Interfun involved phone charge fraud. In 2004, Spanish authorities arrested five suspected fraudsters between the ages of 30 and 36 who employed diallers to defraud some 45 000 Internet

---

1. Similar techniques are used by firms seeking, for example, to protect their programmes from copyright infringements. For example, Microsoft posted a free, cumulative security patch for Windows Media Player (all versions) on its own homepage after hackers penetrated Internet users' systems via Media Player. However, the update did more than just close the security hole; it also contained a revised version of the end user license agreement (EULA). By means of a new passage in the EULA, Microsoft claimed the right in the future to install software on PCs without further inquiry or additional confirmation. With the installed software, Microsoft would be able to prevent the copying or playing of DRM secured files and would also be able to deactivate "other" software (a definition of the term "other" was not offered). Cf.
http://www.freenet.de/freenet/computer_und_technik/betriebssysteme/windows_xp/ms_spionage/index.html (as of: November 2004).
2. In order to counter the deceptions described above, the German regulatory agency for mail and telecommunications is planning to prescribe strict conditions in the form of special consent windows for vendors of diallers. Cf.
http://www.regtp.de/imperia/md/content/mwdgesetz/zustimungsfenster_anhoer ung.pdf (as of: November 2004).

surfers of up to €3 000 each. The Spanish police estimate total damages of some €35 million. In 2003, eighteen apartments and business properties of Interfun GmbH were searched in five different German states based on the suspicion of dialler fraud.[1]

In order to limit dialler abuse, users are asked to consent expressly to the acquisition of the dialler, to its installation and to the establishment of the connection.[2] If possible, consent should not be communicated by means of a simple click but rather through the typing of a word. However, a new generation of diallers circumvents this protection as well. In some cases, there are java applications present on websites offering diallers that enter the letters "OK" in a dialler window on behalf of the user – thus communicating the user's consent. As a result of the intervention of the java programme, the user is unaware of both the installation and of his or her supposed "consent". The user remains ignorant of the existence of the dialler until the phone bill arrives. As the presence of the java application on the computer is only temporary, it is almost impossible to prove foul play.[3]

In order to avoid strict national provisions concerning the use of diallers, some shady providers turn to foreign solutions. For example, in Germany so-called "satellite diallers" have been circulating recently. Instead of using a 0900 number, these diallers call a 0088213 number. In fact, the connection does not function via satellite but rather the Italian gateway operator Telespazio routes the connection via the conventional telephone network.[4]

Computer-related forgery

The above cases illustrate that the forgery of computer data is mostly undertaken in order to commit fraud. However, there are also cases in which forgery is committed for other purposes. In such cases, perpetrators cannot be prosecuted for violating statutes that prohibit fraud; instead, they can only be prosecuted if they are violating statutes prohibiting forgery.

False school transcripts and other documents

Examples of forgery which do not aim at committing fraud are, for example, the forgery of school certificates or certain computer-scanned documents

---

1. Cf. http://www.computerbetrug.de/news/040623_01.php (as of: November 2004).
2. See http://www.regtp.de/aktuelles/pm/02826/index.html (as of: November 2004).
3. Cf. http://www.heise.de/newsticker/meldung/50575 (as of: November 2004).
4. See Urs Mansmann, "Durchs Hintertürchen", *c't Magazin für Computertechnik*, No. 14, 2004, pp. 86-88.

such as transcripts. The altered documents can be used to enhance the offender's private image or to pad the offender's employment or other competitive applications, especially if they are submitted by e-mail or in other electronic form. For example, students in schools in the United States have allegedly hacked school computers in order to alter transcripts.

False identity

Forgery is also committed to conceal the identity of a person on the Internet. The reason for this kind of concealment is often to disguise illegal activities.

> In 2000, millions of America Online (AOL) subscribers were sent spam e-mails containing pornography and get-rich-quick schemes. In order to conceal the true identity of the sender, the offender made it look as though the e-mails were sent by the Internet provider IBM.net.[1]

The falsifying of identity is especially important in cases in which offenders do not simply conceal their identity or choose a fictitious identity under which to commit their acts, but rather where they commit crimes using someone else's identity. This is the case for example if the perpetrator applies for a credit card which he wants to abuse. Whereas a customer who physically goes to the bank runs the risk of being filmed by surveillance cameras, an Internet user who applies for a credit card using another person's access information does not face great risks of being identified by other, for example, non-electronic, means.

Concealment of identity is also important for the distribution of computer worms. Computer worms can be designed to carry a damage function that transforms an infected computer system into a so-called spam relay server. The infected computer system then spread spam e-mails of an unknown third party in some cases to millions of users. For the e-mail recipients, however, the owner of the infected computer system appears to be the spammer. Since the owner of the infected system may pay his Internet provider on the basis of the volume of use, this kind of misuse can cause significant economic damages. The best known worm with this kind of function is the Sobig.F worm that propagates via e-mail attachments and attacks Windows computer systems.[2]

Today, almost all viruses and worms are equipped with a function that falsifies the sender address. To falsify the sender address, viruses and

---

1. Cf. http://news.com.com/2100-1023_3-249758.html?tag=prntfr (as of: November 2004).
2. Antonella Lazzeri, "Nerd is Sobig", *Sun*, 30 August 2003.

worms typically resort to the address books of infected computers and use the e-mail address stored there. As a result, e-mails infected with a virus or worm appear to be sent from a real e-mail address – worse, from an address that may belong to a friend or acquaintance. In the meanwhile, the falsification of e-mail sender addresses has become a mass phenomenon.

Online child enticement and other forms of searching for victims

Online child enticement

A newly developing and serious form of criminal activity on the Internet is that of online child enticement, a problem that has been reported recently in the United States. There, more and more cases have surfaced involving adults who contact minors in Internet chatrooms and convince them to meet privately. In the United States and in other countries, this has led to murder, disappearances, exploitation and abuse. The following crimes committed in recent years illustrate that online offences against children are not isolated events.

> In the UK, a 45-year-old man who used the Internet to stalk his victims was sentenced to five years' imprisonment for the sexual abuse of a 13-year-old girl he met online. The man lured the girl into meeting him after posing as a 15-year-old boy. He managed to obtain her private e-mail address and arranged a private rendezvous. The court heard how he met the girl in his car and took her to his flat where he began a series of indecent assaults.[1]

> In another case in the UK, a man pleaded guilty to a charge of raping a 14-year-old girl whom he had previously met in an Internet chatroom.[2]

> In January 2004, a British citizen was sentenced in the United States (Iowa) to five years in prison after he arranged an in-person meeting with a 14-year-old girl whom he had originally met in an Internet chatroom. He pleaded guilty to enticement of a minor to engage in sexual activity and travelling with intent to engage in sexual activity with a minor.[3]

According to a study undertaken in June 2000 by the Crimes Against Children Research Centre at the University of New Hampshire, approxi-

---

1. See *The Times* (London), 25 October 2000, p. 6.

2. See http://www.qlinks.net/items/qlitem10016.htm (as of: November 2004).

3. Cf. http://www.cnn.com/2004/LAW/01/08/internet.sex.ap (as of: November 2004).

mately one out of every five youths in the United States aged between 10 and 17 who used the Internet regularly received an unwanted sexual solicitation or approach within the last year.[1]

Finding other victims

Criminals use the Internet not only to make contact with children but also to find adult victims. The following cases are illustrative:

> In Germany, the case of the cannibal from Rotenburg attracted a great deal of attention.[2] The offender had placed sixty personal ads on various cannibalism forums with the following content: "seeking young, well-built young man who would like me to eat him. Detailed, full-body photos requested". Additionally, the offender swapped fantasies with like-minded individuals on Internet forums such as "Gourmet" and "Cannibal Café". He arranged meetings with more than thirty potential victims whom he had met via the Internet ads; however, at the last minute, these meetings did not take place. Finally he met one of his victims – who had declared himself in a cannibal newsgroup to be ready and willing to be eaten alive – on one of these websites. In March 2001 he killed this victim in accordance with the offender's and the victim's sexual fantasy. This fantasy involved mutilating the victim, killing him, and dismembering and eating him. Before killing the victim, the cannibal from Rotenburg cut off the victim's penis, fried it, and he and his – still alive – victim tried to eat it. After the killing, the offender met with other potential victims. However these men did not allow themselves to be killed, they only wanted to role-play their fantasies. When the offender took photos of the role-playing and posted them on the Internet, a student from Innsbruck contacted the German National Police in Wiesbaden. The authorities searched the perpetrator's premises and computer systems. On the offender's computer they found fifty stories and instructions about butchering. Among these were essays advocating cannibalism as the solution to overpopulation in the Third World as well as recipes for "breaded boy liver" and "penis with red wine".[3]

> In May 2004, the police found the body of a young woman in a location near Nuremberg. An online flirtation had spelled doom for the 21-year-old; she did

1. This report is one of the first of its kind to assess the extent of the problem of online enticement. It is entitled "Online victimization: a report on the nation's youth" and is available at http://www.unh.edu/ccrc/Victimization_Online_Survey.pdf (as of: November 2004).
2. Cf. http://www.stern.de/politik/panorama/index.html?id=510704 (as of: November 2004). See also Landler, "Eating people is wrong! But is it homicide?", *New York Times*, 26 December 2003, p. 4.
3. Idem.

not survive the first in-person meeting with the man she had met on the Internet.[1]

Only two months later, in July 2004, an unemployed Dane was arrested in Copenhagen on suspicion of raping twenty women. The Dane used the Internet to make contact with his victims, presenting himself as a rich businessman and offering money for sexual services. The victims did not report their experiences immediately because they were ashamed.[2]

Spanish officials have observed "one-off incursions" of organised groups made up predominantly of criminals of Romanian origin. These Romanian criminals place offers of employment opportunities in their country of origin for young persons to work in Spain in computer firms. Once the victims are in Spain, the criminals take away their passports and force them to work in flats belonging to the organisation. Their job is to lure in victims for auction swindles or fictitious sales or to prepare such crimes.[3]

Life-threatening attacks

The computer manipulations described above have not only been used for the purpose of financial gain, they have also been used to carry out life-threatening attacks.

An example for this type of crime is the manipulation of the information system of a Liverpool hospital by a British hacker. The hacker accessed the system in 1994 simply because he wanted to see "what kind of chaos could be caused by penetrating the hospital computer". Among other things, he changed medical prescriptions for patients: a nine-year-old patient who was "prescribed" a highly toxic mixture survived only because a nurse re-checked his prescription.[4]

The potential damage of such acts is high. Disastrous consequences could occur if such manipulations could interfere with city traffic-light control systems, flight control systems or nuclear power plants.

---

1. Cf. http://www.spiegel.de/panorama/0,1518,298352,00.html (as of: November 2004).
2. Cf. http://www.spiegel.de/panorama/0,1518,307919,00.html (as of: November 2004).
3. Government of Spain, reply to the Council of Europe questionnaire on organised crime (2004).
4. Cf. "Bizarre Tat", *Der Spiegel*, 28 February 1994, p. 243.

Content-related offences

In the early 1990s, the triumphant rise of the Internet was accompanied by an exchange of illegal and harmful material that was closely monitored by the press and public. Today, attention is focused primarily on child pornography, racism, hate speech and the glorification of violence on international computer networks.

Child pornography

The possession and dissemination of pornographic illustrations and texts involving children has become a serious problem in recent years, as illustrated by cases that have become known to the general public. An end to this development is not yet in sight; on the contrary, the number of cases is rising annually, and experts are predicting that the expansion of the Internet – in particular into eastern European countries – will further exacerbate the problem. It is feared that the anonymity of the Internet could lead to a spread of organised crime in this area, for example, in the form of better organised paedophile rings. Recent cases illustrate the dimensions of the already existing problem:

> In 1996, the Spanish public was stunned by a case involving the distribution of child pornography. Two students had a collection of over 150 floppy discs with child pornography, all of which had been collected on the Internet. Both had to be released from prison after three days because of a legal loophole in the Spanish Criminal Code.[1]

> In September 1998, a large, internationally co-ordinated police operation successfully uncovered an Internet paedophile ring. Operation Cathedral, which involved law enforcement agencies from 21 countries, spearheaded simultaneous raids in various countries that led police to the trail of over 200 suspects involved in the "Wonderland" paedophile ring, a ring that exchanged images of child pornography on the Internet Relay Chat service. The raids led to the seizure of over a quarter of a million paedophilic images from computers in Europe alone, as well as thousands of videos, CDs and floppy discs.[2]

> Also in 2001, US investigators discovered a business called Site Key, which provided credit card verification services to subscribers of child pornography. The investigation, named Operation Site Key after the business, led investi-

---

1. The law has since been amended.
2. John Twomey, "Tip-off that put police on a trail of worldwide depravity", *Express*, 14 February 2001, p. 6.

gators to 23 000 suspected subscribers in April 2004. To date, 700 arrests have resulted from this investigation.[1]

In another 2001 case, an undercover agent of the FBI identified three so-called eGroups (discussion fora) on the Internet provider Yahoo that disseminated child pornography. As part of Operation Candyman (named after one of the eGroups), 7 000 e-mail addresses were identified – 4 600 addresses in the United States and 2 400 addresses in 84 other countries. Over 100 people were arrested in the United States, and 36 victims were identified.[2]

As part of Operation Artus, homes and businesses were searched in Austria, Canada, Finland, France, Germany, Japan, Spain, Sweden, Switzerland, UK, and the United States in 2002. US Customs officials involved in the operation seized 12 computers, over 600 CDs, floppy discs, external drives and 200 videos.[3]

Furthermore, German National Police carried out the sting Operation Pecunia in 2002. This operation was a follow-up to the investigation of the American business Landslide. Among Landslide's customers were some 1 400 people in Germany who had paid for access to child pornography. Across Germany, homes of suspects were searched, leading to the seizure of some 47 000 data carriers and 25 000 videos.[4]

International investigations conducted by the FBI, the National Hi-Tech Crime Unit in London, Europol and the German National Police led investigators in 2003 to a child pornography ring. Subsequently, homes and businesses in Canada, Germany, Norway, United Kingdom and the United States were

---

1. Cf. http://www.spiegel.de/netzwelt/politik/0,1518,297482,00.html (as of: November 2004) and 'Porn ring has link to Dallas 'The majority of these people don't have a criminal history' FBI, police team up in investigation of child-sex images' by Robert Tharp, staff writer, *Dallas Morning News*, 28 April 2004, section: Metro, at 1B. See also "Datenschutz", *Der Spiegel*, 22 September 2003, p. 192; and Andy Bull, "After the fall", *The Times* (London), 17 July 2004, p. 39.
2. Cf. Benjamin Weiser, "10 arrested in federal investigation of Internet child Pornography, *New York Times*, 10 July 2002, p. 6; and Graham Keeley, "Biggest raids yet on suspected Internet paedophiles", *Evening Standard* (London), 17 December 2002, p. 2.
3. Cf. http://www.usdoj.gov/criminal/ceos/Press%20Releases/PR-Artus.pdf (as of: November 2004).
4. Cf. http://www.heise.de/newsticker/meldung/30888 (as of: November 2004). See also Andy Bull, op. cit.; and Lynette Kalsnes, "Hanover Park man charged with posting child porn on Internet", *Chicago Tribune*, 5 April 2002, at Trib West, p. 5.

searched. In Germany, at least forty members of the ring were identified. Suspicion focused on the ring, which was used to exchange pornographic materials, when members met at a gathering codenamed "Teddy Bear Picnic" in Missouri in 2002.[1]

Also in 2003, over 400 000 pornographic images of children and 16 000 video clips were found in Scotland on the computer of a bricklayer.[2]

On 25 May 2004, persons suspected of possessing child pornography and distributing it on the Internet were searched in co-ordinated raids involving police in Denmark, Finland, Norway and Sweden. The sting, which followed a year-long investigation, led to the arrest of some 350 people. Buyers were traced after they purchased child pornography online with credit cards.[3]

In August 2004, police and large Internet providers in Germany such as AOL, T-Online, MSN and Arcor agreed to work together in the fight against child pornography. When the providers learn of child pornography, they pass their suspicions on to law enforcement agents. In addition, they have begun an information campaign involving a teddy bear that knocks on the computer screen to draw attention to the problem. In the experience of providers, users prefer to report their suspicions to providers than to police.[4] Increasingly, users can also report their suspicions from home via the Internet.[5]

Racism, hate speech and glorification of violence

In the United States, the Ku Klux Klan, the White Aryan Resistance, skinheads and other neo-Nazi organisations had already realised in the 1980s that electronic communication was much more effective than traditional "newsletters".[6] With the growth of the Internet, the dissemination of extreme

---

1. Cf. http://www.heise.de/newsticker/meldung/36680 (as of: November 2004).

2. Cf. http://news.bbc.co.uk/go/pr/fr/-/1/hi/scotland/3227734.stm (as of: November 2004).

3. Cf. Nina Larson, "Hundreds of child porn suspects arrested across Nordic countries", Agence France Presse (English), 25 May 2004. Cf. "Nordic police stage co-ordinated raids on suspected pedophiles", Gazette (Montreal), 26 May 2004, at A25.

4. See "Kampf gegen Kinderpornos", Die Welt, 30 November 2004, http://www.welt.de/data/2004/08/30/325829.html?prx=1 (as of: November 2004).

5. Cf. http://www.polizei-beratung.de/aktionen/kinderpornografie (as of: November 2004).

6. Cf. John Markoff, "Some computer conversation is changing human contact", New York Times, 13 May 1990, p. 1.

right- and left-wing content, incitement to hatred, bomb-making instructions, anti-Semitism and hate music have become more prevalent.[1] Neo-Nazi organisations used electronic communication systems to distribute the names of Jewish "opponents" and to give advice for violent actions. One website that espoused white superiority even went so far as to offer a US$1 000 prize to the student who wrote the best essay on "actionable, practical solutions" for dealing with persons who are not white.[2] In recent years, particularly in the United States, a steep increase in the number of such websites can be seen. This phenomenon is primarily due to the extensive protections afforded to freedom of speech and expression by the US constitution.

In Germany, right-wing and left-wing extremist organisations first used bulletin board systems (BBS) and other electronic communication systems in the early 1990s. Right-wing extremist organisations in particular used the so-called "Thule Network", which consisted of about 10 BBSs. Information about neo-fascist organisations and related propaganda was posted on these BBSs. Electronic means were used for communication within private groups of users as well as for informing the public. Left-wing radical groups (particularly from the anarchist-autonomous scene and from the ranks of the so-called Red Army Faction) have also distributed their plans of action on the Internet, often via the BBS network "Spinnennetz" (cobweb) (material posted on the Spinnennetz is part of an international information exchange fostered by ECN, the European Counter Network).[3]

---

1. Cf. http://www.osce.org/documents/cio/2004/06/3162_en.pdf (as of: November 2004).

2. Cf. http://www.theregister.co.uk/2004/05/10/hate_websites_flourish (as of: November 2004).

3. Cf. Anti-Defamation League of B'nai B'rith, *Hate groups in America*, 1988; Maegerle and Mletzko 1994, No. 5, pp. 1 *et seq.*; Federal Ministry of the Interior (ed.), "Report of the protection of the constitution 1993", p. 23, pp. 147 *et seq.*; Möhrenschlager, in Sieber 1994, p. 108; "Werthebach, Lage der inneren Sicherheit aus Sicht des Verfassungsschutzes", *(1994) Nordrhein-Westfälische Verwaltungsblätter*, pp. 201 *et seq.* (at p. 203); "Response of the Parliamentary State Secretary Lintner of 21 April 1994 to questions of the Member of Parliament Böhm", *Bundestagsdrucksache*, 12/7357; *PC Computing*, December 1989, pp. 146 *et seq.*; *Focus Magazin*, No. 4, 1995, pp. 52 *et seq.*; and for the "Thule-Netz" cf. also *Chip*, No. 3, 1994, pp. 82 *et seq.* "Spinnennetz der Krieger - Die rechtsradikale Szene nutzt die neuen Medien", *Süddeutsche Zeitung*, 22 July 2002, p. 14; and Pfeiffer, *Für Volk und Vaterland. Das Mediennetz der Rechten - Presse, Musik, Internet*, Berlin 2001.

In the meantime, viruses and worms such as the Sober G worm are used in many countries to spread radical right-wing messages via mass e-mailing.[1] Racist groups do not always campaign openly for their goals. Instead, Internet websites may operate under the guise of pseudo-scientific research[2] and make use of supposed co-operation with recognised organisations to propagate their ideas. Increasingly, music CDs and racist video games in which the player discriminates against foreigners and ethnic minorities serve as propaganda material for young people.

> In one such video game, "Concentration Camp Manager", which was distributed mostly via BBS, the player had to decide whether a foreign worker should first be sent to work in a mine or whether he should be gassed immediately.

In addition to racist and xenophobic materials, users seeking to enhance their images also distribute photos of their violent acts on the Internet.

> An example of this kind of behaviour came to the attention of the public in June 2004. In this case, eleven vocational school pupils in Germany tormented one of their fellow classmates from November 2003 to January 2004. In addition to forcing him to eat chalk, chew on cigarette butts and kiss his tormenters' feet, they also hit, kicked and humiliated their victim. They videotaped their abuses in order to post them on the Internet.[3]

News of executions, abductions, abuse and other heinous acts have led to "execution voyeurism" on the Internet.

> For example, Dan Klinker, who lives in the Netherlands, offers websites with video clips of torture, beheadings and shootings. He gets most of his material from Islamic propaganda websites. Users who wish to see grisly details must pay for the privilege.[4]

---

1. Cf. http://www.theregister.co.uk/2004/06/11/german_hate_mail_virus (as of: November 2004).

2. Such as the infamous "Leuchter report" that claims to "scientifically" prove that gas chambers in concentration camps could not have been used as execution gas chambers.

3. Cf. http://www.spiegel.de/panorama/0,1518,302402,00.html (as of: November 2004).

4. Cf. http://www.heise.de/newsticker/meldung/51455 (as of: November 2004).

Soliciting, inciting, providing instructions and offering to commit criminal offences

Not only are crimes committed on the Internet, the Internet can also be used to solicit criminal activity and to provide instructions on how to commit crimes. In fact, users may even use the Internet to advertise their own willingness to commit crimes or other offences. The following examples illustrate the wealth of instructions available on the Internet on how to commit crimes.

Soliciting murder

Examples of solicitation to commit crimes, especially murder, can be found on the Internet. Such appeals, when disseminated via the Internet, reach a potentially huge audience. Solicitations to commit murder target specific victims in a very concrete way and do not, as does hate speech, simply select groups of persons belonging to a particular race or religion.

> Abortion opponents in the United States targeted physicians by name and photo on the Internet. They demanded that the "baby butchers" receive their just deserts. Six doctors, including the New Yorker Barnett Slepian, were murdered. Only hours after he was killed, a line was struck through Slepian's name on the online list.[1]

> In another case, a member of the racist group known as Davids Kampfgruppe (David's Fight Club) used an anonymous website to call for the death of his favourite "Zecke" (jargon for a left-winger).[2]

Inciting and providing instructions regarding rape and child molestation

Inciting crimes on the Internet can also be found with respect to instructions regarding rape and child molestation.

> In March 2000, the German National Police discovered on the homepage of a 26-year-old man seven pages of detailed instructions on how to abduct, rape and murder a 10-year-old girl. The homepage had been visited by many users, some of whom had even requested additional information.[3]

---

1. Cf. http://www.wams.de/data/2002/12/22/27310.html?prx=1 (as of: November 2004).

2. Cf. http://www.welt.de/daten/2000/07/22/0722de181273.htx (as of: November 2004).

3. Cf. http://www.welt.de/daten/2000/08/05/0805h1183881.htx (as of: November 2004).

In Germany a woman offered her 8-year-old daughter for sale on the auction website of eBay. The child was described as "a real working toy". In the sales pitch, the mother expressly stated that the child came with no guarantees and that she was not returnable. Three bids had been registered by the time police removed the offer from the site.[1]

Constructing bombs and providing instructions regarding sabotage

Persons interested in making various types of bombs can easily find instructions on the Internet; a particularly good source for recipes of this nature are the websites of right-wing radicals.

In this vein, Germany's Federal Office for the Protection of the Constitution traced a 17-year-old whose homepage "The Arab stampede" (*Der arabische Sturm*) provided detailed instructions on how to assemble a home-made bomb.[2] In fact, such instructions have actually been followed by Internet users: the youth who bombed a Finnish shopping centre in 2002[3] and the youths who carried out the Littleton, Colorado, school massacre in 1999[4] used devices assembled according to instructions found on the Internet. Both incidents killed and injured numerous people.

Instructions detailing how to sabotage railway lines appeared for the first time in 1996 on the website of the extreme left-wing magazine *Radikal* (a magazine that was removed from normal sales channels by a German agency), which resided on a server in the Netherlands. With the help of instructions entitled "Short guide on the disruption of all kinds of rail transport", users could learn to assemble devices and manipulate railway property in such a way as to slow railway services or bring them to a halt.[5]

In September 2004, French police arrested a computer science student from Alfortville (near Paris). According to the student, he had posted bomb-building instructions on the Internet for fun. After a number of young people in

---

1. Cf. http://spiegel.de/panorama/0,1518,296378,00.html (as of: November 2004).
2. Cf. http://www.welt.de/daten/2000/07/22/0722de181273.htx (as of: November 2004).
3. Cf. http://www.welt.de/daten/2002/10/14/1014vm362212.htx (as of: November 2004).
4. Cf. http://www.wams.de/data/2002/12/22/27310.html?prx=1 (as of: November 2004).
5. Cf. http://www.welt.de/daten/2002/04/18/0418de326873.htx (as of: November 2004).

France were injured when trying to assemble firecrackers according to instructions from the Internet, French police shut down three Internet sites with detailed instructions on how to build explosive devices.[1]

Constructing biological viruses

In addition to instructions on how to build explosive and incendiary devices, information on the genetic structure of biological viruses can also be found on the Internet.

In 2002, a research team in the United States announced that it had successfully constructed artificial life – a polio virus – in the laboratory. The scientists synthesised the virus causing polio, which has been all but wiped out as a naturally occurring disease, using its genome sequence, which is available on the Internet, as their blueprint and genetic material obtained from one of the many companies that sell made-to-order DNA. Some scientists criticised the team for showing terrorists how to construct dangerous pathogens from simple, readily available ingredients.[2]

In the past, access-to-information laws allowed sensitive information to be made available to the public, information that non-law abiding citizens were able to exploit for criminal purposes. In the aftermath of the attacks on the World Trade Centre and the Pentagon in September 2001, many institutions in the United States decided to make less information available, especially via the Internet. For example, the amount of information on the Internet regarding companies that manufacture dangerous substances has decreased, and in mid-October 2001, the World Federation for Culture Collections, a multidisciplinary organisation concerned with the collection, authentication, maintenance, and distribution of cultures of micro organisms and cultured cells, removed data on anthrax from its website.[3]

Obstructing the police, judiciary and administration

Instructions of a different kind – often on the websites of left-wing organisations – can also be found on the Internet.

---

1. Cf. http://www.heise.de/newsticker/meldung/51477 (as of: November 2004).
2. Cf. http://www.welt.de/daten/2002/10/27/1027pg364930.htx (as of: November 2004).
3. Cf. http://www.welt.de/daten/2001/11/06/1106fo293710.htx (as of: November 2004).

On websites, foreigners facing deportation can read about how best to impede the deportation process.[1]

On their own websites or on Internet auctions, Internet users declare themselves willing – for a fee (for example, up to €10 000 per month) to take on someone else's suspended driving privileges and entries in the official register of traffic offenders.[2]

Not only tangible goods can be purchased on the Internet; trade in academic and aristocratic titles is booming.[3] A doctorate is available to everyone, regardless of whether they have finished high school or received a university degree.

Hacking tools and access codes

Many hackers post instructions on how to hack various security programmes. In addition they offer the necessary toolkits for download.

For example, after developing digital watermarks for MP3 files that it considered to be very secure, the SDMI consortium sponsored a hacking contest, providing a US$10 000 reward to anyone who could crack its digital music protection technology. Thereupon, two French hackers cracked the code and posted a detailed explanation of the hacking process on the Internet so that all other users could crack the code as well.[4]

By exploiting a loophole in a US court ruling that prohibited the online publication of the software programme DeCSS (which allows DVD movies to be decoded and played on personal computers), hackers posted graphics on the Internet containing the source code of the programme.[5]

In addition, the dissemination of serial numbers and passwords for programme installation is widespread on the Internet.[6] Security limits of new computer programmes can often be overcome by means of numbers and

1. Cf. http://www.welt.de/daten/2000/08/08/0808h1184272.htx (as of: November 2004).
2. Cf. http://www.welt.de/data/2003/04/04/65409.html (as of: November 2004).
3. Cf. http://www.spiegel.de/panorama/0,1518,295306,00.html (as of: November 2004).
4. Cf. http://www.welt.de/daten/2001/04/04/0404wa245061 (as of: November 2004).
5. Cf. http://www.welt.de/daten/2000/09/20/0920wa191806 (as of: November 2004).
6. Cf. http://www.serialz.to (as of: November 2004).

passwords posted on the Internet shortly after the programmes are released on the market. Furthermore, data permitting access to AVS- (adult verification systems) protected websites are also available on the Internet. The system is supposed to prevent underage web surfers from accessing certain sites, thus protecting minors from content that is dangerous to young people.

Cyberstalking

Cyberstalking is defined as the use of the Internet, e-mail or other electronic communications device to stalk another person. Stalking itself generally involves harassing or threatening behaviour that an individual engages in repeatedly. Cyberstalkers can take advantage of the large amount of personal information available on the Internet to trace their victims, while, on the other hand, the anonymous and impersonal nature of the Internet and its ease of use make it more difficult to trace the offender.[1] In particular, a cyberstalker can send repeated harassing e-mails by the simple click of a button and can also easily dupe third parties into harassing a particular victim.

> In Massachusetts, for example, a man was prosecuted for utilising anonymous re-mailers in a systematic pattern of harassment of a fellow employee that culminated in an attempt to extort sexual favours from the victim under threat of disclosing past sexual activities to the victim's new husband.[2]

> In San Diego, a male university graduate terrorised five female university students over the Internet for more than a year, sending hundreds of violent and threatening e-mails, at times up to five messages per victim per day. More recently, mobile telephones have been used in this way to harass victims with repeated and in some cases threatening text messages.[3]

Libel and the dissemination of false information via the Internet

Not only do Internet users face the prospect of online stalking, they may also be defamed and insulted in cyberspace. Furthermore, false personal or business information disseminated on the web can easily destroy a reputation. Examples of this kind of criminal activity are:

---

1. For the definition of the term see the "US report from the Attorney General to the Vice-President on cyberstalking (1999): a new challenge for law enforcement and Industry", p. 2, available at http://www.cyber-rights.org/documents/cyberstalkingreport.htm (as of: November 2004).

2. Ibid., p. 5.

3. Idem.

An alleged libel case was dealt with by a US court already in 1991.[1] In this case, the defendant, CompuServe, contracted with a third party for that party to conduct a special-interest forum (called "Rumorville") on CompuServe. The plaintiff, Cubby, Inc., claimed that defamatory material about its business was posted by a user in that forum and sued both the forum host and CompuServe. CompuServe was granted summary judgment.[2]

The possible effects of the dissemination of false information on the Internet on the business and privacy rights of individuals can be seen in a 1997 case in Indonesia. There, a posting on the Internet reported the purported death of an influential banker and alleged that his bank was experiencing financial diffi-culties. This led to mass withdrawals of cash from the bank, causing it to ex-perience serious financial problems.

The extent to which the dissemination of pictures on the Internet can affect a person's psychological well-being is illustrated by the following German case. In this case, a boy was invited by his classmates to watch pornographic videos privately. While he was watching the video and masturbating, they secretly filmed him. Subsequently, the classmates circulated the film not only at school but also on the Internet. This brought the victim to the brink of suicide.[3]

In specialised web forums,[4] users can post personal opinions and reports together with intimate (and mostly unflattering) photographs of colleagues, ex-boyfriends and girlfriends, school friends or neighbours. These pages often are widely known by the friends of the victim but not the victim him or her-self. Such acts are now being carried out more and more frequently by means of cellular phones with integrated cameras. In Saudi Arabia, this development has lead to an intensive discussion about whether to prohibit all such cellular phones, particularly in light of the problems surrounding the photographing of unveiled women.

In another case, an Internet user posted for viewing and for sale thirty-three photomontages of the tennis player Steffi Graf on Microsoft Network's German online service. The photos showed Steffi Graf's head superimposed onto a naked body in various pornographic positions. Graf sued Microsoft; a

1. The case was decided in the Southern District of New York, Cubby Inc. v. CompuServe (776 F. Supp. 135, 1991).

2. See http://www.eff.org/pub/CAF/law/libel_1.IW (as of: November 2004).

3. Information on this case was given to the author by a reliable source.

4. For example, http://www.rache-ist-suess.de, which, in the meantime, has been "defused" by the operator.

lower court decision against Microsoft was upheld by a state appeal's court in Cologne in 2002.[1]

In 2004, the hotel heiress Paris Hilton suffered a completely different kind of online injury to her privacy. In this case, Hilton's ex-boyfriend posted a video on the Internet showing the two of them engaging in sexual activity. As a result, the victim claimed, she could no longer live without a bodyguard.[2]

The reputation of a commercial vendor can also be destroyed by just a few sentences on the Internet. In the past, a number of sellers who offer their goods for auction on eBay have taken legal action against negative consumer evaluations.[3] Indeed, both buyers and sellers of goods on the Internet are dependent on a user-evaluation system (in which trading parties post ratings and comments about each other), as there is often no other source of information concerning a potential partner's trustworthiness. However, if an evaluation is not obviously false or if it does not aim at discrediting the contracting party, both buyers and sellers must, as a rule, put up with negative evaluations. The decision to engage in Internet commerce entails a decision knowingly to risk negative evaluations.

Website defacement

Website defacement involves the unauthorised alteration or defacing of third-party websites. Attackers generally obtain access to their target sites by means of hacking methods such as those discussed above or by means of passwords elicited through social engineering. In most cases, defacement is limited to a website's entry or home page. As in the real world, where sprayers leave their tags or a message on buildings, trains, buses, etc., website defacers also tend to leave messages. The messages can be insulting or may simply point out a security hole. In some cases, however, web graffiti contains a political statement. After they are taken offline, some altered sites are saved in various archives so that they can be accessed later.[4]

---

1. OLG Köln, judgment of 28 May 2002 – 15 U 221/01 (LG Köln) in MMR 2002, pp. 548 *et seq.*; and Jon Ashworth, "Graf wins against Microsoft", *The Times* (London), 8 June 2002.

2. http://www.spiegel.de/panorama/0,1518,druck-304056,00.html (as of: November 2004).

3. See Landgericht Düsseldorf, Az.: 12 O 6/04; and AG Koblenz, Az.: 142 C 330/04. See also http://www.jurpc.de/rechtspr/20040217.htm (as of: November 2004).

4. See http://www.zone-h.org/en/defacements (as of: November 2004).

An especially impressive series of website defacements was carried out by a group called Pentaguard in January 2001. The group gained access simultaneously to a large number of government websites in the United States, Great Britain and Australia and left its logo on the homepages of these sites. While the sites were defaced with juvenile references to beer, marijuana, sex and Microsoft, it is also possible that the attacks were politically motivated.[1] In the United States, the Alaska office of the Department of the Interior was affected, pointing to a political motive: at the time of the defacement, it was feared that under the leadership of George W. Bush, nature reserves in Alaska would lose protection against oil prospecting put in place by Bill Clinton.[2]

In May 2004, Portuguese hackers known as the "Outlaw Group" manipulated the homepage of a Microsoft web server. By means of a so-called SQL injection (that is, the planting of commands into an SQL database as a result of the failure by the affected web application properly to screen user entries), the group succeeded in introducing the following greeting into the Microsoft page: "Owned OutLaw Group by Pharoeste e Wolfblack".[3]

Internet gambling

Another activity giving rise to concern in many countries is illegal gambling on the Internet. Internet gambling is a prosperous business for gambling operators. Estimates put the total annual revenue of illegal gambling organisers operating on the Internet in the year 2000 at some US$10 billion.

Although some jurisdictions have very restrictive provisions in this area, gambling operators have located to so-called "safe-havens", and Internet users can access their websites from anywhere in the world. This problematic area is a good example of the fact that the global nature of the Internet means it cannot adequately be regulated by country-specific measures. In light of a 2004 decision of the Dispute Settlement Body of the World Trade Organization (WTO), the punishment of online gambling operators will become even more difficult. The decision demanded that the United States

---

1. Cf. http://www.attrition.org/mirror/attrition/pentaguard.html (as of: November 2004).

2. See "Hackers hit Australian sites", *Daily Telegraph* (Sydney, Australia), 23 January 2001, section: Local, p. 3 and
http://www.theregister.co.uk/2001/01/22/mass_hack_takes_out_govt (as of: November 2004).

3. Cf. http://www.zone-h.org/files/77/microsoft.com.gif and
http://www.heise.de/newsticker/meldung/47645 (as of: November 2004).

abolish restrictions on Internet gambling, including operations located in tax havens, because they would be an unfair limitation on world trade.[1]

> An example illustrating the difficult legal problems in the context of online gambling is the case of a German top model of the 1990s hosting the betting sites Crazyclick and Bet11 in Germany and Austria, although she had only an Austrian licence. Later, she shifted her business entirely to Austria, although she continued the business with German betters via the Internet. In 2001, the Austrian sports betting business Interwetten AG purchased her company.[2]

Offences related to infringement of copyright and related rights

The protection of copyright and related rights has become a fundamental issue for rights holders, investigating authorities and legislatures in the digital age, as reliable conditions for intellectual property owners are necessary for flourishing e-commerce. Computer-related piracy threatens this aim. It concerns all types of digital goods: computer programmes, music and films, databases, books and domains.

Unauthorised reproduction and use of computer programmes

In the 1970s the unauthorised copying and use of computer programmes – often called theft of software or software piracy – was dominated by the copying of individually created software since so-called "standard-software" (such as Microsoft Word) was not yet available. This individually created software frequently contained important internal company know-how. Thus, software theft overlaps with computer espionage in some cases.

> The German "debt collection programme case" (*Inkassoprogramm*), an example of the copying of individual software, led to the German Federal High Court's (*Bundesgerichtshof*) first decision, in 1985, concerning the applicability of copyright protection to computer programmes: because the perpetrator who had copied the central computer programme of a debt collection company was able to sell the programme for a fraction of its original price, the very existence of the debt collection company was threatened.[3]

---

1. See Matthew Garrahan and Frances Williams, "US defeated on online gambling WTO ruling, *Financial Times* (London), 25 March 2004, p. 11.
2. See http://www.welt.de/daten/2000/10/18/1018wa197063.htx and http://www.earlybird.com/en/press/portfolio/122 (as of: November 2004).
3. Cf. Sieber 1986, pp. 699 *et seq.*

The main focus of interest today, however, is the copying of standard software. In the 1980s, the most frequent forms of illegal distribution of software were the sale of programmes in so-called "ant trades" at flea markets (which were organised and overseen by professional gangs).[1] Moreover, the trade in pirated software was largely in the hands of dealers who produced and sold illegal copies of standard software in large numbers. In some cases, commercial operations provided pirated software with the purchase of hardware.[2] However, in the 1990s these methods of illegal sale of computer programmes were considerably reduced due to prosecutions carried out in this field.

Today, the Internet plays the dominant role in the illegal distribution of software and other protected products. Users with writing access to FTP or web servers, whether officially or by hacking, create hidden directories to collect and store huge amounts of illegally copied commercial software. Other Internet services (such as Usenet, IRC, instant messaging and file-sharing systems) are also used to distribute pirated software as well.[3] The software is often stored only for a short time, thus making it difficult to prosecute due to lack of traceable evidence. The advantages of this method of distribution for the perpetrators is its flexibility: The software can be downloaded from the Internet for free and offered again at another web address. The availability of "free web space" to Internet users has encouraged the distribution of pirated software in this way.

In addition, computer programmes are sold on CD-Roms in falsified "original packaging". Computer programmes – such as MS Windows 2000 – are being copied especially by organised crime groups onto CDs and distributed in falsified original packaging so that it is difficult to distinguish between originals and pirate copies. It is usually only the price which identifies a pirate copy, since copies are normally sold for only a fraction of the original's price.[4]

---

1. Cf. von Gravenreuth, "Neue Formen der Softwarepiraterie", *Computer und Recht*, 1995, pp. 309 *et seq.*

2. Cf., for Canada, Piragoff, in Sieber 1994, p. 87.

3. See David Adamczewski, "Piratensport", *c't Magazin für Computertechnik*, No. 20, 2002, pp. 106-13.

4. In software bootlegging, the value of the merchandise seized by the Spanish TCI Brigade in the period 2000-03 could easily be over €5.5 million, Government of Spain, reply to the Council of Europe questionnaire on organised crime, 2004.

In Germany, for example, customs officials seized around 68 000 illegal copies of computer programmes worth over €55.2 million[1] in 1998 when searching a lorry. Follow-up searches uncovered a further 300 000 CD-Roms.[2]

In September 2000, police captured a software pirate who had already provided services to 2 700 customers and had 3 000 burned CDs available for sale. Sales of the pirated copies yielded pure profits of an estimated €125 000 and caused a loss to the industry of some €1 million.[3]

Unauthorised reproduction and use of music and films

The increasing Internet penetration, the arrival of broadband and wireless technology, the increasing size and decreasing cost of hardware memory, and the development of more and more advanced compression processes[4] not only enable the music and film industry to market their products on the Internet but also lead to illegal dissemination of these products, especially via peer-to-peer systems such as BitTorrent, eDonkey, KaZaA, Shareaza and WinMX. As a result, anyone with Internet access can easily download music, movies and all other kinds of digital works, which can then be stored and/or distributed.

> The file-sharing technology firm Napster, set up in 1999 by 19-year-old Shawn Fanning, was the first company to make possible the large-scale, worldwide exchange of copyright-protected music on the Internet. Napster was a centralised system that allowed people to log on and use the Napster search engine to connect with individual hard drives and share music (the precursor of so-called "peer-to-peer" technology). After Napster was successfully sued by the music industry and forced to withdraw its offer from the Internet,[5] the company went bankrupt. However, Napster has already given rise to copycat services such as Freenet, Gnutella and iMesh, which take the Napster concept further. Freenet, for example, is much more sophisticated; it is completely decentralised and no computer, server or person is in control. Moreover, it contains a digital "immune system" that responds to any effort to determine the

---

1. This corresponds to almost DM108 million.
2. See http://www.heise.de/newsticker/meldung/2577 (as of: November 2004)
3. Cf. http://www.golem.de/0211/22761.html (as of: November 2004).
4. For example the MP3 (Motion Picture Experts Group audio layer 3) format or the MPFG 4 format especially for video transmission using low bandwidths with high compression rates.
5. See A&M Records, Inc. v. Napster, Inc., 284 F.3d 1091 (9th Cir. 2002). See also Fagin et al., "Beyond Napster: using antitrust laws to advance and enhance online music distribution", *Boston University of Science and Technology Law*, Vol. 8, 2002, p. 451.

location of a piece of information by spreading the information elsewhere on the network.

In these cases, allegations of unauthorised copying of copyright-protected products are made not only against private individuals offering and copying the protected works but against the telecommunications industry as well. As such, OzEmail, Australia's biggest Internet service provider, has had to answer such allegations: in March 1997, the Australasian Performing Rights Association (APRA), the copyright administrating agency of the Australasian music industry, commenced proceedings against OzEmail in the federal court, claiming that it was infringing copyright by transferring music files to its subscribers via the Internet.[1] Under the terms of a subsequent settlement, OzEmail agreed to make a payment to APRA but did not admit liability in connection with the proceedings. For its part, APRA agreed not to institute further proceedings against OzEmail or any other Internet service provider that joined the litigation settlement agreement.[2]

New forms of data carriers, such as CD-R(W) and DVD, are well suited for the production of pirate copies due to their large storage capacities of up to 700 MB (CD-R(W)) or 8.5 GB (DVD). The fall in prices for CD-R(W) and DVD drives and comparable data carriers has led to the copying and distribution of commercial computer games on a massive scale. The technological development in the field of reproductions especially of digital works has led to an enormous increase of pirated music CDs and movie DVDs. It is estimated that private individuals have burnt more than one billion illegal copies of music CDs.

In Hanover, in 2004, the police put a stop to the activities of a 35-year-old man who had allegedly been selling pirated copies of music CDs and film DVDs on an Internet auction site for six months. A search of his apartment yielded some 600 CDs and 400 DVDs; prior to the search, the suspect had already sold 1 000 copies on the Internet. Damages were estimated at some €250,000.[3]

In another case, in 2004, German police seized two PCs with over 60 000 music titles, including 4 000 complete albums. The music was made available on

1. Shedden, *Weekend Australian*, 27 June 1998, p. 101.
2. See http://www.nmpa.org/nmpa/nv-sf97/apra.html (as of: November 2004); and http://www.copyright.org.au/PDF/Newsletters/N9801.pdf (as of: November 2004).
3. Cf. http://www.chip.de/news/c_news_12083911.html (as of: November 2004).

the FTP server "Lupodata", which was operated by a 56-year-old network technician from Nuremberg.[1]

Copy protection mechanisms and digital rights management systems (DRM) are helpful only to a very limited extent,[2] as tools to outfox copy protection mechanisms and DRM systems are made available on the Internet by both private individuals and commercial enterprises. For example, the software DVDShrink enables the copying of CSS (content scrambling system) protected DVDs.[3] In many cases, companies act more subtly, selling in countries with restrictive laws – such as Germany – copy tools that can only copy DVDs that are not copy protected. At the same time, however, the companies provide information on patches that enable the tool to work on copy-protected DVDs as well.[4]

In November 1999, a group of Norwegian programmers managed to crack the DVD security system and make an illegal copy of a DVD film. A utility called DeCSS that can be used to remove the encryption in a DVD movie was created, allowing for illegal copies to be made. A firmware upgrade has since been introduced by DVD manufacturers.[5]

Unauthorised reproduction of databases

The high value of data in the information society has led to a situation where, in addition to computer programmes, databases and other data collections are also being used illegally. Today, the illegal copying of data ("downloading") affects both providers of online databases as well as distributors of offline databases.

In Germany, for example, there have been several court decisions relating to the sale of CD-Roms that store telephone numbers and addresses. In some cases, the perpetrators simply copied the relevant data by computer, in other cases the data was manually re-typed in China in an attempt to avoid liability

---

1. Cf.
http://www.heise.de/newsticker/result.xhtml?url=/newsticker/meldung/48258 (as of: November 2004).
2. See Stefan Krempel and Volker Zota, "Den Tauschbörsen an den Kragen", c't Magazin für Computertechnik, No. 20, 2002, pp. 24-25.
3. Cf. http://www.dvdshrink.org (as of: November 2004).
4. Cf. http://www.slysoft.com/en/anydvd.html and
http://www.gdata.de/article/articleview/2940/1/160 (as of: November 2004).
5. Cf. Cheng and Waters, Financial Times (London), 14 April 2004, p. 14.

for illegal copying (the attempt proved to be unsuccessful).[1] Ensuing court proceedings held the production of these telephone number CD-Roms to be illegal, both on the basis of violations of competition law as well as on the basis of violations of the personality rights of the telephone users.[2]

Unauthorised reproduction and use of books

Copyright infringements on the Internet are not limited to data in digital form; indeed, print media are also often subject to illegal copying.

> The threat of computer technology and especially the Internet to the traditional print media was illustrated when the book *Le grand secret* by Dr Claude Gubler, the physician of former French President Francois Mitterand, was scanned, translated and published on the Internet, even though it was prohibited in France. In this book Dr Gubler claims that President Mitterand was suffering from cancer right from the beginning of his period as president.

Unauthorised use of websites (framing)

Copyright infringements on the Internet also affect websites. This is especially clear in the context of linking. When a user clicks on a link, the website activated by the link normally takes over the entire browser window, and the browser's address bar shows a new URL. The website shown previously is either closed or hidden behind a newly opened window. The linking of the contents of more than one website is known as framing.[3] Framing enables a web author to divide the browser display area into two or more sections (frames) that can be managed independently of one another by the user. As a result, a newly accessed site does not take over the entire browser window but rather is limited to a single section or frame. As a rule, the address bar continues to show the original address since only a portion of the site has been replaced.

Some users employ framing illegally: for example, one frame may be used to show the contents of a third-party website, such as lists of links or other data. As the address bar still shows the original address and the basic structure of the page has not changed, it is not clear to the user that in fact he or she is looking at information from several different sources. Instead, the

---

1. Cf. http://www.heise.de/newsticker/meldung/14986 (as of: November 2004).
2. See Oberlandesgericht Karlsruhe, "Neue Juristische Wochenschrift", *Computer Report*, 1997, pp. 352 *et seq.*
3. Cf. http://www.heise.de/newsticker/meldung/17841 (as of: November 2004).

user is fooled into thinking that the information on the screen all stems from the original source.

By means of this technique, the provider of the information on the linked site is damaged in a number of ways. First, the user does not come into contact – at least initially – with that provider's home page as only a so-called "deep linking" has occurred. This means that the user may never encounter the site's disclaimer or other significant information. In addition, the accessed information may be shown out of context. Furthermore, copyright issues may arise if the original site presents itself as the author of the linked content and hides or at least obscures true authorship. Finally, financial damages are also possible as framing may lead to the suppression of banner advertisements or other kinds of traffic-based financing.

Unauthorised domain use

Internet-based copyright infringements are not only committed by illegal copying of programmes, music and movie files but rather a new field of activity can be seen in the area of so-called cybersquatting, which is also known as "domain grabbing" or "domain hijacking".

Cybersquatting

Internet users tend to reserve more and more domain names. Often, these domain names are not used but are booked with the sole intent of selling them at a later point to other interested parties. The Internet Corporation for Assigned Names and Numbers (ICANN), which administers the domain-name system,[1] tries to counter these cybersquatting attempts. With the establishment of the Uniform Dispute Resolution Policy,[2] the ICANN has signalled its aim to regulate domain name disputes without recourse to the courts. Parties are encouraged to settle disputes themselves. However, in the case of a (failed) settlement, unsatisfied parties are allowed to take legal action against cybersquatters.[3]

Another measure against illegitimate domain name registrations is taken when new top-level domains are issued (for example, ".info" domains). In a so-called "sunrise period", only parties owning trademarks or similar rights are allowed to register domain names. In the period following the sunrise period (so-called "challenge period"), every registered domain name can be challenged before the World Intellectual Property Organization (WIPO). The

---

1. Cf. http://www.icann.org (as of: November 2004).

2. Cf. http://www.icann.org/udrp/udrp.htm (as of: November 2004).

3. Cf. http://www.heise.de/newsticker/meldung/23256 (as of: November 2004).

WIPO cancels every domain name entry that was registered during the sunrise period without proper authorisation, that is, when the registrants did not own the appropriate trademark, etc.[1]

> At the end of 1999, the World Wrestling Federation (WWF) tried to register the domain www.worldwrestlingfederation.com. However, a US citizen had already reserved the domain and declared that the domain would only be transferred if a fee of US$1 000 were paid. The WWF filed a complaint at the WIPO. Since the domain name and the name of the claimant were identical and the domain name had been reserved with the sole intent of cash generation, the WIPO decided to transfer the rights of the domain name to the WWF.[2]

> A different decision was reached in a case from the year 2000. In this case, online toy vendor eToys.com filed a complaint against the owners of eToy.com. The claimant argued that the owners of eToy.com were cyber-squatting on the domain name and confusing Internet users. However, eToy.com belonged to a group of artists who had registered the domain name a long time before and who used the name for their own presentation. Later, eToys dropped its lawsuit and paid $40 000 for lawyers and other expenses.[3]

Domain hijacking

The term domain hijacking refers to various phenomena. One variation of domain hijacking or the stealing of domains occurs when the owner of a domain forgets to pay for the domain. As a result of the failure to pay, the registrar frees the domain and someone else can register it in his or her name. To this extent, domain hijacking is hardly distinguishable from domain grabbing. Another form of domain hijacking gained notoriety in the following case:

> In August 2004, a student from Germany filed an application to change the provider for the domains google.com, web.de, amazon.de and ebay.de. He

---

1. http://www.legamedia.net/dy/articles/article_14732.php (as of: November 2004).
2. See Jean Eaglesham and John Mason, "Web site wrestler submits to arbitration", *Financial Times* (London), 31 January 2000, section: National News, p. 7 and Cf. http://www.heise.de/newsticker/meldung/7633 (as of: November 2004).
3. See Daniel Lee, "United see red over virtual auctions", *The Times* (London), 14 March 2000, section: Features; Barbara Simons, "Trademarking the Net", *Communications of the ACM*, Association for Computing Machinery, Vol. 43, No. 3, March 2000, pp. 27-28; and Cf. http://www.heise.de/newsticker/meldung/7747 (as of: November 2004).

based his applications on the fact that he was the owner of these domains, and he wished to transfer them to a different web hoster. The DENIC, the central registrar for all domains beneath the top level domain ".de", [1] which carries out provider changes, asked the current providers of the domains via automatic e-mail whether a domain transfer should be carried out. Despite two follow-up letters, the eBay provider located in Canada did not respond.

For such cases, the rules governing provider changes[2] provide that the change be approved if no response is received. As a result of the non-response, the application was approved, and the new provider changed the relevant owner information and rerouted the address to its own server

This led to a situation where entering the address www.ebay.de led the user to the website of a German game clan instead of to the eBay site. Since the new provider was not able to handle the unexpected amount of traffic (users trying to access eBay), the server crashed. After eBay was notified by DENIC, the registrar transferred the domain data back to the original server.

In the meantime, however, auctions continued to take place on the eBay.com site (as opposed to eBay.de) as the address eBay.com was not affected by this incident.[3]

Other domain relevant offences

In addition to the aforementioned criminal offences, offenders engage in numerous activities that involve the misuse of third-party domains in violation of other areas of law, primarily competition law. These activities include the registration of similar sounding[4] or similarly written domain names and the registration of identical domain names at other top level domains, for example, ".ag" (Antigua), which is a common abbreviation in Germany for *Aktiengesellschaft* (corporation), or ".tv" (Tuvalu), which is preferred by television stations. Users who land on these domains by accident often become victims of phishing attacks, or the domain owners use

---

1. Cf. http://www.denic.de (as of: November 2004).

2. Cf. http://www.denic.de/de/domains/verwalten/providerwechsel/index.html (as of: November 2004).

3. Cf. http://www.heise.de/newsticker/meldung/50522 and Spiegel Online, 30 November 2004, http://www.spiegel.de/netzwelt/politik/0,1518,315760,00.html (as of: November 2004).

4. See www.google.com (search engine) vs. www.booble.com ("adult" search engine with similar user interface) (as of: November 2004).

the high frequency of (clueless) visitors to obtain banner advertisements or to advertise for their own (usually pornographic) offers.

Manipulation of search engines

Most users employ search engines such as Google to help them find websites relevant to their areas of interest. Since most users consider only the top 10-20 results provided by a search engine, websites have a very strong interest in being placed high on the list of results for relevant search terms. This may lead website providers to try to manipulate their page-ranking within the individual search engines.

> A phenomenon called "link spam" includes techniques such as cloaking (that is, showing different pages to crawlers than to human visitors) and link farms (a link farm is a large group of web pages created with the intention of creating hyperlinks to one another in order to influence Internet search engine rankings).[1] By means of link spam, the offender tries to achieve a high page-ranking within the search results.

> Other techniques make use of meta tags. A meta tag is a special HTML description within a web page that provides data about the web page such as a description of contents, information about the author of the page, the time the page was last updated, etc. – to search engine robots. Since meta tags are not visible to the user, they can be filled with keywords that do not actually appear on the site. Fraudsters use meta tags not only to include information about the page, but also to include all kinds of information they suspect users use as search phrases thereby increasing the chance to be found in the search engine. In some cases, the names of competitors were included in the meta tags in the hope that a search engine would display their web page instead of the competitor's.

Infringements of privacy

Whereas in the past, the party exhibiting the most interest in the personal data of individuals was the state, today private information is also increasingly sought by commercial operations and private individuals. Both in the area of state and private activities, the borderline between legal data processing and illegal infringements of privacy is often difficult to identify.

---

1. Cf. http://www.jurpc.de/aufsatz/20040259.htm (as of: November 2004).

Infringements of privacy on the Internet can take many forms. The main types of *modus operandi* are accessing, collecting, storing, distributing and linking personal data.

Unauthorised access to personal data

Offenders gain illegal access to personal data mainly by hacking computer systems.

> In order to prove how easy it was to access personal data on networked computers of the city of Hamburg, hackers from Hamburg used standard programmes to break into the network in 1996. After breaking into the network, the hackers made their activities public. The break-in would not only have enabled the whistle-blowers to influence financial transfers and to access sensitive personal data, it also afforded them access to confidential government documents.[1]

> In 2001, hackers gained access to the central computer of the World Economic Forum in Davos. The hackers were able to obtain personal information about government and business leaders who attended the summit, including their credit card numbers.[2]

Unauthorised collection of personal data

Infringements of privacy on the Internet have also increased as far as the unauthorised collection of personal data is concerned. The data can be collected in many different ways.

Collecting data by monitoring and questioning Internet users

In some cases, data are collected from inattentive users without the user's even noticing;[3] in other cases, users are openly asked to provide them. In the latter situation, the user is often asked to provide a great deal of personal information (for example, telephone and fax numbers, mailing address, age,

1. Gunhild Lütge, "Datenschutz: Räuber im Internet", *Die Zeit*, 23 August 1996, p. 35, also available at: http://zeus.zeit.de/text/archiv/1996/35/daten.txt.19960823.xml (as of: November 2004).
2. Gunhild Lütge, "Datenschutz, Verdatet und verkauft: Die Angst vor dem Missbrauch persönlicher Daten droht den E-Commerce zu blockieren", *Die Zeit*, No. 18, 2001, pp. 28 *et seq.*, also available at:
http://zeus.zeit.de/text/archiv/2001/18/200118_datenschutz_inte.xml (as of: November 2004).
3. See under "Collecting data by means of cookies, web bugs and other software".

date of birth, etc.) in specially designed web forms before the user can make use of a particular service offered by a vendor. The most important piece of information in these cases is the user's e-mail address. Data acquired by these means allow commercial enterprises to create user profiles.

Collecting data by means of cookies, web bugs and other software

Users who surf the Internet leave a data trail. Cookies, for example, are a source of especially useful data. A cookie is a message that is given to a web browser by a web server the first time a connection is established and stored by the browser in a text file. When the user re-establishes contact with the web server, the server reads the stored data and, as the case may be, updates it. These data, whose storage is generally unnoticed by users, can be used to create customer profiles or to send targeted e-mail advertisements.

The invisible successors of cookies are so-called web bugs or web beacons. Disguised as small pictures hidden in other graphics, web bugs continuously collect new information about the user. A new software that allows the sender of e-mails to determine whether, when, how long and where a particular e-mail is retrieved functions in a similar manner (sometimes with the help of web bugs). The new development achieved with this software is the ability to track e-mail without alerting the recipient; in other words, the tracking is invisible.[1]

Recently, free programmes available on the Internet have been used more and more frequently to install digital surveillance software on the computer of unsuspecting users. As a consequence, the privacy of Internet users is more and more threatened.

Collecting data by means of discarded PCs, copy machines, etc.

The possibility that sensitive data may be collected by means of harvesting so-called "remaining data" has not yet gained the attention of users. If the storage media have not been properly erased, the sale of computers or computer components or the return of leased units such as copy machines can allow large amounts of sensitive data to land in the wrong hands.

> According to a study conducted by two researchers at the Massachusetts Institute of Technology (MIT), out of 158 hard disk drives (HDD) that were purchased at eBay auctions, only 12 were erased in such a way as to prevent the reconstruction of the data originally saved on them. It was possible to re-

---

1. See http://www.didtheyreadit.com (as of: November 2004).

store data on all the other drives, including pornographic files, love letters and even medical practice data. Account numbers and account balances were retrieved from one of the drives that had presumably been used in an automatic teller machine. [1]

According to data security specialist Ibas, it is even possible to recover sensitive data from discarded copy machines. Many such devices are equipped with internal HDDs to temporarily save data for faster results. When machines are discarded, for example, when leasing contracts end, sensitive data remain in the machine unless the HDDs are properly erased.[2]

Collecting data by working environment surveillance

Another intrusion into privacy occurs when employers unexpectedly monitor employees at work by means of computer programmes or attached hardware. Many national laws prohibit these actions; nevertheless, monitoring still occurs. Surveillance measures at work may include monitoring by registering all key strokes, file operations or programme uses. Furthermore, special programmes allow the taking screenshots at certain intervals or the interception of all outgoing e-mail messages thereby allowing the employer to control all electronic communication. An especially intrusive measure is the use of webcams that can be remote controlled by the employer allowing constant monitoring of the employee. Software used for these purposes is closely related to Trojan Horse software. In order to conceal its actions, both software categories usually save log files in hidden directories and change entries on the affected computers during start up and shut down.[3]

Unauthorised distribution and linkage of personal data

Infringements of privacy on the Internet can also found in the form of unauthorised distribution and linkage of personal data.

The privacy of many people was infringed upon in 1998 when the Internet advertising magazine AdAge sold personal data of its visitors to a new company, Theglobe.com, which offered free homepages. After the sale,

---

1. Simson L. Garfinkel and Abhi Shelat, "Remembrance of data passed: a study of disk sanitization practices", *IEEE Security & Privacy*, January/February 2003, pp. 17-27.
2. Cf. http://www.heise.de/newsticker/meldung/42436 (as of: November 2004).
3. See Detlef Borchers, "Big Brother am Arbeitsplatz", *c't Magazin für Computertechnik*, No. 15, 2002, pp. 132-37.

Theglobe.com sent e-mails to 35 000 Internet advertising experts, in which it offered its services. In addition to a homepage, the e-mail recipients were also sent a password that they had already used at Ad Age.[1]

In 2001, the American Internet advertising company DoubleClick, which sold advertising space on the Internet, opened itself to suspicion. DoubleClick purchased the firm Abacus, an information service that maintained a database of the buying habits of catalogue shoppers, for some US$1.7 billion and in so doing acquired access to data from 88 million US households. DoubleClick wanted to match and merge its own data with the address list from Abacus in order to create detailed user profiles. After a storm of protest from affected parties, the Federal Trade Commission opened an inquiry into the company's practices, leading DoubleClick to abandon its plan.[2]

Special groups of perpetrators

The above analysis shows that cybercrime is one of the major challenges for today's society. The two other major challenges in the field of criminality today are organised crime and terrorism. In order to evaluate the threat of cybercrime it is therefore most relevant, whether and how far cybercrime is combined with these two other major threats and risks of the twenty-first century. The following section will try to seek some answers to this new question.

Organised crime

Overview

Organised crime has already been defined in Chapter 2 of this report. For that reason it is not necessary here to deal with the respective definitions again. The above described definitions can also be applied in this section which looks at the links between organised crime and cybercrime.[3]

---

1. Detlef Borchers, "Daten sind unser Leben", *Die Zeit*, No. 25, 1998, also available at http://www.zeit.de/archiv/1998/25/199825.bulkware.xml (as of: November 2004).
2. http://zeus.zeit.de/text/archiv/2001/18/200118_datenschutz_inte.xml (as of: November 2004).
3. For a discussion of the term "organised crime" and its various forms, see also Sieber and Bögel 1993, pp. 23 *et seq.*, and Susan W. Benner, "Organized cybercrime? How cyberspace may affect the structure of criminal relationships", *North Carolina Journal of Law & Technology*, Vol. 4, No. 1, 2002, http://www.jolt.unc.edu/Vol4_I1/Web/Brenner-V4I1.htm (as of: November 2004).

Until now, investigative authorities of the member states of the Council of Europe have found some links between cyber criminals and organised crime. It is feared that links between cybercrime and organised crime will be seen in the future, especially in the areas of computer fraud, computer-related forgery, child pornography and copyright infringements. An indicator for this development is an analysis of larger cases of child pornography conducted by the Swiss Federal Police Agency, according to which producers and distributors of child pornography are, as a rule, not themselves paedophiles but rather are interested in lucrative business opportunities. According to the study, this is true primarily for criminal organisations in eastern Europe.

Considering the multitude of different types of cybercrime offences, it is obvious that a more detailed evaluation of the question requires a differentiation between the various types of computer-related offences.

Offences against the confidentiality, integrity, and availability of computer data and systems

Up till now, only a few cases are known in which organised crime elements have been active in the area of criminal offences against the confidentiality, integrity, or availability of computer data and systems. Information currently available indicates that perpetrators of hacking – the penetration of otherwise inaccessible computer systems and networks – and computer sabotage, offences commonly committed by means of viruses, worms and Trojan Horses, are usually youths or young adults whose motivation to commit such offences is either a thirst for adventure or curiosity.[1]

However, as can be seen from the following cases, organised hacker groups are also active in this area:

> According to the FBI, its officials discovered a number of organised hacker groups in eastern Europe, primarily the Russian Federation and Ukraine, in 2001. FBI officials identified some forty victims of hacker attacks attributed to these groups; most of the victims were e-commerce or e-banking companies. The hackers always conducted their attacks in the same way: first, they penetrated the company's computer system and downloaded credit card numbers.

---

1. The author of the Sasser and the Netsky viruses was, for example, an 18-year-old German who programmed and disseminated the viruses together with school friends. Cf. http://www.heise.de/newsticker/meldung/47704 (as of: November 2004). The primary author of the Phatbot virus was a 21-year-old unemployed German. Cf. http://www.heise.de/newsticker/meldung/47370 (as of: November 2004).

162

Then they sought to extort money from their victims for "security services". In order to convince victims to comply with their demands, they threatened to post the stolen data on the Internet.[1]

According to police, another kind of cyber extortion was attempted with the help of the Internet in the days leading up to the National Football League's Super Bowl – one of the most important sporting events in the United States – in January 2004: organised groups sent e-mails to online bookies, threatening them with the shutdown of their sites if they did not pay a certain sum of money.[2] This wave of attempts to extort money from online betting agencies by threatening DDoS attacks arrived in Europe in plenty of time for the European soccer championship in 2004. For example, the online betting agency mbet.com received an e-mail threatening the shutdown of its website unless a payment of US$15 000 were made. mybet.com did not pay and the attacker carried out the threat.[3]

In 2004, anti-virus researchers registered an increase in the appearance of viruses and worms produced by organised groups. According to researchers, the linkage between various malicious code programmes indicates that organised structures are behind the authors of these programmes.[4]

Computer-related traditional crimes

The powerful capacity of modern computer and communication systems to store, administer and transfer data is exploited by organised crime groups in many areas. Organised crime groups are especially involved in acts of sophisticated computer fraud, credit card fraud and telephone fraud. Computer data stored and transmitted in encrypted form are also used by drug and arms dealers to carry out their activities. It is assumed that in the

---

1. Cf. Philipp Jaklin, "Cyber-Kriminalität Verursacht Hohe Wirtschaftliche Schäden", *Financial Times* (Germany), 20 August 2001, p. 14, available at
http://www.ftd.de/pw/in/1076893.html (as of: November 2004); and Elise Ackerman, "Companies tally more computer crimes", *San Jose Mercury News*, 12 March 2001, at 1E.
2. Cf. http://www.telepolis.de/deutsch/inhalt/te/16663/1.html (as of: November 2004); and John Jurgensen, "21st century shakedown", *Hartford Courant*, 31 March 2004, at D1.
3. Patrick Brauch, "Geld oder Netz!", *c't Magazin für* Computertechnik, No. 14, 2004, p. 48.
4. Cf. http://www.computerworld.com/printthis/2004/0,4814,95501,00.html (as of: November 2004).

future, electronic money transactions and "cyber money" will be increasingly used for illegal gambling and for money laundering on the Internet.

Computer fraud

The involvement of organised crime groups in the field of computer fraud is illustrated by the following cases:

Already in 1994, a Russian group attacked one of the best known US banks in New York via data networks. Operating from St Petersburg, the group succeeded in causing the computer system of the American bank to transfer over US$10 million to foreign accounts.[1] By monitoring and following the "money trail" of the manipulations, law enforcement agencies ultimately were able to arrest some of the perpetrators. The responsible security officer at the bank concerned told the author of this report that the arrested perpetrators possessed false Greek and Israeli passports and that the quality of the forged documents was such that they could only have been produced in the Russian Federation by members of the former Russian Secret Service, the KGB.

An additional example of the activities of organised groups on the Internet are the so-called Nigerian connection cases.[2] The organisations behind these cases have been sending letters since 1998, first as faxes and later as (virtually daily) spam mails. The letters offer unsuspecting victims payment for help in the (criminal) transfer of money by pretending that members of the organisation are local personalities or relatives of celebrities (for example, the cousin of a former minister) who want to transfer large sums in "frozen" accounts or other valuables out of the country. Victims are asked to pay large sums into foreign accounts for supposed transaction costs, travel costs or other non-existent expenditures.[3] In accordance with the Nigerian Criminal Code provision prohibiting advance fee fraud (No. 419), these groups are also called four-one-niners.[4] In early 2004, police in the Netherlands arrested fifty-two people involved in the Nigeria connection. The police learned about the criminal group because its e-mails were blocking the Dutch cable Internet provider UPC. During the course of the investigation, the police discovered

---

1. Cf. for this *Datenschutz-Berater*, Vol. 10, 1995, p. 23.
2. Cf. http://www.telepolis.de/deutsch/inhalt/te/16665/1.html (as of: November 2004). See also http://server-wg.de:8080/nigeria/nigeria/nigeria/nigeria (as of: November 2004).
3. Cf. http://www.cnn.com/2004/TECH/internet/01/30/dutch.scam.reut/index.html (as of: November 2004).
4. Cf. http://www.nigeria-law.org/Criminal%20Code%20Act-Tables.htm (as of: November 2004).

that the fraudulently acquired funds were used to finance drug smuggling.[1] In a press release in April 2004, the state criminal investigation department of North Rhine-Westphalia stated that damages totalling between €2 and €3 million are caused each year in Germany by scams based on the Nigerian connection model.[2]

Dealing drugs

In addition, organised crime seems to be active in the area of drug dealing using the Internet. According to the 2001 annual report of the International Narcotics Control Board, an independent control organ for the implementation of the United Nations drug conventions, drug dealers are making use of the Internet in a multitude of ways. In addition to making contact in chatrooms with potential (young) customers, drug dealers are disseminating instructions on how to build private drug laboratories, and online pharmacies are selling prescription-only drugs on the web.[3]

Selling stolen goods

In addition, organised groups have used the Internet as a means to dispose of stolen goods.

> In April 2004, a large-scale police action in northern Germany led to numerous arrests of members of two separate criminal groups. Members of one of these groups would follow their victims to swimming pools and fitness studios, steal their car keys out of their lockers, and sell their cars via the Internet to unsuspecting purchasers.

Money laundering

In the future, the Internet will further support money laundering. Depersonalisation of contacts, anonymous data transfers, ease of access and rapidity of electronic transactions and lack of control mechanisms make computer systems and international networks an attractive tool for money laundering. Virtual casinos, auctions, smartcards, online banking, or the possibility to purchase and sell shares, bonds and futures online offer ideal opportunities

---

1. Cf. http://www.computerwoche.de/index.cfm?pageid=254&artid=57546 (as of: November 2004).

2. Cf. http://www.lka.nrw.de/presse/nigeria-connection2.pdf (as of: November 2004).

3. Cf. http://www.telepolis.de/deutsch/inhalt/te/12074/1.html (as of: November 2004); and http://www.incb.org/e/press/2002/press_release_2002-02-27_2.pdf (as of: November 2004).

for money laundering on the Internet. The following cases are examples of money laundering.

> In New Jersey a ring that stole millions of dollars worth of medications, including Zocor, Viagra and Claritin, and resold them on the black market was broken up in March 2004 with the arrests of eleven people. Investigators believe that most of the stolen medications wound up for sale on the Internet, to elderly people who have no prescription drug coverage, and possibly to nightclubs.[1]

> Criminal gangs buy tickets for West End shows and resell the tickets online or through touts in an operation to launder money from stolen credit cards. The perpetrators intercept credit cards in the post and use these to buy tickets for popular shows by telephone or via the Internet. The tickets are converted into cash, for example, by online auction to overseas visitors.[2]

Content-related offences

In the area of content-related offences, organised groups are heavily involved in the production and distribution of child pornography. In addition, organised crime has expanded into a new business area: the running of gambling enterprises on the Internet.

Child pornography

As indicated by the above examples, a large portion of the production and distribution of child pornography is in the hands of organised crime. This has been confirmed by numerous worldwide investigations conducted by law enforcement authorities in this area. Child pornography rings that reach around the entire globe are regularly discovered and disbanded. The following cases illustrate the magnitude of these rings:

> In 2001, German authorities succeeded in crushing an Internet child pornography ring in the context of Operation *Nadelöhr*. Co-ordinated by the German Federal Police, some 200 homes and offices in 12 different countries were searched simultaneously. The authorities learned about this file-sharing ring when German police were called to the scene of an altercation taking place between business partners in the course of which one of the partners sought

---

1. See Robert Hanley, "11 charged with stealing prescription drugs for resale", *New York Times*, 19 March 2004, Section B, Column 5, Metropolitan Desk, p. 5.
2. See Jack Malvern, "Card gangs turn theatre tickets into easy money", *The Times* (London), 26 June 2004, section: Home News, p. 15.

to destroy a computer by throwing it into a sink. The data on the hard disk survived the assault, however, and police were able to seize 16 000 images of child pornography, 300 videos, and 14 address lists with 2 200 file-sharing partners.[1]

In 2003 as part of Operation Marcy, an action co-ordinated by Interpol and the German Federal Police, German police searched the home of the founder of a private child pornography ring. Among other things, they seized some 4 000 e-mail addresses and gathered information concerning other child pornography rings. An investigation of the Internet providers that administered these rings yielded an additional 38 000 e-mail addresses and 26 500 picture files. As a result, it was possible to identify 26 500 suspects in 166 countries, including Europe, the United States and Australia. In Germany, 502 homes and businesses were searched, 745 computers, at least 35 500 CDs, 8 300 disks, and 5 800 videos were seized, and 530 persons were arrested.[2] The entire operation led to the disbanding of 38 child pornography rings.[3]

Additionally, a number of actions against Internet child pornography rings were carried out in Germany in April 2003: in the nationwide operation named Nibelungen that targeted child, violence and animal pornography, 198 homes and businesses were searched, and (among other things) 212 computers, 6 609 data carriers and 522 video-cassettes seized. Investigators learned of the file-sharing ring after searching the computer of a suspect and finding 15 619 e-mails that pointed to active sharing activity with image and video files.[4] Thereafter, 137 homes and businesses were searched on the basis of suspected involvement in child pornography. Police found over 10 000 hidden files and some 1 000 e-mails containing child pornography on the hard drive of a suspect.[5] Finally, the central office of the German Federal Police for Situation-Independent Research in Data Networks (Zentralstelle des Bundeskriminalamtes für anlassunabhängige Recherche in Datennetzen) identified 57 people living in Germany who offered data depicting child pornography on the online file-sharing network KaZaA. Subsequent searches of the homes and/or offices of the suspects led to the seizure by German authorities of 72 computers, 5 144 data carriers and 405 videos.[6]

---

1. Cf. http://derstandard.at/druck.asp?id=776880 (as of: November 2004).

2. Cf. http://www.heise.de/newsticker/meldung/41033 (as of: November 2004).

3. Cf. http://www.heise.de/newsticker/meldung/40619 (as of: November 2004); and Marcus Mueller, "26,500 nabbed in global child porn sweep", *Toronto Star*, 27 September 2003, p. A29.

4. Cf. http://www.heise.de/newsticker/meldung/35935 (as of: November 2004).

5. Cf. http://www.heise.de/newsticker/meldung/36154 (as of: November 2004).

6. Cf. http://www.heise.de/newsticker/meldung/35823 (as of: November 2004).

In Japan, too, a child pornography ring was disbanded in 2003. This ring had been run by the Yakuza (Yamaguchi-gumi gangsters). Eight members of the Yakuza were arrested, and several thousand videos depicting child pornography were seized.[1]

Internet gambling

Organised crime is also active in the area of Internet gambling.[2] The running of online gambling businesses provides organised criminals with the opportunity to launder ill-gotten gains, including profits from unrelated criminal activity. Organised groups engaged in this lucrative business are often located in Caribbean countries because the laws in these countries are less stringent than the laws in, for example, Europe or the United States.[3]

Offences related to infringement of copyright and related rights

An additional source of profit for organised crime syndicates is trafficking in various kinds of pirated material, such as CDs, DVDs and other software.

Professional software pirates – especially in Asia and eastern Europe – are responsible for the lion's share of this illicit market.[4] In these areas, large copy-factories produce pirated copies of commercial software products that are subsequently distributed on the open market.[5] In Kuala Lumpur, for example, Microsoft WindowsXP software – which on the legitimate market costs some US$150 – can be purchased for only US$1.50.[6] Large numbers of illegally produced copies are also sent to Germany. In early 2000, for example, the main customs office at the Frankfurt airport seized 116 000 copies of computer

---

1. Cf.
http://mdn.mainichi.co.jp/news/archive/200311/11/20031111p2a00m0dm015000c.
html (as of: November 2004).

2. Simson Garfinkel, "Codefellas", *Wired Magazine*, December 2003, p. 222.

3. Leonard Stern, "Betting on the Net: with offshore operators, anyone can gamble online, no matter how old you are or where you're from", *Ottawa Citizen*, 8 July 2001, p. C6.

4. Cf. Bob Sherwood, "Market for fakes creates new dangers", *Financial Times* (London), 30 April 2004, p. 26.

5. Cf. http://www.heise.de/newsticker/result.xhtml?url=/newsticker/data/hob-13.01.00-001 (as of: November 2004).

6. Cf. http://www.heise.de/newsticker/result.xhtml?url=/newsticker/data/ps-25.09.01-000 (as of: November 2004).

games.[1] The pirated copies not only offered the same content as did the originals, they exactly imitated the originals as well – all the way down to the design printed on the data carriers and the packaging of the software.

The extent of digital piracy is illustrated in the following on the basis of a number of actual cases: in the context of one of the largest worldwide raids against software pirates, almost 800 homes, businesses and computer centres were searched across Germany on 16 and 18 March 2004. These searches, which took place in Bremen, Frankfurt-on-Main, Cologne, in the Munich area, and in the Ruhr, led to the seizure of 19 Internet servers containing 38 terabyte (38 000 gigabyte) of pirated movies and software. The pirated material was being disseminated even before the official cinematic opening dates, primarily via the Internet. Confiscated films included *Lord of the Rings*, *Finding Nemo* and *The Passion of the Christ*. In addition, 40 000 data carriers and more than 200 computer systems were seized. The investigation focused on piracy enterprises, known as "warez" groups or syndicates, that organise the distribution of pirated copies on the Internet. These piracy enterprises were responsible for the production and dissemination of illegal copies of more than 500 movies in the years 2001-04. The investigation revealed that a hacker group repeatedly penetrated computer centres of firms and institutions, brought several under their control, and subsequently used their memory capacity for the distribution of movies and software.[2] Thereafter, distribution did not take place via the Internet but rather a co-operating group received the pirated copies immediately after they were made and distributed them on DVDs and video-CDs. The data carriers were delivered to salespeople who offered them for sale. The group was highly professional and had specialists supervising the entire production process of the DVDs and CDs. Production was carried out by means of a disk-burning lab with twenty-four high-speed burners. In addition, a special security service hired by the head of the group monitored the person and vehicle traffic in the production zones.[3]

In a similar case, operation Fastlink led to a worldwide co-ordinated raid on the piracy scene on 21 and 22 April 2004, in the course of which 120 searches in 11 countries (including Germany, Spain, United States and the UK) were undertaken. The searches led to the seizure of 200 computers and servers.

---

1. Cf. http://www.heise.de/newsticker/data/cp-13.03.00-000 (as of: November 2004).

2. Cf. http://www.pte.at/pte.mc?pte=040318042 (as of: November 2004). See also Raymond Snoddy, "Film piracy is the latest billion-dollar blockbuster", *The Times* (London), 12 April 2004, p. 20.

3. Cf. http://www.gvu.de/de/presse/presse_m/presse_m_012.php?navid=24 (as of: November 2004).

Pirated computer programmes and computer games, as well as music and movies, valued at €50 million were confiscated. On one server alone – seized in the United States – 65 000 pirated computer programmes, music titles and movies were found. The whole venture was also organised by warez release groups, which made pirated copies available to selected users on special servers. These users then distributed the pirated copies by means of file-sharing systems. According to US investigators, the groups are organised according to a strict hierarchy, whereby the leaders recruit new members.[1]

Organised crime groups have also become involved in another business area: the production of pay TV cards. In large laboratories in eastern Europe, pay TV cards are taken apart and analysed, layer by layer, using the latest technology. After all the layers have been analysed, it is possible to produce imitation cards. Imitation cards produced in this manner are then sold on the market.[2]

Future trends

In the future, cybercrime might in some areas even lead to changes in the structure of organised crime groups. Cybercrime requires less control over a geographical territory, less violence and intimidation, less personal contacts and thus less relationships based on trust and enforcement of discipline between criminals, in short less need for formal organisations. For that reason in certain areas the classical hierarchical structures of organised crime groups may even be unsuitable for organised crime on the Internet. Therefore, cybercrime may favour those organisations which are already based on flat-structured networking. It may also change the characteristics of the offenders: today, legal businessmen engage in organised forms of economic crime. In the future they may be tempted by opportunities offered by cybercrime. This might cause legal commercial entities to organise for cybercrime and become organised cyber criminals.

---

1. Cf. http://www.hartabergerecht.de/index_news5.html?id=211255 (as of: November 2004).
2. Chris Jenkins and Michael Sainsbury, "Payback – Foxtel zaps the illegal card sharp", *Australian*, 7 August 2003, p. 19.

Terrorism

Overview

An analysis of "cyberterrorism" or "the Internet and terrorism" first faces the problem of defining the terms "terrorism" and "cyberterrorism". In the present context an in-depth discussion of various definitions is impossible. Instead, this report will simply give some direction on the meanings of "terrorism" and "cyberterrorism" and stop short of developing a definition that goes beyond a working hypothesis.

Terrorism is a phenomenon that – due to its complexity and political impact[1] – cannot be consolidated in a single definition. The perception of terrorism derives from the French term *terreur* – fright – and terrorists are literally people who frighten others by violence. For this report, it is sufficient to proceed from a broad working hypothesis of what terrorism is, namely, the premeditated, politically motivated perpetration of violence against non-combatant targets by sub-national groups, usually intended to influence an audience.

Cyberterrorism is a menacing and specific new form of modern terrorism. In attempting to define the phenomenon, simply attaching the term "cyber" to the broad definition of terrorism stated above does not yield a meaningful result. Rather, it is necessary to develop a separate, independent definition of cyberterrorism. As a starting point, it is helpful to refer to the proposal for the international convention to enhance protection from cybercrime and terrorism,[2] which provides a definition of cyberterrorism. According to Article 1 of the draft convention:

> Cyberterrorism means intentional use or threat of use, without legally recognized authority, of violence, disruption or interference against cyber systems, when it is likely that such use would result in death or injury of a person or persons, substantial damage to physical property, civil disorder, or significant economic harm.

---

1. The concept of terrorism is a difficult one since terrorism is intrinsically linked to a certain political understanding. This, in turn, explains why there are so many different definitions of terrorism.
2. The proposal is available at the Information Warfare Site http://www.iwar.org.uk/law/resources/cybercrime/stanford/cisac-draft.htm (as of: November 2004). The Convention on Cybercrime itself is available at http://conventions.coe.int/Treaty/en/Treaties/Html/185.htm (as of: November 2004).

A range of other definitions is under discussion.[1]

While there are many other possible definitions of cyberterrorism,[2] this report will assume the draft convention definition given above. However, the links between cyberspace and terrorism go beyond cyberterrorism. Terrorists use computers not only for purposes of sabotage, but also for communication, propaganda, psychological warfare, hate speech, inciting crimes, recruiting and fund raising, and teaching and planning of crimes.

As a consequence, this section on the links between the Internet and terrorism will deal with cyberterrorism or computer sabotage, communication to and manipulation of the public , internal communication and, finally, other crimes such as copyright offences as far as these offences are committed by terrorists.

---

1. See definition by Dorothy Denning, Professor of Computer Science at the Georgetown University in Washington DC, at
http://www.iwar.org.uk/cyberterror/resources/house/00-05-23denning.htm
"Convergence of terrorism and cyberspace. It is generally understood to mean unlawful attacks and threats of attack against computers, networks, and the information stored therein when done to intimidate or coerce a government or its people in furtherance of political or social objectives. Further, to qualify as cyberterrorism, an attack should result in violence against persons or property, or at least cause enough harm to generate fear. Attacks that lead to death or bodily injury, explosions, plane crashes, water contamination, or severe economic loss would be examples. Serious attacks against critical infrastructures could be acts of cyberterrorism, depending on their impact. Attacks that disrupt nonessential services or that are mainly a costly nuisance would not."
See also Gabriel Weimann, "Cyberterrorism. How real is the threat?", in United States Institute of Peace "Special Report 119 (2004)", p. 4, available at www.usip.org, citing Denning.
2. See, for example, the definition of Mark Pollitt, special agent for the FBI: "Cyber terrorism is the premeditated, politically motivated attack against information, computer systems, computer programmes, and data which result in violence against non-combatant targets by sub national groups or clandestine agents", cited in Bonnie N. Adkins, "The spectrum of cyber conflict from hacking to information warfare: what is law enforcement's role?", Air Command and Staff College, Air University, p. 11. Text available at: http://research.airuniv.edu/papers/ay2001/acsc/01-003.pdf (as of: November 2004).

Cyberterrorism

Open questions and contradictions

To date not a single instance of cyberterrorism – as defined above – has been recorded. On the other hand, the mass media, politicians, scholars and even security agencies focus on the subject matter of cyberterrorism. Headlines such as "Information warfare: the perfect terrorist weapon?",[1] "The myth of cyberterrorism",[2] "Cyberterrorism. How real is the threat?"[3] and "www.terror.net – How modern terrorism uses the Internet"[4] demonstrate that the issue has grabbed the attention of the general public.

Discussed *modi operandi*

In the public discussions on cyberterrorism, there are numerous possible scenarios in which terrorists might (mis)use the Internet to commit diverse attacks. As far as the *modi operandi* are concerned, the literature[5] offers broad discussions and speculations of how terrorist groups might cause harm to society's infrastructure. Examples for this are:

> Damage or manipulation of computer systems (for example, DoS attacks[6] on a computer system or network that are designed to bring the network to its

1. Yael Shahar, International Policy Institute for Counter-Terrorism; see http://www.ict.org.il/inter_ter/noncon/infowar.htm (as of: November 2004).
2. Joshua Green, *Washington Monthly*, November 2002, also available at http://www.washingtonmonthly.com/features/2001/0211.green.html (as of: November 2004).
3. Gabriel Weimann, "Cyberterrorism. How real is the threat?", op. cit.
4. Gabriel Weimann, "www.terror.net – How modern terrorism uses the Internet", United States Institute of Peace (USIP), "Special Report 116 (2004)", available at www.usip.org (as of: November 2004).
5. See for example Gabriel Weimann, "Cyberterrorism. How real is the Threat?", op. cit.
6. A Denial of Service (DoS) attack is an attack on a computer system or network that causes a loss of service to users, typically the loss of network connectivity and services. Such attacks are not designed to gain access to the systems, see http://en.wikipedia.org/wiki/Denial_of_service (as of: November 2004).

knees; destruction or manipulation of important data; swarming)[1] is just one example of how terrorists might use common hacking activities.[2]

Another way for terrorists to (mis)use the Internet in pursuit of their goals is to use the hacking weaponry of viruses and worms in order to infect computers and possibly bring about their subsequent collapse.

Discussed targets

According to present literature, cyberterrorism could attack anything that is important to modern society and that is connected to the Internet or accessible via other communication lines. These potential attacks might at best hamper the functioning of power plants,[3] other industrial plants, water supply operations, and traffic and communication lines; at worst, such an attack could bring such operations to a temporary standstill or even shut them down for a longer period of time. Cyber terrorists could also choose military targets. Some examples[4] (not yet caused by terrorists) show that – by negligence only – severe damage and chaos can occur. The impact might be even more severe if terrorists concentrate on infrastructure and damage it intentionally via the Internet or conventionally:

Chicago's O'Hare International Airport was paralysed when a grower of trees in the suburbs cut a cable.

In 1990, a long-distance network of the telephone company AT&T was down for 9 hours due to a deficient software update: during this time, 60 000 people had no telephone service.

---

1. "Swarming" means simultaneous attacks of a designated site by a large number of individuals, see Gabriel Weimann, "Cyberterrorism. How real is the threat?", op. cit., p. 4.
2. Possible types of computer attacks are listed by Bonnie N. Adkins, op. cit., pp. 5-14: cybercrime, hacktivism, computer espionage, computer terrorism and cyber warfare. Text available at: http://research.airuniv.edu/papers/ay2001/acsc/01-003.pdf (as of: November 2004).
3. Working Group Forum on Critical Infrastructure Protection of the North American Electric Reliability Council (NERC, http://www.nerc.com/)
http://www.infragard.net/library/pdfs/ep_action.pdf (as of: November 2004): "An approach to action for the electricity sector", p. 35 (Version 1.0, June 2001).
4. Reported by Patrick Galley, "Computer terrorism: what are the risks?",
http://home.worldcom.ch/pgalley/infosec/sts_en/index.html (English translation) and http://home.worldcom.ch/pgalley/infosec/sts/index.html (French original) (both as of: September 2004).

There are indicators that the Internet worm W32.Lovsan triggered the giant power cut in the US in 2003. The worm was propagating in the Internet at the time of the power cut. The worm also affected other critically important institutions in the United States including Edwards Air Force Base, the test-centre for the B-2 and B-1 bombers.[1]

In September 1991, a group of telephone switches were cut off from power, and the backup generators did not engage. As a result, three airports in the New York area were closed (Kennedy, Guardia and Newark), 500 flights were cancelled, and 500 flights delayed.

Evaluation

Against the above background (lack of reported cyber terrorist attacks), the current "cyber angst" could be considered to be somewhat exaggerated. However, the threat of cyberterrorism should not be underestimated or denied.[2] The threat posed by cyber terrorists is – like the nuclear threat – hardly measurable. Therefore, it has the potential to cause even more fear and can affect our society severely. The new generation of terrorists is now growing up in a digital world, a world in which hacking tools are sure to become more powerful, simpler to use and easier to access.[3] As a consequence, security concepts should definitely include the threats of cyberterrorism.

Communication to and manipulation of the public

In addition to the threat of cyberterrorism in the narrower sense discussed above, there is a considerable threat posed by terrorists using the Internet. The Internet is in many ways ideal for the purposes of terrorist organisations: it is easily accessible all over the world; the information flow is fast and cheap; and terrorist organisations can spread their messages anonymously to a potentially huge international audience. As a consequence,

---

1. See http://www.heise.de/ct/03/18/034/default.shtml (as of: November 2004).

2. Michael A. Vatis, Director of the Institute for Security Technology Studies at Dartmouth College, points out that physical conflict has already led to real cyber attacks: defacement of Indian websites by pro-Pakistan activists, a so-called "cyber battle" between Israelis and Palestinians, and hacking activities during the conflict in Kosovo. "Cyber attacks during the war on terrorism – A predictive analysis", 22 September 2001, pp. 5-9, available at: http://www.ists.dartmouth.edu/ISTS/counterterrorism/cyber_a1.pdf (as of: November 2004).

3. See Gabriel Weimann, 'Cyberterrorism. How real is the threat?', op. cit., p. 12.

terrorists use the Internet as a forum to disseminate propaganda and hate speech, to conduct psychological warfare, to incite the commission of offences, to engage in fund raising, and to mobilise and recruit new members.

Propaganda and psychological warfare

One major field of activity of terrorist organisations on the Internet is propaganda. As it has become very easy to inaugurate websites, propaganda can be spread widely. Although websites can be shut down by providers (or intruding hackers), such actions do not hamper terrorist organisations from moving their content to other sites.

Al Qaeda, for instance, is an organisation that (mis)uses the Internet for propaganda purposes.[1] Pre-recorded (terrorist) videotapes and audiotapes, CD-Roms, DVDs, photographs and announcements are accessible to the public on numerous websites, including sites of sympathetic, aboveground organisations. Despite the massive onslaught it has sustained in recent years,[2] al Qaeda has been able to conduct an impressive scare campaign. Since 11 September 2001, the organisation has festooned its websites with a string of announcements of an impending "large attack" on US targets. These warnings have received considerable media coverage, which has helped to generate a widespread sense of fear and insecurity among audiences throughout the world and especially in the United States. This behaviour pattern is also an example for psychological warfare. Many other terrorist organisations misuse the Internet in the same way.

Psychological warfare is considered one of the most important elements of terrorism.[3] Examples of psychological warfare are threats and executions, such as the decapitations of Nicholas Berg, an American technician, Paul M. Johnson, an employee of Lockheed and Kim Sun-Il, a citizen of South Korea, in Iraq, and the execution of Daniel Pearl, a US journalist, in Pakistan in 2002.[4]

A special propaganda tactic engaged in by terrorists is to interpret economic crises as results of terrorist attacks. Al Qaeda, for example, used the Internet to celebrate the rise in oil prices and the economic and political effects of the

---

1. Cf. Krempl, "terror.web – Das Online-Netz der islamistischen Glaubenskrieger", http://www.heise.de/ct/04/16/052 (as of: September 2004).
2. For example, arrests and deaths of many of its members, dismantling of its operational bases and training camps in Afghanistan, and smashing of its bases in the Far East.
3. Cf. Krempl, op. cit.
4. Ibid.

price increase (especially the effects on the United States) as "success granted us by Allah".[1]

Hate speech

Terrorist groups disseminate claims of responsibility for attacks causing numerous deaths on their websites, and they use their sites to announce planned attacks or to call for the carrying out of such attacks.[2]

In 2004, for example, al Qaeda posted an article on an Internet website explaining the goals of terrorist attacks and of planning terrorist attacks. After the posting, at least four people died in Riyadh, Saudi Arabia, as a result of the planned attack. In a letter, the Haramain Brigade claimed responsibility for the attack.[3] It is estimated that bin Laden's associates have about fifty websites with alternating addresses.[4]

Inciting crimes

The ability to act anonymously in cyberspace facilitates the appeal of committing crimes and exploits one of the unique attributes of the Internet.

In the aftermath of the investigation of the 11 September hijackers and the US attack on Afghanistan, the Internet was used to foment anti-American sentiment in the Islamic world. According to a fatwa (Islamic legal opinion) issued by Sheik Hamûd bin 'Uqlâ' ibn 'Abdullâh asch-Schu'aybî, it is the duty of all Muslims to protect the Taliban from the unbelievers. His fatwa was distributed among Muslims so quickly that the secretariat of the Council of Senior Islamic Scholars (hay'a kibâr al-'ulamâ') intervened, denying asch-Schu'aybî the right to issue a legal opinion. The case became even more delicate when two additional Saudi sheiks, including Sheik 'Abdullâh al-Ghunaymân, himself a member of the Council of Senior Islamic Scholars, issued fataawa (plural of fatwa) containing anti-American and anti-Semitic statements.[5]

In 2003, Hamas disseminated a "wanted" poster in eight languages on the Internet with the pictures of Israeli members of government. The poster was

---

1. Cf. http://www.spiegel.de/wirtschaft/0,1518,302652,00.html (as of: July 2004).

2. Cf. http://www.welt.de/data/2004/06/01/285223.html?prx=1 and
http://www.spiegel.de/politik/ausland/0,1518,302553,00.html (as of: July 2004).

3. Cf. http://www.spiegel.de/politik/ausland/0,1518,296490,00.html (as of: July 2004).

4. Cf. http://www.heise.de/ct/04/16/052 (as of: July 2004).

5. Cf. http://www.bernhard-trautner.de/fatwakrieg.html (as of: July 2004).

an imitation of the US "deck of cards" of fifty-five wanted Iraqi officials that was distributed in Iraq in the aftermath of the war to oust Saddam Hussein.[1]

Recruiting

In addition, the Internet can be used as a recruitment tool for terrorist organisations. Interactive Internet technologies such as chatrooms and cybercafes serve as vehicles for reaching out to potential recruits.[2] New terrorists recruited in this way can even send their attack plans to certain e-mail addresses for evaluation, improvements and distribution.

> In 1995, Ziyad Khalil enrolled as a computer science major at Columbia College in Missouri. He also became a Muslim activist on the campus. He developed links to several radical groups and operated a website that supported Hamas. Due to his Internet activities, he came to the attention of bin Laden and his companions. Khalil became al Qaeda's procurement officer in the United States, arranging purchases of satellite telephones, computers, and other electronic surveillance technologies and helping bin Laden communicate with his followers and officers.[3]

Fund raising

The search for capital by terrorist organisations has also reached the Internet. There are many ways to raise money via the Internet. The most common are direct donations or links to foundations that support certain terrorist organisations.

> Al Qaeda, for instance, has always depended heavily on donations, and its global fundraising network is built upon a foundation of charities, non-governmental organisations, and other financial institutions that use websites and Internet-based chatrooms and forums.[4]

> The Sunni extremist group Hizb al-Tahrir uses an integrated web of Internet sites, stretching from Europe to Africa, which asks supporters to assist the effort by giving money and encouraging others to donate to the cause of jihad.[5]

---

1. Cf. http//www.welt.de/data/2004/07/20/307555.html (as of: July 2004).
2. Cf. Gabriel Weimann, 'www.terror.net – How modern terrorism uses the Internet', op. cit., p. 8.
3. Ibid., p. 8.
4. Ibid., p. 7.
5. Ibid., p. 7.

Internal communication

The Internet is also used to communicate. Powerful encryption tools can be used by terrorists to communicate and to plan crimes.

Communication

Terrorists use many services of the Internet in order to communicate among themselves. For long time, it was reported that al Qaeda operatives kept their communications, especially phone calls or normal e-mail, to a minimum because of their fear of having their messages intercepted. However, as illustrated by recent cases,[1] this fear does not lead the terrorists to renounce completely modern communication.

Mailing lists with frequently changing names[2] distribute hyperlinks to Islamic websites (that frequently change their addresses).[3]

Appeals to demonstrations that are not legal in some countries and the coordination of such events can also be carried out easily on the Internet.[4]

In addition, terrorists conceal photographs of future victims on sport or sex chat sites. Another tactic is to add encrypted messages and instructions to seemingly harmless photographs.[5]

Teaching

The Internet also provides a platform for other terrorist activities. The use of the Internet to teach terrorist offspring to commit crimes or to plan attacks has become common.

It has been reported that hints have been published in the Internet journal *Mu'askar al-Battar* on how to hijack (publicly or covertly) persons.[6] Teaching in

---

1. For example, the arrest of Mohammad Naeem Noor Khan, which revealed his use of e-mail to communicate with other terrorists.

2. Cf. Krempl, op. cit.

3. Weimann estimates that there fifty websites that "suddenly emerge, modify their formats and swiftly dissapear", 'www.terror.net – How modern terrorism uses the Internet', op. cit.

4. Cf. Krempl, op. cit.

5. Cf. http://www.welt.de/data/2004/07/20/307556.html (as of: July 2004).

6. Reported by Florian Rötzer, "Terror.net: 'Online-Terrorismus' und die Medien", 15 July 2004, http://www.telepolis.de/deutsch/special/info/17886/1.html (as of: September 2004).

general with the help of tutorials and handbooks is practised electronically.[1] Instructions on how to build a bomb and how to use chemicals and other dangerous material can easily be found on the World Wide Web.

Planning

Terrorists use the Internet for planning their activities, too. So-called data mining is also relevant in this context.[2]

> An example is the use of readily available information about the Citigroup's headquarters building in Manhattan including 3-D models, maps with construction details, and information concerning the fire rating of materials used in the building.[3] The recent detention of a Pakistani computer expert with suspected ties to al Qaeda, Mohammad Naeem Noor Khan, showed that the organisation kept US financial buildings under surveillance.[4]

> US troops recovered al Qaeda laptops in Afghanistan. They discovered structural and engineering software, electronic models of a dam and information on computerised water systems, nuclear power plants and US and European stadiums. This leads to the conclusion that these terrorists were using the Internet to co-ordinate and plan physical attacks.[5]

Other crimes

It is also probable that terrorist organisations are attempting to make money illegally by committing copyright offences. Although there is as yet no direct proof that terrorist organisations are engaging in trade with pirated copies (software piracy/hardware counterfeiting), there are indications that they are in fact doing so.[6] In 2003, Interpol general secretary Ronald K. Noble

---

1. Cf. Krempl, op. cit.
2. Cf. Timothy Thomas, Analyst at the Foreign Military Studies Office, Fort Leavenworth, Kansas, cited by Krempl, op. cit.
3. Cf. Dan Verton and Lucas Mearian, "Online data a gold mine for terrorists", Computerworld Document No. 48662 (quicklink on http://www.computerworld.com) (as of: November 2004).
4. A computer seized from the suspect contained hundreds of images, including photographs, drawings and layouts of potential US targets, see CNN report at http://www.cnn.com/2004/US/08/02/terror.targets (as of: November 2004).
5. Gabriel Weimann, 'Cyberterrorism. How real is the threat?', op. cit., p. 9.
6. Cf. Interpol General Secretary Ronald K. Noble in his speech delivered on 16 July 2003 before the US Congress, see http://www.interpol.int/Public/ICPO/speeches/SG20030716.asp# (as of: November 2004).

stated that intellectual property crime involving trade with pirated software, CDs and DVDs has become one of the preferred methods of funding for a number of terrorist groups such as al Qaeda, Hezbollah and Chechen separatists.[1]

The impact of cybercrime

In order to determine the extent of computer-related crime, two different approaches are possible: either the relevant statistics provided by the various criminal justice systems can be studied or the situation in the real world can be analysed. The results of these two approaches are quite different.

Criminal justice statistics

Measuring the extent of computer-related crime by using statistical data provided by criminal justice systems poses two problems:

- First, it must be kept in mind that these statistics do not reflect the extent of computer crime in reality but rather only those offences that are dealt with by the reporting judicial system (that is, the statistics do not reflect the so-called dark figure of unreported offences).

- Second, it is important not to overlook the fact that statistics provided by the various criminal justice systems reflect crimes as they are defined by the substantive criminal law of the reporting system (and the systems often do not differentiate between traditional crime and computer-related crime). This also leads to the fact that due to their different offence definitions, statistics provided by various systems often cannot be compared.

Thus, the following data from the answers to the Council of Europe's questionnaire have to be interpreted carefully.

---

1. Cf. http://www.heise.de/newsticker/data/em-16.07.03-001. Noble mentions as an example Chechnya, where a CD manufacturing plant operated by Chechen organised criminals for the benefit of Chechen separatists was broken up in 2000. In another example, a person selling pirated copies of music CDs and computer games to fund a Hezbollah-related organisation was arrested in February 2000.

Analysing the answers to the Council of Europe's questionnaire

In order to help counteract the dearth of useful data and with the preparation of this report in mind, the Council of Europe conducted a survey of its member states in which – among other information – the states were asked to provide data about cybercrime offences. Additionally, the member states were asked to provide information about whether a connection between cybercrime and organised crime is known to the national law enforcement authorities. In the questionnaire, member states were asked to provide information gathered about cybercrime offences from 1999 to 2003. The following cybercrime offences were included:

- illegal access;
- illegal interception;
- attacks against integrity of data;
- attacks against integrity of systems;
- misuse of devices;
- computer-related forgery;
- computer-related fraud;
- child pornography;
- racism and xenophobia;
- copyright offences.

The data requested were divided into three categories:

- offences reported (for example, by the police);
- offences investigated and/or prosecuted;
- offences leading to convictions.

As a rule, information on general crimes (with no relation to computer systems), such as the total number of all reported incidents of fraud, was not considered. However, the situation was handled differently in the context of child pornography, since these offences are often committed by means of the Internet. The following discussion reflects only those member states that responded to the Council of Europe questionnaire.

Offences reported

Arranged by country, the following table shows the various cybercrime offences reported by the national investigative authorities in the years between 1999 and 2003. Empty fields indicate either that no offences were registered in this area or that there are no available data.

Table 3: Offences reported

	Illegal access	Illegal intercep-tion	Attack against integrity of data	Attack against integrity of systems	Misuse of devices	Computer-related forgery	Computer-related fraud	Child porno-graphy	Racism and xenopho-bia	Copy-right offences
Andorra										
Armenia										
Austria	29	4	31			14	107	201		
Belgium	127	cf. illegal access	32	cf. integrity of data		102	999	993 (106 via the Internet)		
Bulgaria	7						1	51		271
Croatia	25	cf. illegal access	cf. illegal acces s	cf. illegal access	cf. illegal acces s			197		
Czech Republic	103	cf. illegal access	cf. illegal acces s	cf. illegal access				173		
Cyprus										
Denmark										
Estonia	21	3	16	3				10		10
Finland	393	814		171				87		286
Germany		3 798	4 709			1 777	49 903		429	
Italy										
Japan[1]	1 89 6									
Latvia	7		6					5		
Lithuania	2		2					4		
Malta	2		2	0			14	5		1
Moldova	26		1							
Norway	245		62	Cf. attacks against integrit y of data	16	227		502	8	13
Poland	975	Cf. illegal access	520	25			1 355	387	49	51 17 6
Portugal	314		84	36			363	140		57
Romania	3	1		1		1	1			

---

1. Non-member state.

	Illegal access	Illegal intercep-tion	Attack against integrity of data	Attack against integrity of systems	Misuse of devices	Computer-related forgery	Computer-related fraud	Child porno-graphy	Racism and xenopho-bia	Copy-right offences
Slovakia	23		6	1						
Slovenia	61		31		9	642		2	18	141
Sweden										
Switzerland										
FYROM[1]	11									
Turkey										
Ukraine	57	49			5					
UK										

Offences investigated and/or prosecuted

Arranged by country, the following table shows, for each category of cybercrime offence under study, the number of incidents from the years between 1999 and 2003 in which the investigative authorities initiated an inquiry or prosecution. Empty fields indicate either that no offences were registered in this area or that there are no available data.

Table 4:   Offences investigated and/or prosecuted

	Illegal access	Illegal intercep-tion	Attacks against integrity of data	Attacks against integrity of systems	Misuse of devices	Computer-related forgery	Computer-related fraud	Child porno-graphy	Racism and xeno-phobia	Copy-right offences
Andorra										
Armenia										
Austria	29	4	31			14	107	201		
Belgium										
Bulgaria	7									
Croatia										
Czech Republic	50	76						92		
Cyprus										
Denmark										
Estonia	9		7					2		4
Finland										
Germany	51	473	50	57		304	11 127	1 616	428	1 430

---

1. "The former Yugoslav Republic of Macedonia".

	Illegal access	Illegal interception	Attacks against integrity of data	Attacks against integrity of systems	Misuse of devices	Computer-related forgery	Computer-related fraud	Child porno-graphy	Racism and xeno-phobia	Copy-right offences
Italy	1 423		Cf. illegal access	Cf. illegal access				9 973		
Japan	123	2 209	46	17		46	210			430
Latvia	4		6					2		
Lithuania										
Malta	2	1					8	0		0
Poland										2 482
Portugal	286		69	24			328	52		49
Romania	3	1		1		1	1			
Slovakia										
Slovenia	50		15		8	633		1	11	81
Sweden										
Switzerland										
FYROM[1]										
Turkey										
Ukraine	33	31			2					
UK										

Convictions

Arranged by country, the following table shows, for each category of cybercrime offence under study, the number of offences from the years between 1999 and 2003 that resulted in a conviction. Empty fields indicate either that no offences were registered in this area or that there are no available data.

Table 5: Convictions

	Illegal access	Illegal interception	Attacks against integrity of data	Attacks against integrity of systems	Misuse of devices	Computer-related forgery	Computer-related fraud	Child porno-graphy	Racism and xeno-phobia	Copy-right offences
Andorra			1							
Armenia										
Austria										
Belgium										

---

1. "The former Yugoslav Republic of Macedonia".

	Illegal access	Illegal interception	Attacks against integrity of data	Attacks against integrity of systems	Misuse of devices	Computer-related forgery	Computer-related fraud	Child pornography	Racism and xenophobia	Copyright offences
Bulgaria	1									
Croatia										
Czech Republic	12	24						22		
Cyprus										
Denmark										
Estonia										
Finland										
Germany	33	307	31	38		239	9 257	1 527		1 089
Italy										
Japan										
Latvia										
Lithuania										
Malta	1		1				0	0		0
Poland	46	17	8	19			143	22	32	4 176
Portugal										
Romania	1									
Slovakia										
Slovenia	3		0		1					
Sweden										
Switzerland										
FYROM[1]										
Turkey										
Ukraine	2	1			0					
UK										

Offender profile

The questionnaire also asked for information on the perpetrators of cyber-crime offences. To the extent that the member states responded, the following picture emerges: in many cases, the offenders are individuals acting alone, especially when youths are involved. Offenders tend to be male adults between the ages of 25 and 55 who are well educated or who are well integrated socially or professionally; another group of offenders is made up of youths. In the area of child pornography, offenders are primarily single

---

1. "The former Yugoslav Republic of Macedonia".

men. The motivation for committing cybercrime is often the pursuit of economic profit, especially for those offences involving the commission of copyright infringement. For younger offenders, the motivation is often the "challenge" of penetrating otherwise inaccessible computer networks.

Conclusion

In light of the variations between the individual member states, evaluation of the questionnaires yields only limited insights. The statistics indicate that national law enforcement authorities in general continue not to focus on special computer offences and that they often do not distinguish between offline and online offences (especially in the area of copyright infringements).

However, on the basis of responses indicating recently completed or ongoing legislative activities, the questionnaires show that many member states recognise the problem of cybercrime, as such.

Long-term country analysis

The data of the judicial systems can be analysed not only in a comparative horizontal way by evaluating the current statistics of a multitude of countries, it is also possible to analyse the development of these statistics over time. Such police and judicial statistics do not show the absolute number of computer-related crime offences because of the number of offences that are unreported. Nevertheless, they point out tendencies if the long-term developments are examined.

Clearly, a country analysis of this kind is only possible for a selected sample of the member states. For the purposes of this report, developments in computer crime will be discussed on the basis of data gathered from 1987 to 2003 in the Federal Republic of Germany.[1] Germany was chosen because it recognised (that is, codified) special computer-related crime offences as far back as 1986. Also, the reporting of such crime has been conducted over a statistically significant period of time. Indeed, developments in other member states, as far as can be seen from available information on computer crime, show similar tendencies.

---

1. From 1987 to 1990, statistics are based on data from the Federal Republic of Germany excluding Berlin and the states of the former German Democratic Republic; from 1991 to 1992 statistics are based on data from the Federal Republic of Germany including Berlin but without the states of the former German Democratic Republic; and beginning in 1993, statistics are based on data from the Federal Republic of Germany including Berlin and the states of the former German Democratic Republic.

The analysis is based on the annual publication "German police crime statistics",[1] which reported computer crime offences separately for the first time in 1987. The publication records all incidents in which the German police carried out investigations. The following computer-related crime offences or groups of offences are recorded:

- fraud by means of illegally obtained debit cards with PIN;
- computer fraud (Section 263a of the German Criminal Code);
- fraud by means of access authorisations for communications services;
- falsification of legally relevant data, deception in legal relations by means of data processing (Sections 269 and 270 of the German Criminal Code);
- data alteration and computer sabotage (Sections 303a and 303b of the German Criminal Code);
- data espionage (Section 202a of the German Criminal Code);
- computer software piracy (private use such as computer games);
- computer software piracy (in a commercial setting).

Additionally, the annual court statistics reporting convictions in Germany will also be analysed (below).

Overall development

The following chart shows the overall development of computer-related crime in the police statistics in Germany.

As can be seen, there has been a constant and rapid increase of incidents since the reporting of computer-related crime began in 1987. In 2003 the number of registered computer-related crime offences had increased by more than 1 900% when compared to the number of such offences registered in 1987. In contrast, the total number of all crimes registered in Germany in 2003 showed an increase of only about 50% over the same time period. In this time period, the computer-related crime category was the fastest growing category of registered crimes in Germany.

---

1. German Police Crime Statistics (*Polizeiliche Kriminalstatistik Bundesrepublik Deutschland*), Bundeskriminalamt (ed.), http://www.bka.de.

Chart 1: Overall development of computer-related crime

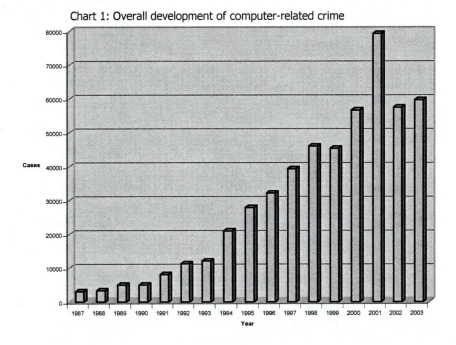

The decrease of offences reported in 2002 is largely due to a change in data collection methods in the category of fraud by means of debit cards (see Chart 3 below).

Development of specific computer crime offences (overview)

The chart shows the development of individual computer crime offences as well as the overall development.

The overall development of computer-related crime offences and developments within the groups of offences listed above show a constant and clear upward tendency in recent years. Computer-related crime offences increased in all categories almost constantly since reporting began (for details see Charts 3 to 10 below). Three categories of crime (fraud by means of illegally obtained debit cards with PIN, computer fraud and fraud by means of access authorisations for communications services) amount to more than 90% of all computer-related crime offences.

Chart 2: Development of specific computer offences (overview)

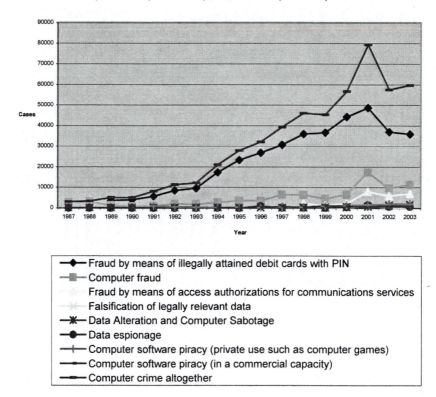

Fraud by means of illegally attained debit cards with PIN
Computer fraud
Fraud by means of access authorizations for communications services
Falsification of legally relevant data
Data Alteration and Computer Sabotage
Data espionage
Computer software piracy (private use such as computer games)
Computer software piracy (in a commercial capacity)
Computer crime altogether

Fraud by means of illegally obtained debit cards with PIN

This chart illustrates fraud by means of illegally obtained debit cards with PIN. Debit cards are cards that enable the holder to withdraw money or to have the cost of purchases charged directly to the holder's bank account.

Before 1989, fraud by means of illegally obtained cards for cash dispensers or pay machines was recorded as computer fraud (see Chart 4). Until 2001, the statistics recorded data concerning fraud by means of illegally obtained cards for cash dispensers or pay machines separately. Since 2002, the category has recorded fraud by means of debit cards with PIN. The reduction of the cases since 2002 is based on an other distribution key. Fraud by means of illegally obtained debit cards with PIN accounts for more than 60% of all computer crime offences.

Chart 3: Fraud by means of illegally obtained debit cards with PIN

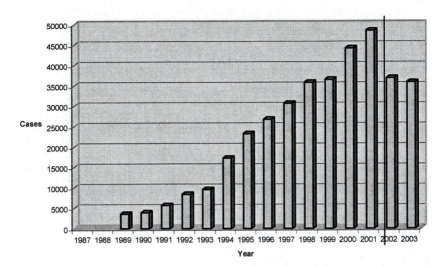

Computer fraud

The following chart illustrates the number of computer fraud offences. Computer fraud (Section 263a of the German Penal Code) penalises the unauthorised influencing of the result of a data-processing operation.[1]

Computer fraud makes up almost 20% of all computer crime offences. Until 1988, this category also included fraud by means of illegally obtained cards for cash dispensers or pay machines; this information has been recorded separately since 1989 (see Chart 3). The reduction of the cases since 2002 is based on an other distribution key. Computer fraud no longer comprises, for example, fraud by means of illegally obtained debit cards with PIN (see Chart 3).

---

1. The relevant part of Section 263a reads as follows: "Whoever, with the intent of obtaining for himself or a third person an unlawful material benefit, damages the assets of another, by influencing the result of a data-processing operation through incorrect configuration of a programme, use of incorrect or incomplete data, unauthorised use of data or other unauthorised influence on the order of events, shall be punished with imprisonment of up to five years or a fine."

Chart 4: Computer fraud

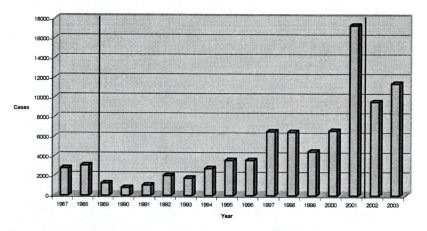

Fraud by means of access authorisations for communications services

The chart illustrates the development of fraud by means of access authorisations for communications services. Communication services are transmis-
sions of speech, text and pictures. They include, for example, access
authorisation by phone cards or passwords.

Fraud by means of access authorisations for communications services was
first recorded in 1998, as the number of offences had grown significantly in
the years before. The number of incidents within this category has increased
rapidly since reporting started; this category now amounts to more than 10%
of all computer-related crime offences.

Chart 5: Fraud by means of access authorisations for communications services

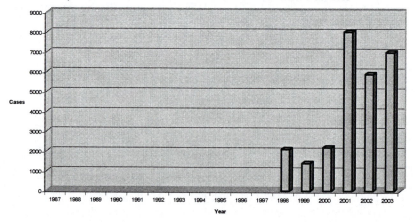

Data alteration and computer sabotage

This figure shows the developments in data alteration and computer sabotage. Data alteration (Section 303a of the German Penal Code) penalises the unauthorised deletion or alteration of data.[1] Computer sabotage (Section 303b of the German Penal Code) penalises interference in data processing either by altering data or by destroying the data carrier.[2]

Data alteration and computer sabotage show the clearest upward tendency of all computer-related crimes. They amount to about 0.03% of all computer-related crime offences.

Chart 6: Data alteration and computer sabotage

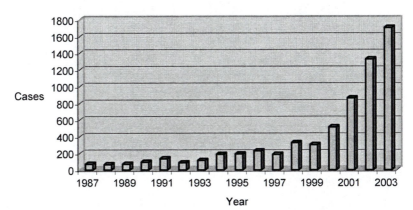

Computer software piracy (private use, such as computer games)

The following chart shows developments in computer software piracy concerning the private use of software; computer software piracy in a commercial setting is examined below. Computer software piracy includes the reproduction of computer software without the consent of the person enjoying the relevant entitlement.

---

1. The relevant part of Section 303a reads as follows: "Whoever unlawfully deletes, suppresses, renders unusable or alters data shall be punished with imprisonment for not more than two years or a fine."

2. The relevant part of Sec. 303b reads as follows: "Whoever interferes with data processing which is of substantial significance to the business or enterprise of another or a public authority by: 1. committing an act under Section 303a or 2. destroying, damaging, rendering unusable, removing or altering a data-processing system or a data carrier shall be punished with imprisonment for not more than five years or a fine."

Chart 7: Computer software piracy (private use, such as computer games)

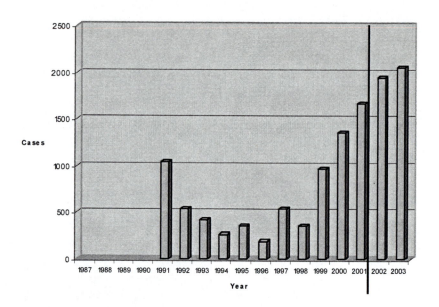

Until 1994, this category included private and commercial computer software piracy. Since 1994, computer software piracy in a commercial setting has been reported separately (see Chart 8). It amounts to about 0.03 % of all computer-related crime offences.

Computer software piracy (in a commercial setting)

This chart shows the development of computer software piracy in a commercial setting.

Prior to 1994, computer software piracy in a commercial setting was not reported separately; instead, it was reported together with computer software piracy for private use (see Chart 7). It is the second smallest group of computer-related crimes and amounts to about 0.01 % of all computer-related crime offences.

Chart 8: Computer software piracy (in a commercial setting)

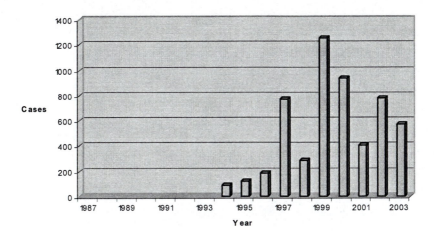

Data espionage

Chart 9: Data espionage

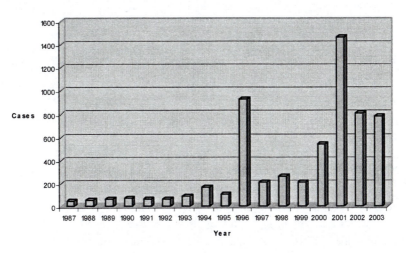

Data espionage (Section 202a of the German Penal Code) penalises the unauthorised obtaining of specially protected data.[1] It amounts to about 0.013% of all computer-related crime offences.

---

1. The relevant part of Section 202a reads as follows: "Whoever, without authorisation, obtains data for himself or another, which was not intended for him and was specially protected against unauthorised access, shall be punished with imprisonment for not more than three years or a fine."

Falsification of legally relevant data

Chart 10 illustrates the falsification of legally relevant data and deception in legal relations by means of data processing (Sections 269 and 270 of the German Penal Code).[1]

Developments in this category have been unusually variable compared to other categories of computer-related crime offences, and it is the only category not showing a significant increase in recent years (except for 2001). As it makes up only 0.004% of all computer-related crime offences, it is the smallest group of computer-related crime offences and has no significant influence on overall developments.

Chart 10: Falsification of legally relevant data

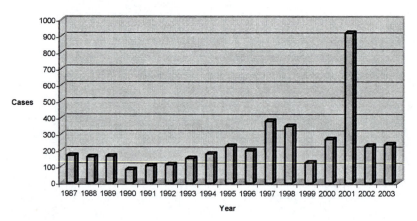

Conclusion

Thus, it can be seen that within only one and a half decades computer-related crime offences have grown from an insignificant number to a major category of crime requiring more and more police resources. The growth has been faster and greater than in any other crime category, although the police assume that only a small percentage of offences are reported and that a considerable number of offences go unreported (such as in the field of

1. The relevant part of Section 269 reads as follows: "Whoever, for the purpose of deception in legal relations, stores or modifies legally relevant data in such a way that a counterfeit or falsified document would exist upon its retrieval, or uses data stored or modified in such a manner, shall be punished with imprisonment for not more than five years."

The relevant part of Section 270 reads as follows: "Falsely influencing data processing in legal relations shall be the equivalent of 'deception in legal relations'."

pirated copies). Therefore, it can be expected that the number of offences will increase noticeably in the future, paralleling the growth in the use of computers and the Internet.

Differences between police statistics and court statistics

In the following, German court statistics[1] will be analysed and compared to German police statistics. The annual court statistics report the number of convictions per year, independent of when the investigations or the court proceedings were begun. As far as computer-related crime offences are concerned, the following offences in the German Criminal Code are relevant:

- computer fraud (Section 263a of the German Criminal Code);
- falsification of legally relevant data, deception in legal relations by means of data processing (Sections 269 and 270 of the German Criminal Code);
- data alteration and computer sabotage (Sections 303a and 303b of the German Criminal Code);
- data espionage (Section 202a of the German Criminal Code).

The following charts show developments in the court statistics as well as in the police statistics to make comparisons easier. For the year 2003, court statistics are not yet available. When comparing these two sources, it is important to keep in mind that court and police statistics for a particular year generally do not refer to the same incidents; this is because convictions often follow months or even years after the police have conducted investigations into a particular incident.

Computer fraud

The chart shows the development of computer fraud.

The number of convictions for computer fraud has increased steadily since 1987. In 2002, the number of convictions was about nineteen times as high as it was in 1987.

---

1. Rechtspflege Strafverfolgung, Fachserie 10/Reihe 3, Statistisches Bundesamt (ed.).

Chart 11: Computer fraud

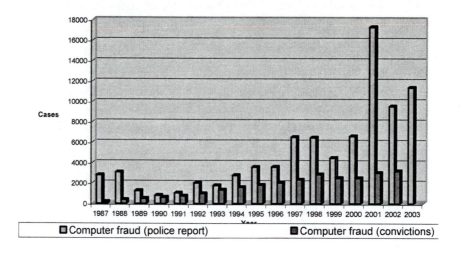

Data alteration and computer sabotage

The following chart illustrates the development of data alteration and computer sabotage.

Chart 12: Data alteration and computer sabotage

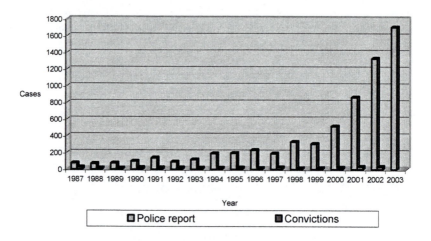

Only a very small percentage of incidents of data alteration and computer sabotage reported to the police lead to convictions in court. The number of convictions has not increased since reporting started in 1987.

Falsification of legally relevant data

This chart shows developments in the falsification of legally relevant data.

Chart 13: Falsification of legally relevant data

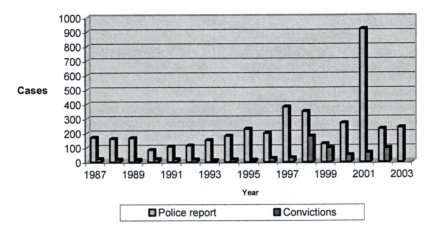

Developments regarding falsification of legally relevant data have been variable. The number of convictions in 2002 is about five times the number of convictions in 1987.

Data espionage (Section 202a of the German Criminal Code)

The following chat illustrates the development of data espionage.

Chart 14: Data espionage

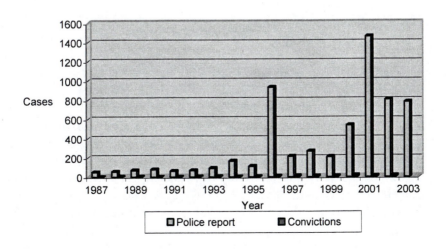

The chart shows that in the case of data espionage as defined by Section 202a of the German Criminal Code – as in the cases of data alteration and computer sabotage – only a very small percentage of incidents reported to the police lead to convictions in court. Again, there has been no increase in the number of convictions since reporting began in 1987.

Conclusion

The court statistics show that only a small percentage of incidents reported to the police lead to convictions. Remarkably, some computer crime offences have not registered an increase in the number of convictions since 1987, although the number of incidents reported to the police has increased significantly.

Yet the lack of increase over time in the number of convictions applies only to the data alteration and computer sabotage offences and to the offences of data espionage. Convictions for these two categories of offences, taken together, make up only a small percentage of the sum of all convictions obtained for the four categories of computer-related crime offences studied here. In contrast, convictions for computer fraud – which make up 95.5% of all convictions obtained for these four computer-related crime categories – increased nineteenfold in a comparable time period (between 1987 and 2002). This increase is approximately the same as the increase in the number of computer-related crime offences reported to the police in the same time period.[1] To this extent, developments in the number of incidents reported to the police and in the number of convictions are comparable.

Studies in the real world

The situation described above as reflected in the statistics kept by the various criminal justice systems is in sharp contrast to the situation that can be analysed by observations and studies in the real world. This becomes especially clear if a distinction is made between the various forms of computer-related crime using the typology developed above.

The following sections deal with the extent and effects of some of the computer-related offences described above. As not all types of offences have been analysed, the following discussion concentrates on those offences for which data, observations or studies are available. As a consequence, these remarks are only a first attempt to measure the extent and effects of computer-related crime independently of the police crime statistics.

---

1. See Chart 1 above.

Computer hacking, interception and other forms of illegal access

In the field of computer hacking, there is some data with respect to the special form of phishing. Phishing has received a great deal of attention lately.

A study conducted in 2004 by the Gartner Group, Inc., a provider of research and analysis of the global information technology industry, shows that e-mail phishing attacks had become more pervasive within the last twelve months.[1] The study is based on survey responses from 5 000 adult Internet users. It is based on a twelve-month period ending in April 2004. The research examined five types of consumer fraud: new account fraud, cheque forgery, unauthorised access to cheque accounts, illegal credit card purchases and fraudulent cash advances on credit cards.

About 19% of the Internet users who replied stated that they had reacted to phishing e-mails, and 3% of those attacked even answered these e-mails and gave their financial or personal information. The study estimates that in just one year 57 million consumers in the United States received phishing e-mails, and some 1.78 million of those attacked revealed such information because of these attacks and suffered financial damage of some US$2.4 billion in 2003. It estimates the costs of phishing e-mails for US banks and credit card issuers at about US$1.2 billion in 2003.

The Anti-Phishing Working Group, an industry association focused on eliminating identity theft and fraud, publishes monthly reports on phishing attacks. The reports are based on phishing attacks reported to the working group via the organisation's website or by email submissions. In most cases companies affected by phishing attacks report to the working group. The monthly report counted 1 974 new phishing attacks in July 2004 alone.[2] The most-targeted companies belong to the financial services and retail sectors. The number of attacks reported has increased considerably since the end of last year. The number of attacks in July 2004 is more than seventeen times higher than the number of attacks in December 2003.

---

1. Cf. http://www4.gartner.com/5_about/press_releases/asset_71087_11.jsp; and http://news.com/2100-7349-5234155.html (as of: November 2004).
2. http://www.antiphishing.org/APWG_Phishing_Attack_Report-Jul2004.pdf (as of: November 2004).

Viruses, worms and Trojan Horses

The Australian Police in co-operation with the Australian High-Tech Crime Centre and AusCERT, the Australian computer emergency response team based at the University of Queensland, produced a computer-related crime and security survey in 2004.[1] The survey questioned 350 public and private organisations and covers a twelve-month period prior to January 2004. The questionnaire asked for information on the extent of security technology used, the extent of electronic attacks harming network and data systems, the impact such attacks had on the organisations and how these organisations manage such attacks. The survey questionnaire could be answered online via a secure website or via a prepaid envelope. Responses to the survey totalled 240,[2] representing over 17 different private industry sectors, plus local, state and federal government sectors. The most represented organisations were from the educational sector (18%), the state government sector (13%) and the manufacturing sector (9%).

The report shows that 88% of the those organisations which responded had detected viruses, worms or Trojan infection.[3] Some 71% of the organisations reported financial losses caused by viruses, worms, and Trojan infection.[4] These led to financial losses of more than AU$7 million in 2003, amounting to about 50% of the total annual losses caused by computer-related crimes.[5] The average loss amounted to AU$116 212. One company suffered damages totalling AU$2 million in a single virus infection. The companies affected by viruses, worms or Trojan infections needed between one and seven days, on average, to repair their computer systems.[6]

A similar result is shown in the 2001 "Cybercrime against businesses" report by the US Department of Justice.[7] The Bureau of Justice Statistics collaborat-

---

1. Australian Computer Crime and Security Survey 2004, http://www.auscert.org.au/download.html?f=114 (as of: November 2004).
2. Not all organisations answered all questions. Hence in the following the exact number of responding organisations will be given in the footnotes.
3. Number of responding organisations: 227; Australian Computer Crime and Security Survey 2004, op. cit., p. 17.
4. Number of responding organisations: 172; ibid., p. 19.
5. Number of responding organisations: 137; ibid., p. 21.
6. Number of responding organisations: 206; ibid., p. 23.
7. 2001 Computer Security Survey, "Cybercrime against businesses", US Department of Justice, Bureau of Justice Statistics, http://www.ojp.usdoj.gov/bjs/pub/pdf/cb.pdf (as of: November 2004).

ing with the US Census Bureau conducted a pilot survey of cybercrime against businesses in the year 2001, which covered a group of 500 businesses throughout the United States. Half of the companies questioned were selected from the largest companies in each industry sector, the other half was randomly selected to represent businesses of all sizes and types. The questionnaire asked for information on the detection of cybercrime incidents and the impact of these incidents. The questionnaire differentiated between six types of incidents: fraud, embezzlement, theft of proprietary information, denial of service attacks, vandalism or sabotage, and a computer virus. Some 208 companies from all industry sectors answered the questionnaire.[1] The report shows that 64% of the companies reported incidents involving computer viruses.[2] Such incidents were the most common cybercrime incidents and caused monetary losses of nearly US$22 million in 2001.[3]

Theft of proprietary information

The 2004 CSI/FBI Computer Crime and Security Survey details the extent of theft of proprietary information.[4] The survey is conducted by the Computer Security Institute with the participation of San Francisco Federal Bureau of Investigation's Computer Intrusion Squad. It is based on a survey of 494 corporations of all sizes and from all industry sectors, government agencies, financial and medical institutions, and universities.[5] The survey asked for information about the security systems used, experiences with computer intrusions during the year 2003 and the impact of such intrusions. It differentiated between ten different kinds of cybercrime incidents, among these theft of proprietary information and computer sabotage. The survey shows that about 10% of those questioned had experienced theft of proprietary information within the last twelve months.[6] The financial damage amounted to more than US$11 million.[7]

---

1. Not all companies answered all questions. Hence in the following the exact number of responding companies will be given in the footnotes.

2. Number of responding companies: 198; "Cybercrime against businesses", op. cit., p. 3.

3. Number of responding companies: 147; ibid., p. 4.

4. Cf. http://i.cmpnet.com/gocsi/db_area/pdfs/fbi/FBI2004.pdf (as of: November 2004).

5. Not all organisations answered all questions. Hence in the following the exact number of responding organisations will be given in the footnotes.

6. Number of responding organisations: 481; 2004 CSI/FBI Computer Crime and Security Survey, p. 9; http://i.cmpnet.com/gocsi/db_area/pdfs/fbi/FBI2004.pdf (as of: November 2004).

7. Number of responding organisations: 269; ibid., p. 10.

Computer sabotage and computer extortion

A study by the San Diego Supercomputer Centre's Cooperative Association for Internet Data Analysis assessed the number and duration of DoS attacks on the Internet. The study is based on a backscatter analysis[1] during a three week period in 2001 and covered about 1/256 of the total number of Internet addresses. The study reveals that DoS attacks against websites occur more than 4 000 times every week. Most attacks last less than one hour. Common targets include Amazon.com, AOL and Microsoft's Hotmail service.[2]

The above-mentioned 2004 CSI/FBI Computer Crime and Security Survey shows that about 20% of the 494 corporations responding had experienced DoS attacks and computer sabotage within the last twelve months, accounting for damages of almost US$27 million.[3]

The above-mentioned "Cybercrime against businesses" report by the US Department of Justice shows similar results: 25% of the 198 companies responding had detected DoS attacks. DoS attacks are the second most common cybercrime incident.[4] The report also shows that computer sabotage or vandalism is the third most common cybercrime incident: of the 198 companies questioned, 19% reported such incidents.[5]

Computer-related fraud

The Internet Fraud Complaint Center (IFCC), a partnership between the American National White Collar Crime Center and the Federal Bureau of Investigation, published the 2002 "Internet fraud report".[6] The report is based on over 75 000 complaints about Internet fraud received by the IFCC via its website during the year 2002. According to the report the number of

---

1. Backscatter refers to the effect whereby a computer attacked sends back replies to every incoming data packet. As the most common DoS attack programmes randomise the address from which the data seems to have come the attacked computer sends replies to each of the random addresses ("scattering back" responses). These responses signal that a computer is under attack.

2. See http://www.caida.org/outreach/papers/2001/BackScatter and http://news.com.com/2100-1001_3-258093.html?tag=prntfr (as of: November 2004).

3. Cf. the 2004 CSI/FBI Computer Crime and Security Survey, pp. 9-10.

4. "Cybercrime against businesses", op. cit.

5. Ibid.

6. IFCC 2002 Internet Fraud Report; http://www.ifccfbi.gov/strategy/statistics.asp See also: http://www.heise.de/newsticker/meldung/36019 (as of: November 2004).

complaints of fraud on the Internet that led to investigations in 2002 was three times higher than in the previous year, when the report was published for the first time. In 2002, 48 252 complaints were referred to law enforcement or regulatory agencies in the United States. The total dollar loss from all referred fraud cases in 2002 was US$54 million, up from US$17 million in 2001.[1]

The above-mentioned "Cybercrime against businesses" report by the US Department of Justice shows that only 11.6% of the 198 responding companies detected computer-related fraud, although computer-related fraud made up almost one third of all monetary losses.[2]

A similar result is shown in studies initiated by the consultancy KPMG: a survey questionnaire in the summer of 2000 among Hong Kong's 1 500 largest companies asked for information about computer fraud experiences in the last two years. Some 8% of the 112 companies responding had experienced computer-related fraud leading to financial losses.[3]

A survey questionnaire in 1999 among Australia's 1 800 largest companies asked for information about the extent and impact of fraud. Some 12% of the 367 companies responding reported computer-related fraud resulting, in most cases, in financial losses or business disruption.[4]

Online child enticement and other forms of searching for victims

A study conducted by the Crimes Against Children Research Centre at the University of New Hampshire (USA) highlights the risk of children being exposed to unwanted sexual solicitations and approaches whilst using the Internet.[5] The study is based on interviews with 1 501 youths aged 10 to 17 regularly using the Internet. The youths were questioned about the way solicitations occurred and how they responded to such incidents. The report

---

1. Cf. http://www.heise.de/newsticker/meldung/36019 (as of: November 2004).

2. "Cybercrime against businesses", op. cit.

3. http://www.kpmg.com.hk/Press%20releases/pressrel_fraud_survey00.html (as of: November 2004).

4. http://www.aic.gov.au/research/fraud/kpmg_aus_1999.pdf (as of: November 2004).

5. This report is one of the first of its kind to assess the extent of the problem of online enticement. It is entitled "Online victimisation: a report on the nation's youth" and is available at: http://www.unh.edu/ccrc/pdf/Victimization_Online_Survey.pdf (as of: November 2004).

revealed that some 20% of youths regularly using the Internet received unwanted sexual solicitations, female youths more often than male youths. In most cases, the youths met the person who solicited them in a chatroom; this was followed by instant messages. Some 3% of the youths were even asked to meet the sexual solicitor. The report found that fewer than 10% of the solicitations were reported to the police.[1]

Child pornography

A study conducted by University College Cork (Ireland) in 1998 claimed that approximately 0.07% of all Internet newsgroups contained "child erotica" or "pornography". However, the study also concluded that it was not possible to estimate with accuracy the amount of child pornography traffic generated on Internet Relay Chat, due to the "organised dynamic nature of paedophile activity".[2]

Experts assume that the number of websites containing child pornography has grown enormously in recent years. According to estimates by Unicef, this market has a business volume of about US$20 billion annually; the German Federal Police estimates a business volume of €5 billion annually. According to the Internet Watch Foundation, 55% of all child pornography websites originate in the United States and 23% in the Russian Federation.[3]

A study conducted by Palisade Systems in 2003 showed a large demand for child pornography: it examined 400 000 files randomly selected from 22 million searches within 3 weeks in a peer-to-peer (P2P) application.[4] Child pornography represented 6% of all search requests, 10% of all video searches, and as much as 24% of all image file searches.[5]

A single case may also illustrate the enormous extent of child pornography: in 2001, following a tip-off from the US Postal Inspection Service, US authorities were able to dismantle the above-mentioned child pornography

---

1. Ibid.

2. Irish Department of Justice, Equality and Law Reform, *Illegal and harmful use of the Internet*, Dublin 1998, at pp. 33 *et seq.*

3. "2003 annual report and statistics", p. 7, available at http://www.iwf.org.uk (as of: November 2004).

4. P2P applications reside on individual computers that can communicate directly with other computers running similar software on a network. When a connection is established, it is possible to share virtually any file between the connected machines.

5. Cf. http://www.palisadesys.com/news&events/p2pstudy.pdf (as of: November 2004).

ring run by a business called Landslide. The business sold child pornography videos and pictures on the Internet and provided access to some 300 child pornography websites. The business, which grossed $1.4 million a month, had some 250 000 customers who paid by credit card and, as a result, were easy to identify.[1] The founder of Landslide was subsequently sentenced by a US court to 1 335 years in prison.[2]

Racism, hate speech and glorification of violence

A report published in the United States in 1999 listed hundreds of hate groups with a presence on the Internet and noted that they are becoming increasingly sophisticated. Many hate sites are openly racist, while others disguise their messages as legitimate information sources. Some even attempt to lure children into their ideology by offering colourful graphics, puzzles and games. The Internet has become a source of revenue for other hate groups.[3]

The Simon Wiesenthal Centre has estimated for the year 2000 that there were well over 2 000 "problematic" websites, including more than 500 extremist sites that originate in Europe but that are hosted on American servers to avoid more stringent laws in Europe.[4]

The web filtering company SurfControl monitors web developments and maintains a database of categorised Internet content. The company reported that hate and violence sites have increased by about 300% since 2000; in the first four months of 2004 the number had grown by 26%.[5]

---

1. Cf. http://www.heise.de/newsticker/meldung/20008 (as of: November 2004).

2. Cf. http://news.bbc.co.uk/go/pr/fr/-/1/hi/uk/3035115.stm (as of: November 2004).

3. Cf. the report "Poisoning the web: hatred online", published by the Anti-Defamation League, available at
http://www.adl.org/poisoning_web/poisoning_toc.asp (as of: November 2004).

4. Cf. http://www.wiesenthal.com (as of: November 2004).

5. Cf. http://www.surfcontrol.com/news/newsitem.aspx?id=650 (as of: November 2004).

Cyberstalking

The number of persons affected by cyberstalking is unknown. A US Government report published in 1999 estimated that some hundreds of thousands of online users in the United States were victims of recent cyberstalking incidents.[1]

A study based on an online survey showed that mostly women were affected and, in contrast to offline stalking, most victims did not know their stalkers as the Internet makes it easy to remain anonymous.[2]

Copyright offences: unauthorised reproduction and use of computer programmes

The extent and effect of unauthorised reproduction and use of other forms of digital and non-digital works is shown by Germany's current market data. According to a 2004 "study of burners" (*Brennerstudie*)[3] conducted by the Society for Consumer Research (Gesellschaft für Konsumforschung), private individuals burned 316 million blank CDs with music in 2003. Furthermore, in the same year, 23.4 million movies were copied onto blank DVDs. Finally, 7.3 million persons carried out a total of 602 million music downloads (assuming that there are 63.6 million Germans aged 10 and above).

According to the "Recording industry commercial piracy report 2004" of the International Federation of the Phonographic Industry (IFPI), some 1.1 billion pirated CDs and CD-Rs were produced and distributed in 2003.[4] In many cases, popular titles were available even before their official release date. The IFPI estimated that commercial piracy of physical formats accounted for US$4.5 billion in 2003.

---

1. "1999 report on cyberstalking: a new challenge for law enforcement and industry", available at http://usdoj.gov/criminal/cybercrime/cyberstalking.htm (as of: November 2004).

2. Paul Bocij, "Victims of cyberstalking: an exploratory study of harassment perpetrated via the Internet", available at http://firstmonday.org/issues/issue8_10/bocij/index.html (as of: November 2004).

3. Cf. http://www.ifpi.de/news/379/index-Dateien/frame.htm (as of: November 2004).

4. Cf. http://www.ifpi.org/site-content/library/piracy2004.pdf (as of: November 2004).

Copyright offences: unauthorised reproduction and use of computer programmes

Currently, standard software is sold on a massive scale, and, as far as the number of crimes are concerned, the predominant offence is the illegal copying of standard software, particularly for use on personal computers. The Business Software Alliance (BSA), a software industry watch-dog, publishes in co-operation with the global market research and forecasting firm IDC an annual "Global software piracy study" assessing the worldwide piracy rate and total revenue lost by the software industry due to piracy.[1] In 2003, this total loss of revenue worldwide as a result of software piracy amounted to US$28.79 billion. This represents a world piracy rate of 36% (the market share of illegally copied software). Eastern Europe was the region with the highest piracy rate, at 70%, while the North American region continued to have the lowest rate, at 23%, and western Europe had the second lowest rate, at 36%. According to the BSA and IDC figures, the retail software revenue lost to piracy in the member states of the Council of Europe and other states having signed or ratified the Convention on Cybercrime (as far as listed) in 2003 was as indicated in the table below.

The BSA has been conducting the study annually since 1994 (in co-operation with the IDC for the first time in 2003), and although the overall world piracy rate has gradually declined from 1995 (45%) to 1999 (36%), the small increase in 2000 and 2001 (to 40%) and the small decrease in 2003 (to 36%) would suggest that it now appears to be levelling out. Indeed, those regions with the lowest piracy rates are showing the least progress in reducing the figure further. There therefore appears to be a core piracy problem that is becoming entrenched and will be difficult to overcome. This view is supported by a survey carried by the BSA in 2002 of consumers who download software from the Internet: 25% of those questioned said that they would never pay for software.[2]

A study of fifty-seven countries (including numerous member states of the Council of Europe) conducted by the market research institute IDC in 2003 shows that software piracy is not only a microeconomic problem affecting the software industry but rather that it is a macroeconomic problem affecting the economy as a whole.[3]

---

1. Cf.
http://www.bsa.org/globalstudy/loader.cfm?url=/commonspot/security/getfile.cfm&pageid=16947&hitboxdone=yes (as of: November 2004).
2. Cf. http://www.bsa.org/resources/2002-05-29.117.pdf (as of: November 2004).
3. Cf. http://global.bsa.org/germany/piraterie/pics/idc2003.pdf.

Table 6: Software piracy rates and revenues lost

Country	Piracy rate	Retail software revenue lost (in million US$)
Austria	27%	109
Belgium and Luxembourg	29%	240
Bulgaria	71%	26
Canada	35%	736
Croatia	59%	44
Cyprus	55%	8
Czech Republic	40%	106
Denmark	26%	165
Estonia	54%	14
Finland	31%	148
France	45%	2 311
Germany	30%	1 899
Greece	63%	87
Hungary	42%	96
Ireland	41%	71
Italy	49%	1 127
Japan	29%	1 633
Latvia	57%	16
Lithuania	58%	17
Malta	46%	2
Netherlands	33%	577
Norway	32%	155
Poland	58%	301
Portugal	41%	66
Romania	73%	49
Russian Federation	87%	1 104
Slovakia	50%	40
Slovenia	52%	32
South Africa	36%	147
Spain	44%	512
Sweden	27%	241
Switzerland	31%	293
Turkey	66%	127
Ukraine	91%	92
United Kingdom	29%	1 601
USA	22%	6 496

According to the study, countries with low piracy rates have faster growing IT sectors. The study claims that this results in a greater tax basis and more jobs. It estimates that if the piracy rate of the countries studied could be reduced by ten percentage points over four years, the IT sector would be supported and could grow by 49% – namely, fifteen points faster – between 2001 and 2006, as opposed to the current estimate of 34%. A ten point drop in worldwide piracy over four years could add 1.5 million jobs in the IT sector, US$64 billion in tax revenues and US$400 billion in additional economic growth. In addition, according to the IDC, high piracy countries could achieve the highest benefits from piracy reduction (the Russian Federation, for example, could double its IT sector by the year 2006). However, these findings are controversial. The study does not consider that the average customer in countries with high piracy rates is not able to pay the prices charged for legal software copies. Perhaps, a reduced piracy rate will not lead to more sales volume but to less use of actual software. The growth of the IT sector could hence be less than calculated. Furthermore it should be noted that more sales volume does not automatically lead to more jobs.

General issues

Computer crimes are not limited to certain industries or economic sectors. The Australian Computer Crime and Security Survey 2004[1] and the CSI/FBI Computer Crime and Security Survey 2004[2] show that across the board both the public and the private sectors are affected by computer crimes. Similarly, the "Cybercrime against businesses report" of the US Department of Justice points out that companies from all industry sectors are affected.[3]

The damage caused by computer crimes is said to be increasing constantly. The Australian Computer Crime and Security Survey 2004[4] shows that the damage reported for the 2004 survey is about three times as high as the damage reported for the first survey conducted in 2002.

As far as total losses caused by computer crimes are concerned, the CSI/FBI Computer Crime and Security Survey 2004,[5] for example, indicates that 269 responding corporations and government agencies suffered a damage of some US$141 million in one year. According to the "Cybercrime against businesses" report, 147 companies suffered monetary losses of some US$61 million in 2001; recovery costs amounted to one third of the total losses.[6]

Conclusion

The above-mentioned studies, reports and surveys vary greatly in regard to the methods used and the extent to which they explore the phenomena of the various computer crime offences. Often, no information about the

---

1. Cf. Australian Computer Crime and Security Survey 2004, op. cit., p. 4.
2. Cf. 2004 CSI/FBI Computer Crime and Security Survey, op. cit., p. 2,
3. "Cybercrime against businesses".
4. Cf. Australian Computer Crime and Security Survey 2004, op. cit., p. 4,
5. Cf. 2004 CSI/FBI Computer Crime and Security Survey, op. cit., p. 10.
6. "Cybercrime against businesses", op. cit.

criminological method or the criminological criteria used is available. Thus, some of the studies should be viewed with great caution.

However, all analyses indicate that the extent of computer crime in reality is much higher than police and judicial reports show. This is highly plausible and largely due to the fact that computer crime offences are often not reported to the police for the following reasons.[1] Many computer users do not even notice that they have become the victim of a computer crime attack. Victims are too embarrassed to reveal their levity in use of the Internet. To the extent that companies are victims, they often fear that the publicity resulting from reporting an offence to the police will have an adverse effect on their public image. Therefore, companies are quite reluctant even to answer anonymous surveys, such as those mentioned above.[2] The "Cyber-crime against businesses" report shows that only about 14% of the companies affected reported incidents to law enforcement agencies.[3]

Although an overall study on the extent of computer crime does not exist, the available studies and cases allow the conclusion to be drawn that computer crime seems to be virtually omnipresent where there are computers and a possibility to use the Internet. In order to get reliable data it would be advisable to conduct a serious criminological study on the extent of computer crime.

Conclusion and consequences

The vulnerability of the information society

The starting point of this chapter on cybercrime has been the vulnerabilities of the information society. These are primarily due to the fact that it processes most of its important economic and social transactions by means of computer systems and computer networks and is therefore highly dependent on the efficiency and security of modern information technology. In addition, in the age of the Internet and other electronic communication systems, these intangible values can be attacked not only by perpetrators

---

1. Cf. for the problem of the "dark figure": Sieber 1986a, p. 33.
2. Only 137 of 250 questioned organisations for the Australian Computer Crime and Security Survey 2004 (about 55%) responded to questions on computer crimes and financial losses, similarly only 269 of 494 questioned organisations for the 2004 CSI/FBI Computer Crime and Security Survey (about 54%) answered such questions; the "Cybercrime against businesses" report shows that only 198 out of 500 questioned companies (about 40%) responded.
3. "Cybercrime against businesses", op. cit.

within victimised companies but also by external perpetrators, even from abroad. Moreover, the technical software applications necessary for the flexible administration of these systems are so complex that total security cannot be guaranteed, especially since the systems must be accessible to numerous users via telecommunication facilities. In short, technological developments have created societies that are extremely dependent on computer systems and especially vulnerable to all kinds of computer-based attacks.

The threat analysis of this chapter did not only confirm this hypothesis, it also showed special features of computer-related crime which make the new threat of cybercrime particularly serious. The features of modern information technology shape common characteristics of computer-related crime:

- Computer and telecommunication technology has spread into nearly all areas of life including the administration of important social infrastructures. The same is true for computer-related crime. Moreover, the people using computers have changed: the computer of the 1950s and 1960s was still an exclusive "device of power" in the hands of the state or of particular enterprises. Today it is available to every citizen. This led to changes concerning computer offences both on the side of the criminals as well as victims. As a consequence, computer crimes can nowadays be committed by nearly everybody and threaten – just as the other dangers of the "risk society" – every citizens. With this, computer crime has become more frequent, more diverse and more dangerous.

- Computer systems and networks as well as all other networks for digital devices are powerful instruments for commercial, private and public use – but the same powerful technological infrastructure can also support and intensify criminal purposes. As a consequence, the Internet, in particular, offers perfect conditions not only for the exchange of useful information but also for the exchange of illegal content such as child pornography. A single file with child pornography offered in the Internet can – at least in theory – easily be accessed by millions of users. And web-based file sharing systems, for example, can be used to access millions of copyright-protected music and video files or software files. The illegal exchange in these systems seriously damages the profit of the entire software, music and movie industries. The same principle applies with respect to attacks against computer systems and networks. The Internet contains large amounts of illegal content which means that millions of victims are just a mouse click away. Thus, a single attack in one country can affect millions of computer systems in other countries. This relation between a single action and serious consequences is illustrated by spam e-mails, which not only are an inconvenience to millions of users but may also pose serious threats due to viruses or Trojan Horses hidden within attached files. And it is especially dangerous if terrorist attacks are directed towards the Internet itself or against the above-mentioned important infrastructures of our societies, for example, conventional power stations, nuclear power plants, or air traffic or defence systems.

- Computer data are hard to control. This is due to the multitude of data in modern computer systems, their encryption and the many different kinds of computer systems (which often cannot be handled by the police). Control deficits are also caused by the fact that many computer networks are open and decentralised, that is, without central control instruments. Actually, the Internet has been designed to resist influence from the outside as far as possible. In order to protect the system, no central control instrument was integrated in the network architecture so as to preclude the possibility of an attack against a central control unit influencing the functioning of the entire network. This makes it difficult to control illegal network operations. As a consequence, it is also difficult to identify offenders who use the Internet in order to commit crimes. Since even a simple data exchange procedure such as opening a web page involves more than one provider, the identification of offenders and the collection of evidence needs special routines.

- Computer networks are global and connect computers all over the world. Even in a data exchange process between two computers in a single country the information may pass through one or more other countries if no direct connection is available. The international character of the Internet in turn leads to the global character of cybercrime: using computer networks, crimes committed in one country can have effects in another country. Computer viruses, computer worms, and Trojan Horses – such as the "I love you virus" or the "Blaster Worm" – can spread around the globe within hours and affect millions of computer systems. Similarly, illegal content on servers in a "computer crime haven" can be accessed from most countries of the world. Terrorists can exchange encrypted information and messages worldwide and hide these messages even in multimedia files such as pictures. One can argue about whether cyberspace is really virtual since Internet servers are always located in the real word. However, at least one can say that cyberspace is an international space where it is often unclear which country is being used to store or transfer the relevant data.

- Computer and computer networks are fast. Whereas in some cases traditional data collections (such as those kept in file systems) offered a certain amount of protection simply on the basis of their physical size, digital data can be gathered quickly, searched, analysed and copied – all without leaving a trace. Also, information via vulnerable points in security systems can spread much more quickly than was the case with traditional means (for example, publications). Thus, in early 2004 the average period of time between the discovery of a security hole and the appearance of corresponding code exploiting that weakness was less than six days.[1] For firms, this means that their personnel must continually monitor security mailing lists and must be able to patch all affected systems extremely quickly.

These characteristics of computer-related crime explain the above-analysed developments: the high number of computer-related crimes, their damages, the increasing links between cybercrime and organised crime as well as the use of the Internet by terrorist groups. These developments also prove that the security of computer systems and computer networks and the prevention of their misuse have become central challenges for today's information society.

Responding to these new threats, it should be clear that the main means to protect society against computer-related crime are the education of computer users about the relevant risks as well as the development of technical security measures which go beyond the topic of this report. However, it is also essential to have an effective criminal law system which enables investigation and prosecution of these new types of crime. The present empirical threat analysis does not include the analysis of these legal aspects. However, it showed that there are considerable problems for effective prosecution of cybercrime.

The contradiction between computer-related crimes and criminal law systems

The new problems of cybercrime for the criminal justice system are not just caused by the practical difficulties of dealing with computer-related crime. More important is the fact that the new characteristics of cybercrime are in complete opposition to the characteristics of traditional law. Based on the

---

1. See "Symantec Internet security threat report", op. cit.

above analysis of the characteristics of computer-related crime, the following points describe just a few of the main aspects of this tension:

- Traditional criminal law deals primarily with the protection of clearly defined tangible goods against human attacks. In contrast, computer crimes frequently violate new intangible values, which depend on a difficult balance of interests and which are difficult to define by means of general terms and blanket clauses. Examples of these difficult balancing acts are copyright law (balancing the economic interests of creators and the justifiable information demands of society), privacy law (balancing the protection of privacy and the freedom to process information), as well as the legal regulation of harmful content (balancing the protection of minors, minorities, racial groups with the right to freedom of information of adults).

- Traditional systems of criminal law are based on the idea of national sovereignty; thus, the direct scope of their decisions is limited to their national territory. In contrast, the Internet is a truly global medium. Geographical aspects – such as the location where information is physically stored – are of minor importance. Transferred information passes through countries and regions regardless of borders and boundaries.

- Traditional systems of criminal law are slow: decisions made by the police often need to be confirmed by a judge; in many cases the accused has the right to be heard, judicial decisions can be appealed and transnational proceedings are highly formalised. In contrast, the Internet is an extremely fast system: whereas the transfer of national decisions of criminal law takes weeks or months, computer data can be transferred to a foreign country in milliseconds. The speed of the transfer process and the multinational interaction represent a challenge for all national legal systems and national legal institutions. Data can be erased or altered in milliseconds around the globe; log files are often only kept for a certain period of time and traffic data revealing the origin of a communication chain are only stored for a short period of time. This tension can have disastrous consequences for effective investigations. While the police start to search a computer system in premises A, the perpetrator can easily erase the relevant data in the storage devices in premises B. Or, when the police receives the traffic data of one Internet service provider, the next Internet service provider in the investigated chain of communication no longer stores the traffic data necessary to identify the sender of data.

- In a criminal prosecution, the perpetrators of crime must be identified and robust proof of their actions must be provided. These requirements make the prosecution of computer-related crime in computer networks difficult as especially the Internet is hard to control and provides – at least for skilled users – a high level of anonymity. International computer networks (with anonymous re-mailers or free access devices to Internet service providers) offer anonymity to perpetrators which can only be lifted if all countries crossed by the communication decide to co-operate. In addition, computer and communication systems are increasingly offered together with strong encryption and possibilities to hide data. Today, standard software is able not only to encrypt data but also to hide data, for example in pictures (steganography). Obtaining the necessary information to prosecute successfully in this area is especially difficult since many constitutions limit access to sensitive user information that is necessary to identify offenders. Any proposal that tries to limit this anonymity faces criticism from proponents of data protection and telecommunication secrecy and is criticised for supporting "big brother like" surveillance.

New challenges for criminal law systems

The foregoing analysis and description of the tension between computer-related crime and traditional criminal law indicates how difficult it is for criminal law to adequately address computer-related crime and explains why cybercrime, in particular, is one of the most significant challenges facing the traditional criminal law.

Nevertheless, these general observations also shed light on future solutions for traditional criminal law systems. In order to deal with the new challenges posed by cybercrime, criminal law must adapt to the new phenomena:

- Substantive criminal law must not only cover new forms of attacks against traditional corporeal values, it must also protect the new (especially intangible) values of today's information society, and, specifically, it must deal with the civil law questions of copyright and data protection as well as with the protection of minors. Although in recent years international and supranational institutions as well as national legislatures at least in the western world have tried hard to reform the substantive law to meet the new challenges posed by cyberspace, there are still important legislative gaps in this field, namely, in the areas of the criminalisation of hacking tools, the safeguarding of minors, the fight against spam and fraud, and the protection of digital rights management systems.

- Procedural law and law enforcement must tackle the problems of anonymity, lack of evidence, and the need for new coercive powers and new investigative computer tools. Many practitioners consider this to be a battle already lost. However, this seems to be far too pessimistic. In addition to creating new problems for the prosecution of crimes, information technology also creates new opportunities. Information technology can be a powerful instrument not only for criminals but also for police and prosecutors who can build new analysis and surveillance tools and strategies. Thus, the challenge in the future will be to build and use these new instruments while at the same time balancing the needs of effective prosecution with conflicting privacy interests.

- International co-operation agreements must find new solutions in order to ensure co-operation between different jurisdictions and their national prosecution authorities. The contrast between the global nature of computer crime and the national limitations of criminal law make international co-operation between prosecuting agencies indispensable. Thus, international mutual assistance treaties should allow the same actions as national procedural law.

- International criminal law must find new answers to questions of how to apply criminal law to the virtual cyberspace. Although corporeal parts of networks and computer systems can be located in the territory of states, the traditional rules on the territorial application of law are not sufficient with respect to the global virtual cyberspace. In addition, supranational law, harmonisation of law, improved co-operation procedures, and new rules for the international application of criminal law have to be developed as answers to the new global challenges posed by cybercrime.

Wide ratification of the Council of Europe's Convention on Cybercrime and its protocol, as well as the implementation of other existing international instruments and recommendations dealing with computer-related crime, would be important steps towards addressing these challenges.

Chapter 4 – Summary and threat assessment

Organised crime as a threat to human rights, democracy and the rule of law has been on the agenda of the Council of Europe for at least two decades and in particular following the 2nd Summit of Heads of State and Government in 1997.

Organised crime and other forms of economic and serious crime are likely to remain priority concerns of European societies for the foreseeable future. However, as the nature of crime changes and as new threats emerge, policies against crime will need to adjust.

The purpose of the 2004 organised crime situation report is therefore:

- to point at new threats and the main issues of concern;
- to help policy makers in Europe take more informed decisions on anti-crime policies.

The report is based on contributions from thirty-five member states as well as a range of other sources. The chapters on the organised crime situation have been prepared by the Department of Crime Problems (Directorate General of Legal Affairs) of the Council of Europe, while the chapter on cybercrime was written by Professor Dr Ulrich Sieber and his collaborators at the Max Planck Institute for Foreign and International Criminal Law (Freiburg) and the University in Munich, Germany.

The threat of organised crime

The framework

The United Nations Convention on Transnational Organized Crime reflects a globally agreed upon concept of organised crime. Nevertheless, ambiguities remain rendering analyses of organised crime and reporting on the organised crime situation in the forty-six member states of the Council of Europe rather difficult. In particular, the links between certain forms of economic crime and organised crime, and the distinction between these two concepts require further clarification. Such ambiguities carry the risk that organised crime is everything or nothing and that countermeasures against organised crime, on the one hand, and human rights standards, on the other, are not well balanced.

European countries share many common features and values, but at the same time also reflect asymmetries in terms of human development and governance. Such differences are likely to persist and will continue to facilitate organised crime. Related push and pull factors contribute to making human beings a profitable commodity exploited by organised crime groups and networks.

Globalisation will continue to facilitate transnational organised crime, and in particular economic crime at transnational levels, if no adequate safeguards are put in place. The capacity of national governments to respond to transnational and rapidly changing challenges is limited. The international regulatory framework is only slowly taking shape; and even where instruments exist they are not always efficiently implemented.

Crime markets

Organised crime in Europe takes many forms and involves a large variety of criminal activities. However, there are three crime markets which are common to and considered to be major threats in most European countries:

1. Fraud and other forms of economic crime

    In contrast to previous years, many central and eastern European countries now also report economic crime as a major issue of organised crime. Economic crime accounts for a large share of organised crime cases detected in 2003. In Estonia, Moldova and Serbia and Montenegro, it was the main category of organised crime recorded. In countries like Belgium, Bulgaria, the Netherlands and Slovakia, economic crime was the primary activity of 24% or more of organised crime groups and networks. Economic crime comprises a – not very well-defined – range of crimes. Value added tax fraud, fraud related to public procurement and privatisation, subsidy fraud, investment fraud, fiscal and customs offences and corruption in particular have been mentioned. The proceeds and the material damage of economic crime exceed those of other forms of crime by far. For example, in Germany, economic crime accounted only for 1.3% of all crimes recorded but for 57% (or €6.8 billion) of the material damage caused by crime in 2003.

    Economic crime poses a particular threat to Europe. More than other forms of organised crime, it involves legal commercial structures and direct interaction with legal public and private institutions. It is believed to be structural crime distorting market mechanisms and undermining trust and confidence in economic and legal systems. In the light of the increasing power of corporations in the context of globalisation, economic crime may furthermore weaken public trust in democratic institutions, above all when combined with corruption.

2.   Drug production and trafficking

Europe is probably the most profitable drug market globally. Not only the EU 15 with between 1 and 1.5 million problem drug users, but also some of the new EU members, as well as other central and eastern European states, are important drug consuming countries. Prevalence rates are highest or among the highest in the world in the Russian Federation for heroin, in Spain, Ireland and the United Kingdom for cocaine, in the Czech Republic and the United Kingdom for cannabis, in Ireland, the United Kingdom and Denmark for amphetamines, and in Ireland, the Czech Republic and the United Kingdom for ecstasy. In about one third of the member states, drug trafficking is considered the most important activity of organised crime groups and networks. Seizures of heroin have been highest in the United Kingdom, Italy and Turkey, of cocaine in Spain and the Netherlands, and of amphetamine-type substances (ATS) in the United Kingdom. However, seizures also increased in central and eastern European countries. The main producers of amphetamines and ecstasy are located in Europe, in particular the Netherlands. Almost all heroin consumed in Europe is based on opium produced in Afghanistan.

Organised crime-related drug production and trafficking will remain a major threat in Europe, in particular with regard to amphetamine-type substances and heroin.

3.   People as a commodity in the form of smuggling of persons and trafficking in human beings

People are exploited as a commodity by organised crime primarily in the forms of trafficking in human beings and smuggling of persons, and both forms have serious human rights implications.

Often ignored in the past, trafficking in human beings is now reported to be an important market of organised crime in about half of the member states. This is reflected in the large number of cases recorded and organised crime groups and networks and suspects involved. While the concept of trafficking may cover different forms of exploitation, most victims in Europe are trafficked for sexual purposes in connection with prostitution. Most of them are women and girls who are foreign to the countries in which they are exploited. Moldova, Romania, Ukraine, the Russian Federation, Bulgaria and Lithuania are the most often quoted countries of origin. Children account for a considerable share of victims. South-Eastern Europe remains of particular importance with regard to trafficking. Violence and intimidation against victims are frequent; and corruption is reported to be widespread as a tool facilitating trafficking. It would seem that often trafficking in human beings is treated as a question of illegal immigration, which means that victims are deported rather than provided with support and protection and that the organised crime background is ignored.

An increasing number of European countries report organised crime in connection with smuggling of persons. In some countries – such as Croatia and Slovenia – smuggling of persons represents the category with the highest number of organised crime-related cases, and in the United Kingdom it is considered one of the main threats of organised crime. Many countries believe that smuggling of persons – as one expression of illegal migration – will remain or become a major threat in the coming years. Different routes are used to smuggle people to the well-off countries of western Europe. The risks to the lives of people are ever increasing. Several thousand people have died in recent years when trying to reach southern Europe, in particular Spain and Italy. As legal entry to the European Union becomes more difficult and border controls more tight, not only economic migrants but also refugees rely on smuggling organisations to arrange their transport.

Smuggling of persons and trafficking in human beings are likely to expand with negative impact on human rights, and they will continue to generate political controversies.

Smuggling in cigarettes and other commodities, trafficking in arms and a wide range of other activities of organised crime groups and networks are important in different member states. However, the above three markets are the most common ones and are likely to remain the main markets exploited by organised crime in Europe in the near future.

The common denominator of all organised crime and of most other forms of serious crime is the pursuit of profit. Criminals need to launder the proceeds of crime in a way that they become indistinguishable from legitimate money. Europe is a major stakeholder in global money laundering as a source and destination of criminal proceeds, and – through its financial markets – as an actor in different stages of the money laundering process.

With the creation of financial intelligence units throughout Europe in recent years, the number of suspicious transaction reports has multiplied. In many countries, fraud, embezzlement and other forms of economic crime are the predicate offences for the largest number of investigations into money laundering. As criminals encroach on the legal institutions of society by investing their proceeds in legal commercial entities, the boundaries between legal and illegal structures of societies become ever more blurred.

Organised crime groups and networks

Reports received in 2004 reflect an important shift in the understanding of what constitutes an organised crime group. Organised crime groups as ethnically homogeneous, formally and hierarchically structured, multifunctional bureaucratic criminal organisations which confront society now appear to be the exception. The notion of clearly defined hierarchical organisations is being replaced by one of criminal networks – consisting of individual criminals or cells of criminals as well as legal entities and professionals which are more or less loosely affiliated and co-operate in varying compositions for particular criminal enterprises. The identification of such networks is very difficult, unless network analyses and financial investigations are applied systematically. These difficulties are reflected among other things by the fact that some countries report none or very few organised crime groups, while some others indicate more than one thousand groups operating on their territory.

Modi operandi of organised crime groups and networks include:

- Violence and intimidation. Violence is still widely used by organised crime groups and networks to enforce discipline within their group or to confront competing groups. Moreover, intimidation and violence against victims are an intrinsic part of specific offences, such as robbery, extortion and racketeering, as well as trafficking in human beings. In most European countries, organised crime groups and networks avoid open confrontation with public authorities. However, there are exceptions, such as the violence used against state bodies by some of the Mafia-type organisations in Italy, by organised crime groups and networks in Albania and Lithuania, as well as in Serbia as reflected in the assassination of Prime Minister Djindjic in 2003.

- Use of corruption and influence. Symbiotic relationships – nurtured by corruption, nepotism, patron-client relationships, family and clan ties – with public officials, politicians, criminal justice representatives, media but also private sector representatives appear to be the preferred *modi operandi* to facilitate criminal activities or to ensure protection from law enforcement. With the expansion of economic crime, corruption as a primary tool of organised crime is likely to gain importance throughout Europe, not only with regard to public-private corruption but also in relation to corruption in the private sector.

- Shielding practices. Organised groups make use of practices to shield criminal activities such as coded communications and the use of shell companies as well as legal commercial entities. This does not only include sectors which are close to the activities of such groups – such as import/export, sex industry, gambling – but also investments in financial holdings, shares in foreign companies, investment in the oil industry, interests in banks and others.

- Transnational operations. Nationals from a large range of countries operate in Europe. In Belgium, for example, more than seventy different nationalities were identified in 2003 in connection with organised crime investigations. However, throughout Europe the majority of suspects of organised crime are nationals of the country in which the crimes are committed, and they network with criminals in other countries to carry out activities involving different countries.

- Information and communication technologies. The use of ICT has gained in importance not only to facilitate communication among members of organised crime groups and networks and shielding through encryption, but also as tools to commit "old forms" of crime more efficiently and at a lower risk as well as to move into new fields of crime.

Cybercrime – a threat for Europe?

The Internet has a tremendous impact on societies all over the world. From 300 million Internet users in 1999, the number doubled to 600 million in 2002.[1] E-commerce has taken off. Americans are expected to spend more than US$200 billion online in 2004, and Europeans are beginning to follow suit.[2] There is thus no doubt that today's societies depend on ICT and are vulnerable to attacks.

---

1. Figures from INSEAD/World Economic Forum: "Network Readiness Index 2003–2004".

2. *Economist*, 15 May 2004.

Cybercrime challenges the fundamental values that Europe stands for – human rights, democracy and the rule of law. However, given the nature of cybercrime, it would be misleading to look at cybercrime as a threat to Europe in isolation – in fact it is a global threat which can only be addressed globally.

Cybercrimes

Cybercrime comprises a wide range of offences and its meaning has changed considerably since the 1960s when it basically meant an infringement of privacy.

Today, cybercrimes can be divided into the following types of offences:

- Offences against the confidentiality, integrity and availability of computer data and systems (so-called CIA offences). These include illegal access to computer systems by computer hacking, wiretapping and deceiving Internet users (for example, by spoofing and phishing), computer espionage (including Trojan Horses and other techniques), computer sabotage and extortion (for example, using viruses and worms, DoS attacks, spamming or mail bombing).

- Computer-related traditional crimes, such as computer-related fraud (ranging from classical fraud such as invoice manipulations or manipulations of accounts and balance sheets within companies, to online manipulations, fraudulent auctions and online order services, illegal use of ATM cards, abuse of credit cards, etc.), computer-related forgery, online grooming of children and other forms of searches for victims, as well as attacks on life through manipulation of flight control systems or hospital computers.

- Content-related offences, in particular child pornography, racism and xenophobia, as well as soliciting, inciting, providing instructions and offering to commit crimes, ranging from murder, to rape, torture, sabotage and terrorism. This category also includes cyberstalking, libel and the dissemination of false information through the Internet, and internet gambling.

- Offences related to infringement of copyright and related rights, such as unauthorised reproduction and use of computer programmes, audio/video and other forms of digital works, or of databases and books.

225

- Infringement of privacy, including unauthorised access to systems containing personal data, the collection, distribution and linkage of personal data or the collection of data by cookies, web bugs and other software.

Official statistics on cybercrime are far from being realistic since many offences are simply not reported or because cybercrimes are not reported as separate offences or because cyber offences are not (yet) criminalised in the same way in all countries. Nevertheless, it would seem that cybercrimes represent the fastest growing category of crime in many countries. For example, an analysis of data in Germany indicates that the number of registered computer crimes has increased tremendously since 1987. Fraud by means of illegally obtained debit cards with PIN codes, computer fraud and fraud by means of access authorisations for communication services account for 90% of all computer-related offences.

Data and surveys carried out in different regions of the world in 2004 show, among other things, that:

- Throughout the world, phishing attacks for personal and financial data have increased considerably during the first eight months of 2004, resulting in high damages.

- 71% of private and public organisations questioned in Australia and 64% of companies questioned in the United States in 2004 reported incidents related to viruses, worms and Trojan Horses as well as theft of information.

- 20% of some 494 corporations questioned in the United States in 2004 were subjected to attempted computer sabotage and extortion, among others means through DoS attacks.

- Different surveys show increasing economic losses attributable to computer-related fraud.

- Websites promoting racism, hate and violence reportedly increased by 300% between 2000 and 2004. Most of these sites are hosted in the United States but many may originate in Europe.

- With regard to copyright offences, the share of pirate software among users in Council of Europe member states in 2003 ranged from 27% in Austria and Sweden to 71% in Bulgaria, 73% in Romania, 87% in the Russian Federation and 91% in Ukraine.

- Child pornography represents one of the fastest growing markets. It is estimated that child pornography has an annual business volume of about US$20 billion globally. Some 55% of the material is reported to stem from the USA and a further 23% from the Russian Federation. Surveys in 2003 suggest that child pornography accounts for 24% of image searches in peer-to-peer applications.

Cybercrime and organised crime

Data on connections between organised crime and cybercrime are still scarce and do not permit a reliable analysis. The separation of law enforcement units dealing with cybercrime from those investigating organised crime may help explain this scarcity of data. On the one hand, most cyber criminals are individual offenders, often juveniles or young adults. This is particularly true for CIA offences such as hacking, and distribution of viruses, worms and Trojan Horses. On the other hand, cases are known where criminals have organised themselves for fraud schemes on the Internet, theft of credit cards and cyber extortion. It is very likely that organised crime groups and networks will attempt to exploit the opportunities offered by e-commerce on a large scale.

Available information suggests the following:

- As economic crime is already a primary activity of organised crime, ICT will further facilitate offences such as credit card, "pump-and-dump" schemes and other kinds of fraud, money laundering, counterfeiting, but also modern forms of traditional crimes such as electronic bank robberies or cyber extortion. Depersonalisation of contacts, ease of access and rapidity of electronic transactions make ICT an attractive tool for money laundering. Virtual casinos, auctions, smartcards, online banking, or the possibility to purchase and sell shares, bonds and futures online offer ample opportunities for money laundering. With regard to counterfeiting in March 2004, for example, the search of 800 premises in Germany led to the confiscation of 19 Internet servers, 200 computers, 40 000 CDs and DVDs and 38 tera-byte of pirate videos and software which had been made available for sale through the Internet. In April 2004, co-ordinated searches in eleven countries led to the seizure of software, CDs and DVDs with a value of €50 million.

- Organised crime exploits the vulnerability of societies, public institu-tions, the business sector and of individuals using the Internet. Not only corporations engaged in e-commerce and business-to-business operations, but also individuals using online banking or participating in e-commerce become victims of electronic theft and phishing. Victims include children as the most vulnerable group of society. Child pornography seems to have become an important activity of organised criminals. Several major cases uncovered in different countries of Europe since 2001 showed that offenders were not only members of networks of paedophiles exchanging images, videos and data of victims, but also criminals organising child pornography for profit.

- ICT offer anonymity, facilitate the logistics and reduce the risks for organised criminals to be prosecuted. It permits remote controlled operations, covert activities, transnational operations, networking and encrypted communication. The penetration and infiltration of banks and corporations or online "bank robberies" through the Internet are far less risky than in the real world. Already ten years ago Russian groups were known to have caused banks to transfer money to foreign accounts of criminals. Modern computer and communication networks have developed specific characteristics which are useful for criminal perpetrators and difficult to overcome for prosecutors: international computer networks (with anonymous remailers or free access devices to Internet service providers) offer anonymity to perpetrators which can only be lifted if all the countries involved in the communication decide to co-operate. Moreover, computer and communication systems are increasingly offered together with strong encryption and possibilities to hide data. Current standard software is able not only to encrypt data but also to hide data, for example, in pictures (steganography).

- ICT are tools for global outreach and the search for potential victims. An example is the Nigerian fraud schemes which have proliferated through the Internet and under which people all over the world are lured into making advance payments for dubious money transfer schemes.

- ICT are likely to change the shape of organised crime, that is, the way people organise themselves to carry out crimes. Cybercrime does not require control over a geographical territory, and requires less personal contacts and thus less relationships based on trust and enforcement of discipline between criminals, in short less need for formal organisation. The classical hierarchical structures of organised crime groups may even be unsuitable for organised crime on the Internet. ICT may favour those organisations which are already based on flat-structured networking. ICT may also change the characteristics of offenders. In the real world legal businessmen engage in organised forms of economic crime; and, *modus modendi*, the opportunities offered by ICT may tempt legal commercial entities to organise for cybercrime, that is, become organised cyber criminals.

Cyberterrorism

The possible link between cybercrime and terrorism is an issue of much controversy. The definition of cyberterrorism raises difficulties, but – at least for working purposes – it may mean:

> unlawful attacks and threats of attack against computers, networks, and the information stored therein when done to intimidate or coerce a government or its people in furtherance of political or social objectives. Further, to qualify as cyberterrorism, an attack should result in violence against persons or property, or at least cause enough harm to generate fear. Attacks that lead to death or bodily injury, explosions, plane crashes, water contamination, or severe economic loss would be examples. Serious attacks against critical infrastructures could be acts of cyberterrorism, depending on their impact. Attacks that disrupt nonessential services or that are mainly a costly nuisance would not.[1]

Some argue that "cyber attacks" on electricity power lines, transmission facilities and control systems could cause blackouts, that attacks on control systems of surface transportation could lead to the collision of trains, attacks on the control systems of water facilities could lead to contamination, that attacks on energy supply systems could lead to energy shortages, that attacks on financial infrastructure could disrupt financial markets, information systems of armed forces could be taken over or disrupted, that nuclear power stations could be manipulated, or the source codes of missile guidance programmes be stolen, and so on.[2]

Others argue that the threat of cyberterrorism has been "over-hyped"[3] and is rather limited and unlikely to occur when compared to real life threats such as blackouts caused by faulty power grids, or problems in different control

---

1. See definition by Dorothy Denning, Professor of Computer Science at the Georgetown University in Washington DC, available at http://www.iwar.org.uk/cyberterror/resources/house/00-05-23denning.htm. See also Gabriel Weimann, "Cyberterrorism. How real is the threat?", op. cit., p. 4.

2. http://zdnet.com.com/2102-1105_2-955293.htm. See also Institute for Security Technology Studies at Dartmouth College, op. cit.

3. http://newsvote.bbc.co.uk//mpapps/pagetools/print/news.bbc.co.uk /2/hi/tech285041.st

systems caused by flawed software. Terrorists are more likely to use bombs or physical means to attack critical infrastructure.

It would thus seem that the actual and potential threat of cyberterrorism and the many hypotheses related to this question require further analyses.

However, apart from cyberterrorism in a narrow sense, already today it is safe to say that computer systems and the Internet play an important role in terrorist activities. Terrorists use the Internet for propaganda purposes (for example, the posting of images of the decapitation of Paul Marshall Johnson in July 2004) and they deface websites to spread disinformation. They also use the Internet for the distribution of hate speech, inciting serious crimes, teaching, recruiting and fund raising. Like organised criminals they may also use ICT for secure communication and the planning and financing of activities.

Challenges for criminal justice

ICT and cybercrime not only lead to new threats but also to a new environment of crime and to new problems concerning criminal law and criminal prosecution. These are not merely practical difficulties of dealing with computer crime. More important is the fact that the characteristics of cybercrime are in complete opposition to the characteristics of traditional law. For example:

- Traditional criminal law deals primarily with the protection of clearly defined tangible goods against human attacks. In contrast, computer crimes frequently violate new intangible values,[1] which depend on a difficult balance of interests and which are difficult to define by means of general terms and blanket clauses.

- Traditional systems of criminal law are based on the idea of national sovereignty; thus, the direct scope of their decisions is limited to their national territory. In contrast, the Internet is a truly global medium.

- Traditional systems of criminal justice and law enforcement are slow. In contrast, the Internet is an extremely fast system. Whereas the transfer of national decisions of criminal justice takes weeks or months, computer data can be transferred to a foreign country in milliseconds.

---

1. See Sieber 2001, pp. 1-29.

- In a criminal prosecution, the perpetrators of crime must be identified and robust proof of their actions must be provided. However, the Internet is hard to control and provides a high level of anonymity. Moreover, finding a proper balance between limiting anonymity and protecting personal data and telecommunication remains a difficult issue.

Broad ratification of the Convention on Cybercrime and its protocol would represent an important step towards addressing these challenges.

References

Amnesty International (2004), "Kosovo (Serbia and Montenegro): 'So does it mean that we have the rights?' Protecting the human rights of women and girls trafficked for forced prostitution in Kosovo", London.

Bell, I. and Pickar, A. (2003), "Report on trafficking in children in the Czech Republic".

Black, C., Vander Beken, T., Frans, B. and Paternotte, M. (2001), *Reporting on organised crime. A shift from description to explanation in the Belgian annual report on organised crime*, Maklu, Antwerp.

Bonn International Center for Conversion (2004): *Conversion Survey 2004: Global Disarmament, Demilitarization and Demobilization*, Baden-Baden.

Bundesamt für Polizei (2004): *Bericht Innere Sicherheit der Schweiz 2003*. Bern.

Bundeskriminalamt (2003), *Lagebild Organisierte Kriminalität 2002*, Wiesbaden.

Bundeskriminalamt (2003a), *Jahresbericht Wirtschaftskriminalität 2002*, Wiesbaden.

Bundeskriminalamt (2003b), *Rauschgiftjahresbericht 2002*, Wiesbaden.

Bundeskriminalamt (2003c), *Wirtschaftskriminalität und Korruption. BKA Herbsttagung 2002*, Munich.

Bundeskriminalamt (2004), *Bundeslagebericht Wirtschaftkriminalität 2003*, Wiesbaden.

Cartier-Bresson, J. (1997), "Etat, marchés, réseaux et organisations criminelles entrepreneuriales" (extract from "Criminalité organisée et ordre dans la société" – Colloquy, Aix-en-Provence, 5-7 June 1996), Paris.

Castells, M. (2003), *The rise of the network society*, Malden, Oxford, Victoria.

Clifford, M. (1998), *Environmental crime*, Aspen Publication, Gaithersburg, Maryland.

Commission of the European Communities, COM (2003), "Protection of the financial interests of the Communities and the fight against fraud. Annual report 2002", Brussels.

Correia, Z. and Wilson, T. (1997), "Scanning the business environment for information: a grounded theory approach".
http://www.shef.ac.uk/~is/publications/infres/paper21.html

Council of Europe (1986), Recommendation No. R (86) 8 on crime policy in Europe in a time of change, Strasbourg.

Council of Europe (1997), Recommendation No. R (97) 13 on intimidation of witnesses and the rights of the defence, Strasbourg.

Council of Europe (2002), "Trafficking in human beings and corruption" (PACO Programme, TP 28 rev), Strasbourg.

Council of Europe (2003), Demographic yearbook 2003, Council of Europe Publishing, Strasbourg.

Council of the European Union/Multi-disciplinary Group on Organised Crime (2003), "The smuggling of manufactured tobacco products in the European Union and its links with organised crime", Brussels (CRIMORG 90).

Davis, I., Hirst, C. and Mariani, B. (2001), Organised crime, corruption and illicit arms trafficking in an enlarged EU, London, Saferworld.

European Monitoring Centre for Drugs and Drug Addiction (EMCDDA) (2003), "Annual report 2003 – The state of the drugs problem in the European Union and Norway", Lisbon.

EMCDDA (2003a), "Annual report 2003 – The state of the drugs problem in the acceding and candidate countries to the European Union", Lisbon.

Entorf, H. and Spengler, H. (2002), Crime in Europe – Causes and Consequences, Springer, Heidelberg.

Europol (2002): "Computer-related crime within the EU: old crimes new tools; new crimes new tools", The Hague.

Europol (2003), "2003 European Union organised crime report".

http://www.europol.eu.int/publications/EUOrganisedCrimeSitRep/EUOr ganisedCrimeSitRep2003.pdf (15 December 2003).

Financial Action Task Force, FATF (2004), "Report on money laundering and terrorist financing typologies 2003-2004", Paris.

Findlay, M. (1999), *The globalisation of crime*, Cambridge University Press, Cambridge.

Gambetta, D. (1994), *The Sicilian Mafia*, Harvard University Press, Cambridge, Massachusetts.

Garfinkel, S. and Spafford, G. (1996), *Practical Unix and Internet security*, Sebastopol.

Grabosky, P., Smith G.R. and Dempsey, G. (2001), *Electronic theft: unlawful acquisition in cyberspace*, Cambridge University Press.

Hafner, K. and Markoff, J. (1993), *Cyberpunk. Die Welt der Hacker*, Düsseldorf and Vienna.

Hughes, D.M. (2002), "The use of new communications and information technologies for sexual exploitation of women and children", *Hastings Women's Law Journal*, 13 (1), winter 2002.

International Centre for Migration Policy Development, ICMPD (1999), "The relationship between organised crime and trafficking in aliens" (study prepared by the secretariat of the Budapest Group), Vienna.

International Organisation for Migration, IOM (2002), "Trafficking for sexual exploitation: the case of the Russian Federation", Geneva.

Interpol (2003), "Global situation of criminal organizations and illicit drug trafficking 2002", International Criminal Police Organisation, Lyons.

Joosens, L. and Raw, M. (1998), "Cigarette smuggling in Europe: who really benefits?", *Tobacco Control*, (7) 1998, pp. 66-71.

Kaufmann, D., Kraay, A. and Mastruzzi, M. (2003), "Governance Matters III: Governance indicators for 1996-2002", The World Bank, Washington, 30 June.

Kovacich, G.L. and Boni, W.C. (2000), *High-technology-crime investigator's handbook: working in the global information environment*, Butterworth-Heinemann, Oxford and Boston.

Leshin, C.B. (1997), *Internet investigations in criminal justice*, Prentice Hall, New Jersey and Columbus, Ohio.

Levi, M. (2002), "The organization of serious crime", in Maguire et al., pp. 878-913.

Levi, M. and Naylor, T. (2000), "Organised crime, the organisation of crime, and the organisation of business", DTI Crime Foresight Panel Essay 2000. http://www.cf.ac.uk/socsi/whoswho/levi-orgcrime.pdf (12 October 2003).

Loader, I. and Sparks, R. (2002), "Contemporary landscapes of crime, order, and control: governance, risk, and globalization", in Maguire et al., pp. 83-111.

Maegerle, A. and Mletzko, M. (1994), *Terrorism, extremism, organized crime*, No. 5, pp. 1 *et seq.*

Matveeva, A. et al. (2003), *Macedonia: guns, policing and ethnic division*, Saferworld/Bonn International Center for Conversion (BICC), London and Bonn.

Maguire, M., Morgan, R. and Reiner, R. (eds) (2002), *The Oxford handbook of criminology*, Oxford University Press, Oxford.

McClure, S., Scambray, J. and Kurtz, G. (2001), *Hacking exposed: network security secrets and solutions*, 3rd edition, Berkeley.

Morrison, J. (1992), "Environmental scanning", in M. Whitely et al. (eds), *A primer for new institutional researchers*, The Association for Institutional Research, Tallahassee.

National Criminal Intelligence Service, NCIS (2003), "UK threat assessment – The threat from serious and organised crime 2003", London.

Nelken, D. (2002), "White-collar crime, in Maguire et al., pp. 844-76.

Nicolic-Ristanovic, V. et al. (2004), "Trafficking in people in Serbia", Victimology Society in Serbia and the OSCE, Belgrade.

Open Society Institute, OSI/EU (2002), *Monitoring the EU accession process: corruption and anti-corruption policy*, Budapest and New York.

Passas, N. (1998): "Globalisation and transnational crime: effects of criminogenic asymmetries", in Williams, P. and Vlassis, D. (eds), *Combating transnational crime. Concepts, activities and responses*, and *Transnational Organised Crime*, Vol. 4, Nos. 3 and 4, autumn/winter.

Pearson, G. and Hobbs, D. (2001), *Middle market drug distribution*, Home Office, London.

Regional Intelligence Liaison Office for Western Europe, RILO (2001), *LASSO 2000 – Review of cigarette smuggling in Europe*, Cologne and Rotterdam.

Royal Canadian Mounted Police, RCMP (2002), "Environmental scan 2002". http://www.rcmp.ca/enviro/scan2003june_d_e.htm (15 October 2003).

Save the Children UK (Serbia Programme) (2004), *Protecting children from trafficking in human beings*, Belgrade.

Sieber, U. (1977 and 1980), *Computerkriminalität und Strafrecht*, Cologne, Berlin, Bonn and Munich.

Sieber, U. (1985), *Informationstechnologie und Strafrechtsreform – Zur Reichweite des künftigen Zweiten Gesetzes zur Bekämpfung der Wirtschaftskriminalität*, Cologne, Berlin, Bonn and Munich.

Sieber, U. (1986), "Bilanz eines 'Musterverfahrens' – Zum rechtskräftigen Abschluß des Verfahrens BGHZ 94, 276", (Inkassoprogramm), Entscheidungs besprechung, *Computer und Recht*, pp. 699-701.

Sieber, U. (1986a), *The international handbook on computer crime*, Chichester.

Sieber, U. (1992), *The international emergence of criminal information law*, Cologne, Berlin, Bonn and Munich.

Sieber, U. (ed.) (1994), *Information technology crime*, Cologne, Berlin, Bonn and Munich.

Sieber, U. (2001), "The emergence of information law", in Lederman and Shapira (eds), *Law, information and information technology*, Kluwer Law International, The Hague, London and New York.

Sieber, U., for further references see:
http://www.iuscrim.mpg.de/info/leute/sieber/sieber.html

Sieber, U. and Bögel, M. (1993), *Logistik der Organisierten Kriminalität*, Wiesbaden.

Stiglitz, J. (2002), *Globalization and its discontents*, London and New York.

Swedish National Criminal Investigation Department (2004), "Organised crime in Sweden 2004", Stockholm.

Transparency International (2004), *Corruption Perception Index 2004*, Berlin.

Transcrime (2004), *Trafficking in persons and smuggling of migrants into Italy*, Trento.

Union des Fabricants (2004), *Counterfeiting and organised crime report*, Paris.

United Nations (2002), United Nations Convention against Transnational Organized Crime and the protocols thereto, United Nations Office for Drug Control and Crime Prevention/Centre for International Crime Prevention, Vienna and New York.

United Nations Development Programme (2003), *Human development report 2003*, New York.

United Nations Development Programme (2004), *Human development report 2004*, New York.

United Nations International Drug Control Programme (2000), *World drug report 2000*, Vienna.

United Nations Office on Drugs and Crime/Centre for International Crime Prevention (2002), *Seventh United Nations survey of crime trends and operations of criminal justice systems, covering the period 1998-2000*, Vienna.

United Nations Office on Drugs and Crime (2004), *World drug report*, Vienna.

United Nations Office on Drugs and Crime (2004a), *Drugs and crime trends in Europe and beyond*, Vienna.

UNODC 2004b: *Afghanistan opium survey 2004*. Vienna.

United States Department of State (2004), *Trafficking in persons report*, Washington.

Van der Heijden, T. and Landman, R. (2004), *Oost-Europese zware of georganiseerde criminaliteit en EU-uitbreiding. Verslag van een deelproject in het kader van het nationaal dreigingsbeeld* (eastern European organised crime and EU enlargement. Results of an analysis for the National Threat Assessment), KLPD-dienst Nationale Recherche Informatie, Zoetermeer.

Van Dijk, J. (2003), "A criminal divide: the unequal burdens of victimization across the globe", paper presented at the XI International Symposium on Victimology, University of Stellenbosch, South Africa, 17 July 2003.

Van Duyne, P., Pheijffer, M., Kuijl, H., Van Dijk, A. and Bakker, G. (2001), *Financial investigation of crime*, The Hague.

Von Lampe, K. (2001), "The illegal cigarette market in Germany: a case study of organized crime" (paper presented at the 1st annual meeting of the European Society of Criminology, Lausanne, Switzerland, 6 September 2001).

Von Lampe, K. (2001a), "Not a process of enlightenment: the conceptual history of organized crime in Germany and the United States of America", *Forum on Crime and Society*, 1 (2), pp. 99-116.

Waters, M. (1995), *Globalization*, Routledge, London.

Williams, P. (2001), "Transnational criminal networks", in Arquillo, J. and Ronfeldt, D.F. (eds), *Networks and netwars: the future of terror, crime, and militancy*, RAND, Santa Monica.

Williams, P. (2001a): "Organised crime and cybercrime: synergies, trends and responses", *Global Issues*.
http://usinfo.state.gov/journals/itgic/0801/ijge/gj07.htm (15 December 2003).

Williams, P. and Godson, R. (2002), "Anticipating organised and transnational crime", *Crime, Law and Social Change*, Vol. 37, No. 4.

World Bank (2005), *World development report 2005*, Washington.

World Health Organization Regional Office for Europe (2004), "Young people's health in context. Health behaviour in school-aged children (HBSC) study: international report from the 2001/2002 survey", Copenhagen.

Walker, J. (1998), *Modelling global money laundering flows – Some findings.*

WODC (2003), *European sourcebook of crime and criminal justice statistics – 2003*, The Hague.

Appendix: Octopus interface – The challenge of cybercrime

Programme

Octopus interface 2004

Conference on the Challenge of Cybercrime

15 to 17 September 2004
Council of Europe
Palais de l'Europe, Strasbourg, France

Background

Computer networks are turning the world into a global information society in which any kind of information is available to Internet users almost anywhere and in which electronic commerce may soon exceed hundreds of billions of euros. However, this process is accompanied by an increasing dependency on such networks and a growing vulnerability to criminal intrusion and misuse. Networks facilitate illegal access to information, attacks on private or public computer systems, distribution of illegal content as well as cyber laundering and possibly cyberterrorism.

Cybercrime thus poses new challenges to criminal justice and international co-operation. In order to counter cybercrime and protect computer networks, governments must provide for:

- effective criminalisation of cyber offences. Legislation of different countries should be as harmonised as possible to facilitate co-operation;
- investigative and prosecutorial procedures and institutional capacities which allow criminal justice agencies to cope with high-tech crime;
- conditions facilitating direct co-operation between state institutions, and between state institutions and the private sector;

- efficient mutual legal assistance regimes, allowing direct co-operation among multiple countries and the establishment of inter-governmental emergency networks.

In November 2001, the Convention on Cybercrime (ETS No. 185) of the Council of Europe was opened for signature. Its implementation will help parties cope with these challenges. So far (as at 8 September 2004), the convention has been signed by thirty-eight states – including Canada, Japan, South Africa and the United States which are non-member states – and ratified by seven.

The Additional Protocol to the Convention on Cybercrime, concerning the criminalisation of acts of a racist and xenophobic nature committed through computer systems (ETS No. 189) of January 2003 has been signed by twenty-two states and ratified by one.

Efforts are urgently required to accelerate broad ratification and implementation of these important instruments. The conference is designed to support such efforts.

Objectives

The aims of the conference are:

1. to encourage wide and rapid ratification of and/or accession to the Convention on Cybercrime and its protocol;

2. to involve leading chief executives with a professional interest in "e-matters" in the global fight against cybercrime, and encourage public-private partnership in this area;

3. to draw the attention, at the highest political level, to the fact that the fight against cybercrime (including cyberterrorism) should be strengthened, as societies (largely "computer-dependent") are increasingly vulnerable to cyber attacks;

4. to ensure effective implementation of the Convention on Cybercrime.

Participants

Participants should be professionally involved in issues related to cyber-crime, and include representatives of:

1. States

-   forty-five Council of Europe member states (one cybercrime expert to be funded by the Council of Europe, others at the expense of the member state);
-   all Observer states, states having participated in the elaboration of the convention or considering accession to the convention, and the members of the Organization of American States (OAS).

2. Parliamentary Assembly of the Council of Europe

3. European Union (including the Secretariat General of the Council, the European Commission, Eurojust and Europol)

4. Other international institutions

-   United Nations (including the United Nations Office on Drugs and Crime);
-   Interpol;
-   Organization for Security and Co-operation in Europe;
-   Organisation for Economic Co-operation and Development.

5. Relevant private sector institutions and associations

Participation will be by invitation only.

Organisation

Following an opening session and a general update on new developments related to economic and organised crime, the conference will focus on three themes, namely:

-   the threat of cybercrime;
-   legislation and institutions against cybercrime;
-   co-operation against cybercrime.

Each theme will be introduced in the plenary and subsequently discussed in parallel workshops. The results of the workshops will then be presented in the plenary sessions.

On the third day, a high-level round table discussion will be held adding a political dimension to the conference.

The conference will furthermore offer an opportunity for states to sign the Convention on Cybercrime or its protocol or to deposit the instruments of ratification.

The conference will be open to the media.

Contact

For any questions, please contact:

Department of Crime Problems
Directorate General I – Legal Affairs
Council of Europe
F-67075 Strasbourg Cedex, France

Alexander Seger
Tel   +33 (0) 3 9021 4506
Fax   +33 (0) 3 8841 3955
e-mail   alexander.seger@coe.int

Programme

Wednesday, 15 September 2004

Plenary session	Room 1

9.30 a.m.	**Opening session** Setting standards against crime (Mr Guy De Vel, Director General of Leal Affairs)

10 a.m.	**Standard setting, monitoring, technical co-operation – Update** Summary of new developments in Europe (Mr Roberto Lamponi, Director of Legal Co-operation, Council of Europe) The Convention on Cybercrime – Current state of implementation (Mr Rik Kaspersen, Netherlands)
11 a.m.	*Coffee break*
11 a.m.	**Introduction to theme 1: the threat of cybercrime** The cybercrime situation (Professor Ulrich Sieber, Max Planck Institute, Freiburg, Germany) Human rights and the Internet (Ms Isabelle Rorive, ULB, Belgium)
1 p.m.	*Lunch break*

Workshop sessions	Room 1	Room 2
2.30 p.m.	**Workshop 1 a:** ■ Offences against confidentiality, integrity and availability, and computer-related offences (Mr Rik Kaspersen)	**Workshop 1 b:** ■ Child pornography (Ms Isabelle de Schrijver, Child Focus) ■ Xenophobia and racism (Mr Carlo Sarzana Di Sant'Ippolito, Honorary Deputy President, Court of Cassation, Rome, Italy) ■ The emergence of new types of content-related computer crimes (Mr Roderic Broadhurst, Centre for Criminology, University of Hong Kong)

4.15 p.m.	Coffee break	

4.30 p.m.	**Workshop 1 c:**	**Workshop 1 d:**
	▪ Cyber laundering and cyberterrorism (Ms Simona Mulinari, Price-waterhouse-Coopers, Milan, Italy)	▪ Copyright violations (Mr Ilias Chantzos, Symantec, Belgium) ▪ New types of crime (Mr Peter Grabosky, Research School of Social Science, Regulatory Institution Network, Australia)

6 p.m.	End of day 1

Thursday, 16 September 2004

Plenary session		*Room 1*
9.30 a.m.	Summary of the previous day's workshops **Introduction to theme 2: legislation and institutions against cybercrime**	

Workshop sessions	*Room 1*	*Room 2*
10.30 a.m.	**Workshop 2 a: legislation**	**Workshop 2 b: institution building and investigation**
	▪ Crimes committed against the confidentiality, integrity and availability of data or computer systems (Mr Anatoly Vorobiev, Head of Section, Federal Security Service, Russian Federation) ▪ Computer-related offences (Mr Stein Schjolberg, Chief Judge, Moss Tingrett Court, Norway)	▪ Setting up specialised law enforcement institutions (Mr Wolfgang Schreiber, BKA, Germany) ▪ The investigative tools to combat cybercrime (Andy Letherby, Acting Manager, Tactical & Technical Support, National Hi-Tech Crime Unit)

1 p.m.	Lunch break

Plenary session	Room 1
2.30 p.m.	Summary of the workshop discussions **Introduction to theme 3: co-operation against cybercrime** International co-operation (Mr Christopher Painter, US Department of Justice) Public-private co-operation (Ms Magda Popescu, Business Software Alliance, Romania)

Workshop sessions	Room 1	Room 2
3.30 p.m.	**Workshop 3 a: international co-operation** <ul><li>International co-operation – Provisions of the Convention on Cybercrime (Mr Eugenio Selvaggi, Prosecutor, Italy)</li><li>Practical experiences of international co-operation in fighting cybercrime (Ms Betty Shave, US DoJ)</li><li>Cybercrime as a challenge to international co-operation (Mr Boris Miroshnikov, Ministry of the Interior, Russian Federation)</li></ul>	**Workshop 3 b: public-private co-operation** <ul><li>Regulating the cyberspace: private-public partnership (Ms Magda Popescu)</li><li>Improving co-operation between ISPs, law enforcement authorities and other states' bodies to fight cybercrime (Mr Detlef Eckert, Chief Security Officer EMEA, Microsoft)</li></ul>
6 p.m.	*Cocktail reception (Restaurant Bleu at the Council of Europe)*	
6 p.m.-7 p.m.	Opportunity for signature and/or ratification of the Convention on Cybercrime (ETS No. 185) and its Additional Protocol concerning the criminalisation of acts of a racist and xenophobic nature committed through computer systems (ETS No. 189)	

Friday, 17 September 2004

Plenary   Room 1
session

9.30 a.m.	Summary and conclusions of plenary and workshop discussions
10 a.m.	**High-level round table discussion** ▪ Moderator: Mr Riz Khan, journalist ▪ Mr Terry Davis, Secretary General of the Council of Europe ▪ Mr Marko Starman, State Secretary, Ministry of Justice of Slovenia ▪ Mr Ryuichi Shoji, Consul General, Permanent Observer of Japan to the Council of Europe ▪ Mr Boris Miroshnikov, Ministry of the Interior, Russian Federation ▪ Mr Mark Richard, Former Deputy Assistant Attorney General of the United States ▪ Mr Giuseppe Verrini, Vice-President, Europe, Middle East, Africa, Symantec
12.30 p.m.	Conclusion of the meeting

Conclusions of the conference

The conference had a very clear purpose: to promote ratification and implementation of the Convention on Cybercrime and its protocol. The conference made an impressive contribution to that effect.

It brought together the main stakeholders from the private sector, "industry", associations dealing with content-related crime, state institutions involved in drafting legislation, law enforcement and information society issues, and not only representatives from Europe, but also those from the Americas, Africa, Asia and Australia. The event served as an "interface" between different institutions and continents. It will facilitate linking up, exchanges of experience, co-operation and provision of support to further efforts against cybercrime.

Presentations and discussions provided a large number of reasons to support the convention and the protocol such as:

National legislation and legal systems are not incompatible with the provisions of the convention and no major obstacles are expected for their implementation in national law. Further exchanges of experience are needed to tailor the convention to the specific needs of each country.

Although technology keeps changing, the Convention on Cybercrime will not be outdated in the short term as the provisions describe conduct rather than technology.

Cybercrime affects all groups of society, including the most vulnerable one, namely children. Child pornography should thus be criminalised in all countries in line with Article 9 of the convention. Multi-disciplinary action, prevention and awareness raising will need to complement legal measures.

The protocol to the convention provides a response to xenophobia, racism and hate speech on the Internet, which are threats to the basic values of European societies. The boundaries between these crimes, on the one hand, and freedom of expression, on the other, are not always easy to determine. The notion of "harmful content" needs to be developed further. However, as many countries as possible should sign and ratify this instrument as well.

The Internet provides vast opportunities for money laundering. The procedural measures of the Convention on Cybercrime will help address a number of problems related to the prevention and control of cyber laundering.

While there is little evidence of actual cyberterrorism, there is a considerable potential for attacks on critical infrastructure and loss of life. Information and communication technologies are already used by terrorists for communication and the planning of activities. This requires all stakeholders to be alert and keep an open mind. The discussion on cyberterrorism is controversial, but it has at least contributed to sensitise policy makers, law enforcement and the private sector to improve cyber security. Cybercrime in general and cyberterrorism are not necessarily the same issues, but the tools for prevention and control are similar. Implementation of the convention is therefore essential to cope with cyberterrorism. Additional discussions at international level on cyber security in order to protect critical infrastructure may be required.

The provisions of the convention on intellectual property right violations will provide an important basis for criminal and civil law measures as well as effective law enforcement. Public-private partnerships can build on this.

Whenever there is profit to be made on the Internet or through information and communication technology, criminals will try to exploit this opportunity. New types of cybercrime are therefore likely to appear and require individuals and companies to minimise opportunities. Particular attention should be paid to wireless communication. "Cyber paradises" should be avoided by spreading the principles of the Convention on Cybercrime around the world.

Cybercrimes require a global legal framework. An historical overview of international discussions showed that the Convention on Cybercrime is a milestone. Global application is desirable. The actions undertaken by the Asia-Pacific Economic Cooperation (APEC) forum and the Organization of American States highlight initiatives to develop a common approach in a given region in line with the principles set out in the convention. This should be followed by these countries' accession to the convention if at all possible. This approach could also be followed by countries in Africa and the Middle East.

The Council of Europe and other donors should provide technical assistance to such countries to bring their legislation and institutions in line with the requirements of the convention.

The provisions on international co-operation are among the most important ones of the Convention on Cybercrime. They are based on several "mother conventions" which have been in operation in Europe for almost fifty years.

These provisions also contain innovative elements which serve as examples for other instruments on judicial co-operation.

The round the clock network of contact points is a useful mechanism for co-operation in emergency cases. It is a "rough-and-ready" tool for investigators which should not be overburdened with too many rules. Practice has shown that it is less complicated to establish such contact points than it may seem.

Public-private partnerships are essential for preventing and controlling cybercrime. Many opportunities and examples of such partnerships were discussed at the conference. Such partnerships require a clear legislative and regulatory framework (such as competition legislation, anti-trust regulations, criminal law provisions, in particular on corporate criminal liability, freedom of information laws and personal data protection legislation), as well as awareness raising and training.

In order to improve standards, responses, innovation, vertical co-operation and technical training, partnerships within the industry are of key importance. An example is the Global Infrastructure Alliance for Internet Safety.

A change of mind in the private sector is evident. The private sector is now seeking stronger partnerships with government, including law enforcement agencies.

The conference helped create a new momentum for ratification and implementation of the Convention on Cybercrime and its protocol. The conference will also have an impact in the future.

The media, which reported extensively on this conference, made a major contribution to help spread the message around the globe.

Participants were all experts in cybercrime issues and are in positions of responsibility. They will therefore be able to carry the message back to their institutions and influence the process of ratification or application of the convention in practice.

The ratification process is now very much on track; additional ratifications in the coming months can be expected.

The Secretariat of the Council of Europe will see this conference and the commitment shown by participants as encouragement to provide the necessary support for this effort.

Participants in the conference

State and intergovernmental organisations

Country	Name	Institution
Albania	Mr Elvis Cirko	Director IT Department Council of Ministers Tirana
Albania	Ms Lidra Zegali	Director Press Information and IT Department Ministry of Foreign Affairs Tirana
Armenia	Mr Robert Grigoryan	Police Officer Department of the Fight against Organised Crime Police of the Republic of Armenia Yerevan
Armenia	Mr Vaner Harutyunyan	Third Secretary Legal Department Ministry of Foreign Affairs Yerevan
Austria	Mr Christian Bohm	Judge Directorate for Penal Legislation Federal Ministry of Justice Vienna
Azerbaijan	Mr Ramin Hasanov	Second Secretary International Law and Treaties Ministry of Foreign Affairs Baku
Azerbaijan	Mr Fuad Safarov	Head of Division Ministry of National Security Baku
Belgium	Mr Frederik Decruyenaere	Legal Adviser Legislation, Fundamental Rights and Freedoms Ministry of Justice Brussels

Belgium	Ms Isabelle Rorive	Professor of Law University Libre de Bruxelles Brussels
Bosnia and Herzegovina	Mr Gildzana Tanovic	Adviser International Law Department Ministry of Foreign Affairs Sarajevo
Bulgaria	Ms Antonia Angelova	Chief Expert International Legal Co-operation Department Ministry of Justice Sofia
Bulgaria	Mr Peter Rashkov	Director International Legal Co-operation and International Legal Assistance Directorate Ministry of Justice Sofia
China	Mr Roderic Broadhurst	Professor Centre for Criminology University of Hong Kong Hong Kong
Croatia	Mr Drazen Dragicevic	Head of Legal Informatics Department Faculty of Law University of Zagreb Zagreb
Croatia	Ms Mirjana Vukovic	Police Officer Department for Economic Crime and Corruption Ministry of the Interior Zagreb
Cyprus	Mr Philippos Vrontos	Chief Inspector Financial Crime Unit Police Headquarters Nicosia
Czech Republic	Ms Magdalena Zindulkova	Legal Expert Security Policy Department Ministry of the Interior Prague
Estonia	Mr Andrus Aidla	Leading Police Inspector IT Crime Division

		Tallinn
Estonia	Mr Ardo Annist	IT Expert Security Police Board Tallinn
European Commission	Mr Roger Holla	Administrator DG Information Society European Commission Brussels
Europol	Mr Louis Maatman	First Office Serious Crime Department High Tech Crime Centre Europol The Hague
France	Mr Alain Tourne	Commissaire Divisionnaire Honoraire de Police Chef de service Service informatique de la Police Judiciaire Paris
Georgia	Mr Kakha Koberidze	Deputy General Prosecutor General Prosecutor's Office Tbilisi
Georgia	Mr Shalva Tsiskarashvili	Second Secretary International Law Department Ministry of Foreign Affairs Tbilisi
Germany	Dr Angelika Laitenberger	Staatsanwältin Bundesministerium der Justiz Berlin
Germany	Mr Wolfgang Schreiber	Bundeskriminalamt Wiesbaden
Greece	Mr Theodore Mitrakos	Attorney-at-law Hellenic Ministry of Justice Athens
Hungary	Mr Sandor Dusik	Principal Counsellor Ministry of the Interior Budapest
Iceland	Mr Hallgrimur Asgeirsson	Member of the Criminal Law Committee Legal Affairs Department Ministry of Justice Reykjavik

Interpol	Mr Bernhard Otupal	IPSG Financial and High Tech Crime Unit Lyons
Ireland	Mr Paul Gillen	Detective Inspector Garda Siochana (Irish Police) Garda Bureau of Fraud Investiagtion Dublin
Ireland	Mr James Madden	Detective Sergeant Garda Siochana (Irish Police) National Bureau of Criminal Investigation Dublin
Italy	Mr Biagio Roberto Cimini	Magistrate Director of Ufficio I (International and Legal Affairs) General Directorate Criminal Justice Ministry of Justice Rome
Italy	Mr Carlo Sarzana di Sant'Ippolito	Honorary Deputy President Court of Cassation Department of Judicial Affairs Ministry of Justice Rome
Japan	Mr Ryuichi Shoji	General Consul Consulate General of Japan Permanent Observer of Japan to the Council of Europe Strasbourg
Japan	Mr Takashi Garcia Sato	Superintendent Assistant Director Cybercrime Division National Police Agency Tokyo
Japan	Mr Yoichi Kumota	Assistant Director National Police Agency High-Tech Crime Technology Division Information Communications

		Bureau Tokyo
Japan	Ms Mai Inamura	Official Minister's Secretariat Global Issues Department International Organised Crime Division Ministry of Foreign Affairs Tokyo
Japan	Mr Naoyuki Iwai	Consul (attorney) Consulate General of Japan Permanent Observer of Japan to the Council of Europe Strasbourg
Japan	Ms Françoise Nadia Richer	Assistant Consulate General of Japan Strasbourg
Latvia	Mr Vladislavs Gedjuns	Inspector Economic Police Latvian State Police Riga
Liechtenstein	Mr Patrick Ritter	Deputy Permanent Representative of Liechtenstein to the Council of Europe Office for Foreign Affairs Vaduz
Luxembourg	Ms Anne Kayser	Deputy Permanent Representative of Luxembourg to the Council of Europe Strasbourg
Malta	Mr David Agius	Police Sergeant Police Department Cybercrime Unit Home Affairs
Mexico	Mr Carlos Manuel Salazar-Diez de Sollano	Deputy Permanent Representative of Mexico to the Council of Europe Strasbourg
Mexico	Mr Juan Carlos Mendez Vital	Director of Technology of the Information Procuraduría General de la

		República Federal Agency of Investigation
Mexico	Ms Ilina Patricia Ramirez Mazon	Subdirección Projectos Normativas Procuraduría General de la República
Moldova	Mr Stepan Grabovschii	Head of the Department of Information and Security Chişinău
Moldova	Mr Tudor Nicorici	Chief Adviser Information and Transfrontier Crime Department Ministry of Internal Affairs Chişinău
Monaco	Ms Corinne Laforest de Miniotty	Conseiller au cabinet du Ministère d'État Secrétariat Général du Ministère d'État CCIN Monaco
Monaco	Mr Rémi Mortier	Administrateur Bureau des Affaires Européennes Direction des Relations Extérieures Représentation Permanente de la Principauté de Monaco auprès du Conseil de l'Europe Strasbourg
Netherlands	Mr Pascal Hetzscholdt	Strategic Adviser Dutch High-Tech Crime Project Dutch National Police Agency (KLPD) Schiphol Airport
Netherlands	Mr Taco Stein	National Prosecution Service Rotterdam
Netherlands	Mr John Stienen	Policy Adviser Ministry of the Interior and Kingdom Relations

		Public Sector Innovation and Information Policy Department The Hague
Netherlands	Ms Nienke Van den Berg	General Manager Dutch High-Tech Crime Project Dutch National Police Agency (KLPD) Schiphol Airport
Netherlands	Mr Paul Van der Flier	Senior Legal Adviser Ministry of Justice The Hague
Norway	Mr Magnar Aukrust	Deputy Director General Police Department Ministry of Justice Oslo
Norway	Mr Stein Schjolberg	Chief Judge Moss Tingrett Moss
OSCE	Ms Detelina Stambolova-Ivanova	Chief Expert Human Rights Department Ministry of Foreign Affairs Sofia
OSCE	Mr Drino Galicic	Programme Officer Legal Adviser OSCE Mission to Serbia and Montenegro Legislation and Institution Building Section Podgorica
Poland	Mr Andrzej Adamski	Expert Ministry of Justice Professor of Criminal Law and Computer Law Nicolaus Copernicus University Torun
Portugal	Mr Pedro Verdelho	Assistant State Prosecutor Public Prosecution Department Departamento de Investigaçao e Acçao Penal de

		Lisboa Lisbon
Romania	Ms Cristina Schulman	Legal Adviser Department of International Relations and Human Rights Ministry of Justice Bucharest
Romania	Mr Virgil Spiridon	Head of Cybercrime Unit Romanian National Police Bucharest
Russian Federation	Mr Ernest Chernukhin	Third Secretary New Challenges and Threats Department Ministry of Foreign Affairs Moscow
Russian Federation	Mr Alexander Fedorov	Foreign Intelligence Service Moscow
Russian Federation	Mr Boris Miroshnikov	Head of Department Ministry of the Interior Moscow
Russian Federation	Mr Anatoly Vorobiev	Head of Division Federal Security Service Moscow
Serbia and Montenegro (Serbia)	Ms Marija Savic	Network Security Expert ICT Department Ministry of Foreign Affairs Belgrade
Serbia and Montenegro (Montenegro)	Mr Dejan Djurovic	Chief Inspector Department for Protection against Organised Crime Ministry of the Interior Podgorica
Slovakia	Mr Robert Stevik	Senior Police Officer Computer Crime Unit Ministry of the Interior Bratislava
Slovenia	Ms Ivana Lipovec	Counsellor Ministry of Justice Ljubljana
Slovenia	Mr Marko Starman	State Secretary Ministry of Justice Ljubljana
Slovenia	Mr Klemen Ticar	Counsellor

		Ministry of Information Society Ljubljana
Spain	Mr Fernando Fernández	Police Inspector Brigada de Investigación Tecnológica Cuerpo Nacional de Policia Madrid
Sweden	Ms Gunnel Lindberg	Director Department of Penal Law Ministry of Justice Stockholm
Sweden	Mr Stefan Kronqvist	Head of Unit Information Technology Crime Squad National Criminal Investigation Department Stockholm
Switzerland	Ms Eva Bollmann	Analyst CYDC Federal Office of Police Federal Department of Justice and Police Berne
"The former Yugoslav Republic of Macedonia"	Mr Zarko Kamcev	Head of Department Ministry of Justice Skopje
"The former Yugoslav Republic of Macedonia"	Mr Ljubomir Manev	Chief Inspector Organised Crime Department Ministry of the Interior Skopje
Turkey	Mr Nihat Caylak	Expert International Relations Department Radio and Television Supreme Council Ankara
Turkey	Mr Mehmet Bora Sönmez	Expert International Relations Department Radio and Television Supreme Council Ankara

Ukraine	Mr Vitaliy Butuzov	Head of Section for Hi-Tech Offences Department of Economic Crime Ministry of Internal Affairs Kyiv
Ukraine	Mr Borysovich Rhlevytskyi	Deputy Head of Department Security Service of Ukraine Kyiv
United Kingdom	Mr Kevin McNulty	Hi-Tech Crime Team Organised and Financial Crime Unit Home Office London
United Kingdom	Ms Caroline Povey	Manager National Hi-Tech Crime Unit Tactical and Technical Support London
United States	Mr Marc Goodman	Programme Analyst International Cyber Crimes Staff US Department of State Washington
United States	Mr Sean Kanuck	Science and Technology Officer US Embassy Oslo Department of State Oslo
United States	Mr Christopher Painter	Deputy Chief Computer Crime and Intellectual Property Section Chair of the Technical Crime Subgroup US Department of Justice Washington
United States	Mr Mark Richard	Council for European Union and Internal Criminal Matters US Mission to the European Union Brussels
United States	Ms Betty-Ellen Shave	Senior Counsel/Co-ordinator for International Computer

		Crime Matters Computer Crime and Intellectual Property Section US Department of Justice Washington

Other organisations and the private sector

Institution	Name	Address
ABA CEELI	Ms Albena Panainte	Staff Attorney Criminal Law Reform Program Central European and Eurasian Law Initiative American Bar Association Sofia
ABA CEELI	Ms Iryna Zaretska	Legal Adviser Criminal Law Reform Program in Ukraine Central European and Eurasian Law Initiative American Bar Association Kyiv
Adalat Law Firm	Mr Mukhtar Mustafayev	Lawyer Adalat Law Firm Baku
Australia	Mr Peter Grabosky	Professor Regulatory Institutions Network Research School of Social Sciences Australian National University Canberra
Azleks Law Firm	Mr Abbas Atakishiyev	Lawyer Azleks International Law Firm Baku
Child Focus	Mr Tom Van Renterghem	Operating Officer New Tech and Multimedia Team Child Focus Brussels

Consultant	Mr Andre Fofana	Consultant Ettlingen, Germany
DBB Akademie	Ms Mary Ann Siara-Decker	International Project Manager DBB Akademie Bonn
DELO	Ms Helena Vignevic Kocmur	Journalist DELO Ljubljana
Fujitsu Limited	Mr Shinnosuke Date	General Manager Strategic Alliance Fujitsu Limited Tokyo
INHOPE	Ms Jennifer Siebert	Lawyer, Project Manager Jugendschutz.net/INHOPE Mainz, Germany
INACH	Ms Suzette Bronkhorst	Secretary General INACH Amsterdam
INACH	Mr Ronald Eissens	Director Magenta Complaints Bureau for Discrimination on the Internet Amsterdam
Max Planck Institute	Ms Nadine Gröseling	Researcher Foreign and International Penal Law Penal Law Department Max Planck Institute Freiburg
Max Planck Institute	Mr René Kieselmann	Researcher Foreign and International Penal Law Penal Law Department Max Planck Institute Freiburg
Max Planck Institute	Mr Roland Kniebühler	Researcher Foreign and International Penal Law Penal Law Department Max Planck Institute Freiburg
Max Planck Institute	Ms Francesca Possenti	Researcher Foreign and International

		Penal Law Penal Law Department Max Planck Institute Freiburg
Max Planck Institute	Ms Johanna Rinceanu	Attorney-at-Law and Researcher Foreign and International Penal Law Max Planck Institute Freiburg
NTV	Mr Kayhan Karaca	Journalist/TV Programme Producer NTV + CNBC-e European Affairs Department Strasbourg
Pricewater-houseCoopers SpA	Ms Simona Mulinari	Senior Consultant Global Risk Management Solutions Anti-Money Laundering Services Milan
Save the Children	Mr Mats Albinsson	Internet Analyst Save the Children Sweden Vasteras
Tokyo Electric Power Company	Mr Yoshio Kubota	Senior Adviser Tokyo Electric Power Company Tokyo
Tokyo Electric Power Company	Mr Atsushi Koya	Corporate Systems Department Tokyo Electric Power Company Tokyo
University of Munich	Dr Marco Gercke	Senior Researcher University of Munich Cologne
University of Trento	Mr Roberto Flor	Assistant New Technologies Criminal Law Faculty of Law University of Trento Trento
University of	Ms Stefania	Ph.D. in Criminal Law

Trento	Tabarelli de Fatis	Faculty of Law University of Trento Trento
University of Zurich	Mr Christian Schwarzenegger	Professor Faculty of Law University of Zurich Zurich
University of Zurich	Ms Sarah Jane Summers	Research Assistant Faculty of Law University of Zurich Zurich

Speakers and participants in the round table

Institution	Name	Address
University of Hong Kong	Mr Roderic Broadhurst	Professor Centre for Criminology University of Hong Kong Hong Kong
Symantec Corporation	Mr Ilias Chantzos	GMEA Government Relations Manager Government Relations Department Symantec Corporation Wemmel, Belgium
Child Focus	Ms Isabelle de Schrijver	Chief Research and Prevention Officer Brussels
Microsoft	Mr Detlet Eckert	Chief Security Adviser Diegem, Belgium
Australian National University	Mr Peter Grabosky	Professor Regulatory Institutions Network Research School of Social Sciences Australian National University Canberra
Moderator of the round table	Mr Riz Kahn	Journalist
Faculteit	Mr Henrik Kaspersen	Professor of Computer Law

Rechtsgeleerd heid		Computer/Law Institute Vrije Universiteit Amsterdam Faculteit Rechtsgeleerdheid Amsterdam
National Hi-Tech Crime Unit	Mr Andrew Letherby	Acting Manager Tactical and Technical Support National Hi-Tech Crime Unit London
Ministry of the Interior	Mr Boris Miroshnikov	Head of Department Ministry of the Interior Moscow
Pricewater-houseCoopers SpA	Ms Simona Mulinari	Senior Consultant Global Risk Management Solutions Anti-Money Laundering Services Milan
US Department of Justice	Mr Christopher Painter	Deputy Chief Computer Crime and Intellectual Property Section Chair of the Technical Crime Subgroup US Department of Justice Washington
Business Software Alliance	Ms Magda Popescu	Attorney-at-Law Business Software Alliance in Romania Bucharest
US Mission to the European Union	Mr Mark Richard	Council for European Union and Internal Criminal Matters US Mission to the European Union Brussels
University of Brussels	Ms Isabelle Rorive	Professor of Law University Libre de Bruxelles Brussels
Ministry of Justice	Mr Carlo Sarzana di Sant'Ippolito	Department of Judicial Affairs Court of Cassation Rome
Moss Tingrett	Mr Stein Schjolberg	Chief Judge Moss Tingrett Moss, Norway

Bundeskrimi-nalamt	Mr Wolfgang Schreiber	Bundeskriminalamt Wiesbaden, Germany
Procura Generale presso la Corte di Appello	Mr Eugenio Selvaggi	Deputy District Attorney General Procura Generale presso la Corte di Appello Rome
US Department of Justice	Ms Betty-Ellen Shave	Senior Counsel/Co-ordinator for International Computer Crime Matters Computer Crime and Intellectual Property Section US Department of Justice Washington
Max Planck Institute	Mr Ulrich Sieber	Director Max Planck Institute Freiburg, Germany
Symantec Corporation	Mr Giuseppe Verrini	Vice President Europe, Middle East, Africa Symantec Corporation Wemmel, Belgium
Federal Security Service	Mr Anatoly Vorobiev	Head of Section Federal Security Service Moscow

Secretariat

Institution	Name	Details
Council of Europe	Mr Terry Davis	Secretary General Strasbourg
Council of Europe	Mr Guy De Vel	Director General of Legal Affairs Strasbourg
Council of Europe	Mr Roberto Lamponi	Director of Legal Co-operation DG I – Legal Affairs Strasbourg
Council of Europe	Ms Margaret Killerby	Head of the Department of Crime Problems DG I – Legal Affairs Strasbourg
Council of Europe	Mr Gianluca Esposito	Department of Crime Problems

		DGI – Legal Affairs Strasbourg Tel: +33 (0) 3 88 41 28 41 Fax: +33 (0) 3 88 41 27 94 E-mail: gianluca.esposito@coe.int
Council of Europe	Mr Alexander Seger	Department of Crime Problems DG I – Legal Affairs Strasbourg Tel: +33 (0) 3 90 21 45 06 Fax: +33 (0) 3 88 41 39 55 E-mail: alexander.seger@coe.int
Council of Europe	Mr Roman Chlapak	Department of Crime Problems DG I – Legal Affairs Strasbourg Tel: +33 (0) 3 90 21 43 61 Fax: +33 (0) 3 88 41 39 55 E-mail: roman.chlapak@coe.int
Council of Europe	Ms Carole Steinmetz	Department of Crime Problems DG I – Legal Affairs Strasbourg Tel: +33 (0) 3 88 41 28 78 Fax: +33 (0) 3 88 41 39 55 E-mail: carole.steinmetz@coe.int
Council of Europe	Ms Jacqueline Bloice	Department of Crime Problems DG I – Legal Affairs Strasbourg Tel: +33 3 90 21 54 94 Fax: +33 3 88 41 27 94 E-mail: jacqueline.bloice@coe.int

Sales agents for publications of the Council of Europe
Agents de vente des publications du Conseil de l'Europe

AUSTRALIA/AUSTRALIE
Hunter Publications, 58A, Gipps Street
AUS-3066 COLLINGWOOD, Victoria
Tel.: (61) 3 9417 5361
Fax: (61) 3 9419 7154
E-mail: Sales@hunter-pubs.com.au
http://www.hunter-pubs.com.au

BELGIUM/BELGIQUE
La Librairie européenne SA
50, avenue A. Jonnart
B-1200 BRUXELLES 20
Tel.: (32) 2 734 0281
Fax: (32) 2 735 0860
E-mail: info@libeurop.be
http://www.libeurop.be

Jean de Lannoy
202, avenue du Roi
B-1190 BRUXELLES
Tel.: (32) 2 538 4308
Fax: (32) 2 538 0841
E-mail: jean.de.lannoy@euronet.be
http://www.jean-de-lannoy.be

CANADA
Renouf Publishing Company Limited
5369 Chemin Canotek Road
CDN-OTTAWA, Ontario, K1J 9J3
Tel.: (1) 613 745 2665
Fax: (1) 613 745 7660
E-mail: order.dept@renoufbooks.com
http://www.renoufbooks.com

CZECH REPUBLIC/
RÉPUBLIQUE TCHÈQUE
Suweco Cz Dovoz Tisku Praha
Ceskomoravska 21
CZ-18021 PRAHA 9
Tel.: (420) 2 660 35 364
Fax: (420) 2 683 30 42
E-mail: import@suweco.cz

DENMARK/DANEMARK
GAD Direct
Fiolstaede 31-33
DK-1171 COPENHAGEN K
Tel.: (45) 33 13 72 33
Fax: (45) 33 12 54 94
E-mail: info@gaddirect.dk

FINLAND/FINLANDE
Akateeminen Kirjakauppa
Keskuskatu 1, PO Box 218
FIN-00381 HELSINKI
Tel.: (358) 9 121 41
Fax: (358) 9 121 4450
E-mail: akatilaus@stockmann.fi
http://www.akatilaus.akateeminen.com

FRANCE
La Documentation française
(Diffusion/Vente France entière)
124, rue H. Barbusse
F-93308 AUBERVILLIERS Cedex
Tel.: (33) 01 40 15 70 00
Fax: (33) 01 40 15 68 00
E-mail: commandes.vel@ladocfrancaise.gouv.fr
http://www.ladocfrancaise.gouv.fr

Librairie Kléber (Vente Strasbourg)
Palais de l'Europe
F-67075 STRASBOURG Cedex
Fax: (33) 03 88 52 91 21
E-mail: librairie.kleber@coe.int

GERMANY/ALLEMAGNE
AUSTRIA/AUTRICHE
UNO Verlag
Am Hofgarten 10
D-53113 BONN
Tel.: (49) 2 28 94 90 20
Fax: (49) 2 28 94 90 222
E-mail: bestellung@uno-verlag.de
http://www.uno-verlag.de

GREECE/GRÈCE
Librairie Kauffmann
28, rue Stadiou
GR-ATHINAI 10564
Tel.: (30) 1 32 22 160
Fax: (30) 1 32 30 320
E-mail: ord@otenet.gr

HUNGARY/HONGRIE
Euro Info Service
Hungexpo Europa Kozpont ter 1
H-1101 BUDAPEST
Tel.: (361) 264 8270
Fax: (361) 264 8271
E-mail: euroinfo@euroinfo.hu
http://www.euroinfo.hu

ITALY/ITALIE
Libreria Commissionaria Sansoni
Via Duca di Calabria 1/1, CP 552
I-50125 FIRENZE
Tel.: (39) 556 4831
Fax: (39) 556 41257
E-mail: licosa@licosa.com
http://www.licosa.com

NETHERLANDS/PAYS-BAS
De Lindeboom Internationale Publikaties
PO Box 202, MA de Ruyterstraat 20 A
NL-7480 AE HAAKSBERGEN
Tel.: (31) 53 574 0004
Fax: (31) 53 572 9296
E-mail: books@delindeboom.com
http://home-1-worldonline.nl/~lindeboo/

NORWAY/NORVÈGE
Akademika, A/S Universitetsbokhandel
PO Box 84, Blindern
N-0314 OSLO
Tel.: (47) 22 85 30 30
Fax: (47) 23 12 24 20

POLAND/POLOGNE
Głowna Księgarnia Naukowa
im. B. Prusa
Krakowskie Przedmiescie 7
PL-00-068 WARSZAWA
Tel.: (48) 29 22 66
Fax: (48) 22 26 64 49
E-mail: inter@internews.com.pl
http://www.internews.com.pl

PORTUGAL
Livraria Portugal
Rua do Carmo, 70
P-1200 LISBOA
Tel.: (351) 13 47 49 82
Fax: (351) 13 47 02 64
E-mail: liv.portugal@mail.telepac.pt

SPAIN/ESPAGNE
Mundi-Prensa Libros SA
Castelló 37
E-28001 MADRID
Tel.: (34) 914 36 37 00
Fax: (34) 915 75 39 98
E-mail: libreria@mundiprensa.es
http://www.mundiprensa.com

SWITZERLAND/SUISSE
BERSY
Route de Monteiller
CH-1965 SAVIESE
Tel.: (41) 27 395 53 33
Fax: (41) 27 395 53 34
E-mail: bersy@bluewin.ch

Adeco – Van Diermen
Chemin du Lacuez 41
CH-1807 BLONAY
Tel.: (41) 21 943 26 73
Fax: (41) 21 943 36 05
E-mail: info@adeco.org

UNITED KINGDOM/ROYAUME-UNI
TSO (formerly HMSO)
51 Nine Elms Lane
GB-LONDON SW8 5DR
Tel.: (44) 207 873 8372
Fax: (44) 207 873 8200
E-mail: customer.services@theso.co.uk
http://www.the-stationery-office.co.uk
http://www.itsofficial.net

UNITED STATES and CANADA/
ETATS-UNIS et CANADA
Manhattan Publishing Company
468 Albany Post Road, PO Box 850
CROTON-ON-HUDSON,
NY 10520, USA
Tel.: (1) 914 271 5194
Fax: (1) 914 271 5856
E-mail: Info@manhattanpublishing.com
http://www.manhattanpublishing.com

Council of Europe Publishing/Editions du Conseil de l'Europe
F-67075 Strasbourg Cedex
Tel.: (33) 03 88 41 25 81 – Fax: (33) 03 88 41 39 10 – E-mail: publishing@coe.int – Website: http://book.coe.int